CELEBRATION

A Celebration of 100 Years of Statehood

A sea of colorful balloons was released during Oklahoma's State Capitol dome dedication ceremony, which served as the unofficial kickoff to the state's Centennial celebration.

OKLAHOMA '07 CENTENNIAL

CELEBRATION

A Celebration of 100 Years of Statehood

*This book was designed and written by Ackerman McQueen
and published with the generous assistance
of the Oklahoma Centennial Commission and Oklahoma Events.*

This book was made possible
thanks to the generous assistance of
the Oklahoma Centennial Commission and Oklahoma Events.
Designed and written by Ackerman McQueen.

Library of Congress Cataloging-in-Publication Data
The Oklahoma Centennial – 1st ed.
ISBN: 978-0-615-23589-9

There were more than 1,000 Centennial activities and events
that took place throughtout the state. Included in this
book are only those projects that received public or private
funding through the Oklahoma Centennial Commission.

As we pay tribute to our first century,
we honor all who came before us.
Their efforts, their endeavors, their achievements
created Oklahoma's unique history and its promise for
an extraordinary future.

THE CELEBRATION OF A CENTURY

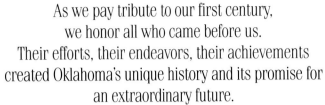

1

PREMIER EVENTS

2

NOTABLE PROJECTS

3

STATEWIDE ACTIVITIES

4

SPECIAL THANKS

ON THE INSIDE COVERS *A multitude of commemorative items were produced in honor of the Oklahoma Centennial. Merchandise ranged from shirts, hats and glasses to keepsake plates, beautifully bound books, custom-designed ornaments and other timeless treasures. **Ryan O'Toole** served as director of marketing and merchandise and collaborated with **Oklahoma Events** and **USA Screen Printing and Embroidery**, who produced many of the products. All served as wonderful, lasting mementos of the state's historic celebration.*

On November 16, 1907,
President Theodore Roosevelt issued Proclamation 780
admitting Oklahoma as the 46th state.
In his annual message on December 3, 1907,
President Roosevelt announced to Congress,
"Oklahoma has become a state,
standing on full equity with her elder sisters,
and her future is assured by her great natural resources."

A STATE IS BORN

OKLAHOMA

1803
*U.S. acquires most
of Oklahoma in
Louisiana Purchase.*

1811
*George C. Sibley, a U.S. Indian
agent at Fort Osage on the Missouri
River, explores the Salt Plains of the
Cimarron and Salt Rivers.*

1800 **1810**

1817
*Fort Smith is established
as military post.*

The land that now comprises Oklahoma was first discovered by Spanish explorer Francisco Vasquez de Coronado in 1541. Most of the area was later acquired by the United States in the 1803 Louisiana Purchase, with the remaining western panhandle region becoming U.S. territory following the 1845 annexation of Texas.

Designated as Indian Territory in 1834, the land served as home to many tribes, including those known today as the Five Civilized Tribes: Choctaw, Creek, Chickasaw, Seminole and Cherokee. After the Civil War ended in 1865, much of this land was ceded to the U.S. government, which assigned it to other tribes. The Organic Act of 1890 helped to create a new territory that would eventually encompass the occupied and unoccupied federal lands west of these Indian nations; it was known as Oklahoma Territory.

1700s
*The land that would be Oklahoma is
claimed by French explorers in the 1700s.*

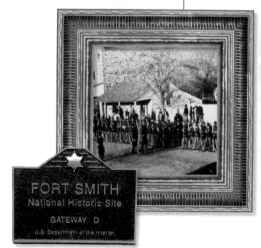

FORT SMITH
National Historic Site
GATEWAY D
U.S. Department of the Interior

BOOMERS AND SOONERS. As western expansion reached the region in the late 1800s, a movement arose by groups, called "Boomers," who wanted to settle the Unassigned Lands. The government finally relented to their pressure and opened up two million acres for settlement in 1889.

Settlers came from across the nation for the land run; it was the first of five to be held between 1889 and 1895. Later land openings were conducted by means of a lottery or sealed bids as some of the early homesteaders – aka "Sooners" – had jumped the gun and

1824
Fort Gibson is established as first fort in Oklahoma.

1845
Western panhandle region becomes U.S. territory with annexation of Texas.

1860s
Buffalo soldiers fight for the North all across Indian Territory – land that later would become the state of Oklahoma.

1863
One of many Civil War battles that took place in Oklahoma erupted in the small town of Honey Creek, in eastern Oklahoma. U.S. Major General James G. Blunt defeated the Confederate forces over a three-day period.

| 1820 | 1830 | 1840 | 1850 | 1860 | 1870 |

1830-40
The forced relocation of the Five Civilized Tribes (Cherokee, Chickasaw, Choctaw, Creek and Seminole) from the south-eastern U.S. to Indian Territory is commonly called the Trail of Tears because of the great suffering they endured in route to their destinations.

1843
Captain Nathan Boone, son of Daniel Boone, makes a second exploring expedition through the valleys of the Arkansas and Cimarron and their tributaries.

1851
Fort Arbuckle is established near the Wichita Mountains.

Fort Arbuckle, Oklahoma

1870-72
First railroad to cross Oklahoma is built.

already staked their claims before the land was officially opened for settlement. On November 16, 1907, Indian Territory and Oklahoma Territory combined to form the state of Oklahoma – it became the 46th state to join the union.

BLACK GOLD AND BLACK TOWNS. It wasn't long before the nation's newest state became the place to strike it rich. Oklahoma's teeming oil fields drew fortune seekers from around the world as cities such as Tulsa, Ponca City, Bartlesville and Oklahoma City flourished. The prosperity of the '20s can still be seen today in spectacular art deco architecture.

As the 20th century wore on, many different groups flooded into the state. Black towns – comprised of African Americans who chose to live separately from whites – sprouted and grew. In fact, nowhere else in America did so many black men and women come together to create, occupy and govern their own communities. Greenwood, located in north Tulsa, was one of the most successful of these towns and became known as America's "Black Wall Street."

By the 1930s, as the nation was struggling through the Great Depression, Oklahoma was forced to battle another opponent: Mother Nature. Severe droughts coupled with record heat and high winds caused massive dust storms to blow throughout the state. This Dust Bowl, immortalized by John Steinbeck in *The Grapes of Wrath*, resulted in major agricultural damage and widespread crop failure.

The winds of change blew in better times in the form of Route 66 – America's Main Street was paved end to end in 1937. Stretching from Chicago to Los Angeles, it ran right through the heart of Oklahoma and inspired a nation to "get its kicks." Route 66 spawned unique roadside attractions such as the Round Barn, Blue Whale, the Belvidere Mansion and Totem Pole Park – many of which can still be seen today.

HEARTACHE IN THE HEARTLAND. Oklahoma's history since has included the renewed rise of tribal sovereignty and enterprise, the development of Tinker Air Force Base, extensive urban growth and, in 1971, the opening of the Oklahoma portion of the Arkansas River Navigation System that gave Muskogee and Tulsa direct access to the sea. More recently, the state experienced a second oil boom in the '80s.

Tragedy struck in 1995, when Oklahoma became the scene of our nation's largest act of domestic terrorism at that time. A bomb blast destroyed the nine-story Alfred P. Murrah Federal Building in downtown Oklahoma City, killing 168 people including 19 children. The community's response was as instantaneous as the act that precipitated it. Their support of the rescue workers, survivors and families of victims was so genuine and so overwhelming it was given a name: the "Oklahoma Standard." Those words today symbolize the highest level of compassion and caring.

1889
Indian Territory's first land run is held April 22 at high noon.

1895
The fifth and final land run occurs May 23.

1892
Third land run is held April 19.

1879
Will Rogers was born on a large ranch in the Cherokee Nation near what later would become Oologah. An Indian, a cowboy and a national figure, Oklahoma's favorite native son was a star of Broadway and 71 movies of the 1920s and 1930s. He was a popular broadcaster and writer of more than 4,000 syndicated newspaper columns.

1880

1890

1893
The largest and most spectacular run in northern Oklahoma, the Cherokee Strip, is held on September 16.

1891
Second land run is held September 21.

1890
Territorial capital is established at Guthrie.

Oklahoma Land Run of '91
A Lincoln County Centennial Salute

HARPER'S WEEKLY

1880
Captain David L. Payne began settlement efforts in Oklahoma Territory despite being turned back repeatedly by federal troops. From lobbying lawmakers in Washington, D.C., to leading numerous groups of settlers, often in the hundreds, Payne became the figurehead for the Boomer movement, the land grab that eventually led to the land runs.

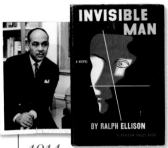

1914
African-American writer and teacher, Ralph Waldo Ellison, is born. He later achieved international fame with his first novel, The Invisible Man.

1905
One of the most successful oil fields in American history, known as the Glenn Pool, is discovered just outside of Tulsa.

1915
The Phillips family continues to enrich the community with thriving businesses and generous philanthropy.

1935
Will Rogers and Wiley Post die when their small airplane, piloted by Post, crashes in Alaska Territory.

1937
Route 66 is paved from Chicago to L.A. via Oklahoma.

1930-60
Five Oklahoma natives, Maria Tallchief, Marjorie Tallchief, Yvonne Chouteau, Rosella Hightower and Moscelyne Larkin, dominate ballet stages throughout the world as star attractions with some of the most famous dance companies of all time. Larkin later founded the world-renowned Tulsa Ballet Company with husband Roman Jasinski.

1900 · 1910 · 1920 · 1930 · 66 · 1940 · 1950 ›››

1907
Oklahoma and Indian Territories are combined to create the 46th state of the union, Oklahoma, on November 16.

1930
The Dust Bowl hits the Great Plains states.

1943
Oklahoma! the musical opens on Broadway.

1900-30
The bustling cities of Tulsa, Bartlesville and Oklahoma City, to name a few, continue to thrive, quickly becoming the economic center for all things oil and gas.

1940
The final openings in the Pensacola Dam are completed, creating one of Oklahoma's favorite attractions, Grand Lake. The dam remains the largest multiple-arch dam in the world, spanning almost a mile, with 51 arches and 21 spillways.

NATIVE SONS AND NATIVE DAUGHTERS. Oklahoma entered the 21st century with unbridled hope and optimism. The state's nearly century-old roots had sown a people of character and valor, of dogged dedication and drive. Many went on to make their mark on the world, and will forever be remembered as Oklahoma's cherished sons and daughters.

Will Rogers could be considered a composite of Oklahoma's finest traits – "The Cherokee Kid" was a winsome cowboy who was honest, open, optimistic and friendly. So friendly, in fact, that Rogers famously "never met a man he didn't like." Over a career that spanned trick roping and political commentary, Rogers was a pioneer of his day and set the stage for many other Oklahoma pioneers to come.

Athlete Jim Thorpe gained worldwide fame with double gold medal victories in the 1912 Olympics. Aviator Wiley Post pushed back the boundaries of aviation and space, paving the way for Gordon Cooper to become the fourth American to orbit the Earth. A few years later, Thomas Stafford commanded the Apollo 10 and Shannon Lucid logged more time in space than any woman in history.

Oklahoma sports heroes live forever in hearts as well. Some of the state's unforgettable names include baseball legends such as Mickey Mantle, Bobby Murcer, Johnny Bench, Allie Reynolds, Carl Hubbell, Warren Spahn, the Waner brothers – Lloyd and Paul – and Pepper Martin; rodeo hall-of-famers Bill Pickett, Tom Ferguson and Jim Shoulders; football Heisman Trophy winners Billy Vessels, Steve Owens, Billy Sims, Barry Sanders and Jason White; plus legendary coaches such as Barry Switzer and world-champion gymnasts Shannon Miller and Bart Conner.

An astonishing and ever-expanding wealth of homegrown musical talent is a well-known phenomenon, from Gene Autry and Woody Guthrie to "The Singing Rage" Miss Patti Page and "King of the Road" Roger Miller. Enid's own Leona Mitchell is a star of the New York Metropolitan Opera. Plus, superstars such as Reba McEntire, Vince Gill, Garth Brooks, Toby Keith and Carrie Underwood join a list that gets longer and longer every year.

DAWN OF A NEW CENTURY. These pioneers introduced a nation to a state just getting started. They were proud caretakers of the land, with great faith in its bright future. Now, as the next generations inherit the state's vast resources and collective life's work, they will be entrusted with its gifts and its momentum. And upon this unique history, Oklahoma will begin to write new chapters of what promises to be a truly extraordinary future.

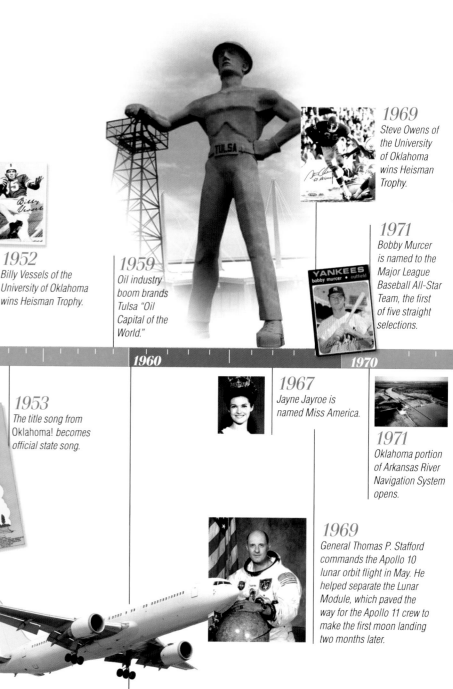

1969
Steve Owens of the University of Oklahoma wins Heisman Trophy.

1971
Bobby Murcer is named to the Major League Baseball All-Star Team, the first of five straight selections.

1952
Billy Vessels of the University of Oklahoma wins Heisman Trophy.

1959
Oil industry boom brands Tulsa "Oil Capital of the World."

1950 *1960* *1970*

1953
The title song from Oklahoma! becomes official state song.

1967
Jayne Jayroe is named Miss America.

1971
Oklahoma portion of Arkansas River Navigation System opens.

1969
General Thomas P. Stafford commands the Apollo 10 lunar orbit flight in May. He helped separate the Lunar Module, which paved the way for the Apollo 11 crew to make the first moon landing two months later.

1960-70
Oklahoma's economy grows to include aeronautics and other advanced technology industries. Two large electronics plants and an aeronautics center are established in Oklahoma City. Tulsa becomes the site of a new space equipment factory. Large industries expand to include automobiles and computers. Thousands of people move into Oklahoma.

19 OKLAHOMA 76
CK-9148
1776 BICENTENNIAL 1976

1976
Oklahoma celebrates America's bicentennial.

1984
Reba McEntire begins her four-year reign as the Country Music Association's "Female Vocalist of the Year."

1988
Barry Sanders of Oklahoma State University wins Heisman Trophy.

1990
Oklahoma's Native American population is largest in the nation at 252,420.

1996
Shannon Miller takes home the Olympic gold medal in the balance beam as part of the U.S. gymnastics team. She now ranks as the most decorated gymnast, male or female, in U.S. history.

2002
Commander John Herrington becomes the first Native American in space, traveling aboard Endeavor, the 16th Shuttle mission.

2005
Oklahoma float appears in the first of three Macy's Thanksgiving Day Parades.

2007
Oklahoma celebrates its 100th birthday.

1980 **1990** **2000**

OKLAHOMA '07 CENTENNIAL

1981
Susan Powell is named Miss America.

1978
Billy Sims of the University of Oklahoma wins Heisman Trophy.

1984
Vince Gill is named Top New Male Vocalist by the Academy of Country Music.

1996
Shawntel Smith is named Miss America.

1993
Toby Keith enters the country music scene with his debut single "Should've Been a Cowboy." It shot to #1 on the Billboard country singles chart and his self-titled debut album was certified platinum.

1990
Garth Brooks releases his second album, "No Fences." It would spend 23 weeks at #1 on the Billboard country music chart and would go on to become his highest-selling album.

2003
Jason White of the University of Oklahoma wins Heisman Trophy.

2002
New State Capitol Dome is completed.

2006
Jennifer Berry is named Miss America.

2006
A 10-foot-tall bronze statue of James Garner is unveiled in Norman on April 21.

2006
Tulsa kicks off Oklahoma's year-long Centennial celebration.

2007
Two Oklahoma floats and the Oklahoma All★Star Centennial Band appear in the Rose Parade.

2007
Lauren Nelson is named Miss America.

2006
The "Oklahoma Rising" anthem by Jimmy Webb and Vince Gill debuts.

As Oklahoma neared its 100th anniversary of statehood, an undercurrent of excitement began to rise. It was time to make plans for the

CELEBRATION
OF A LIFETIME

From town to town, border to border, a sea of grand-scale plans were designed to captivate, commemorate, excite and entertain. With them came a growing sense that this monumental milestone would open the world's eyes to the state we know and love. A place of boundless, unbridled potential. One outsiders would hardly recognize.

With each dedication and each generous and ingenious new contribution, the celebration gained momentum. Soon, it became clear that Oklahoma's Centennial would be more than the celebration of a lifetime; it would be thunderous proof that this mighty state had arrived.

CREATION OF THE CENTENNIAL COMMISSION. Planning for this historic occasion began well in advance — more than a decade in fact. It started with the formation of the Oklahoma Centennial Commission, a state agency created in 1996. Guided by a 42-member board comprised of citizens, legislators, state agency directors and mayors, its role was to direct a commemoration that was geographically and ethnically inclusive, that reflected Oklahoma's history and heritage, and that left a lasting legacy for future generations.

In 1999, Gov. Frank Keating tapped J. Blake Wade, then the executive director of the Oklahoma Historical Society, to fill the executive director position at the commission. By 2002, with Oklahoma wrapping up touches on its new State Capitol dome, Wade had begun a search for someone to head up the dome dedication ceremony. His short list had just one name on it: Lee Allan Smith. Responsible for coordination of the 1982 Oklahoma's Diamond Jubilee and the 1989 Olympic Festival, Smith had the extensive event-planning experience Wade was seeking. Not only did Smith put together a successful dome dedication celebration, he went on to serve as chairman of projects and events for the Centennial Commemoration Commission.

OKLAHOMA CENTENNIAL COMMISSION BOARD OF DIRECTORS

Chickasaw Nation	Mrs. Lou Kerr
Gov. Bill Anoatubby	Mrs. Nancy Leonard
Lt. Gov. Jari Askins	Mr. Tom McDaniel
Former Gov. Henry Bellmon	Mr. Paul Meyer
Speaker of the House	President Pro-Tempore
Chris Benge	Mike Morgan
Mrs. Judy Benson	Mrs. Betty Price
Dr. Bob Blackburn	Lawton Mayor John Purcell Jr.
Former Gov. David Boren	Sen. Jeff Rabon
Mr. Leroy Bridges	Mr. Carl R. Renfro
Co-President Pro Tempore	Mr. John Richard
Glenn Coffee	Mr. Bob Rollins
Mr. Don Coffin	Canute Mayor David Root
Oklahoma City	Muskogee Mayor Wren Stratton
Mayor Mick Cornett	Rep. Daniel Sullivan
Mrs. Julie Daniels	Tulsa Mayor Kathy Taylor
Mr. Charles Ford	Ms. Ann Thompson
Mrs. Jane Jayroe Gamble	Durant Mayor
Gov. Brad Henry	Jerry Tomlinson
Rep. Jeff Hickman	Ms. Barbara Warner
Rep. Shane Jett	Mr. Hardy Watkins
Former Gov. Frank Keating	Sen. Jim Wilson
Mr. Steve Kelley	Mr. Daniel J. Zaloudek

GOV. FRANK KEATING *As early as his 1996 State of the State Address, Gov. Keating was looking ahead to Oklahoma's 100th anniversary. "The Oklahoma Centennial is just 11 years away," noted Keating. "Let us work together, starting now, to make it a true celebration of greatness."*

PLANNING THE PERFECT EVENT. The job of the Oklahoma Centennial Commission was an enormous one – that of planning a birthday celebration for three million people. It began in grand fashion with the completion of the State Capitol dome in 2002, and only grew from there. For the next five years, funds were raised. Historic restorations begun. New cultural centers conceived. Events developed. Festivals planned. And once-in-a-lifetime celebrations set in motion.

To encourage broad statewide participation, communities and individuals were invited to submit their project or event for recognition as an "official" Centennial activity. Criteria to receive this recognition included appropriateness, timeliness and community support.

There were two levels of Centennial projects – those that received funding support and recognition, and those that received recognition alone. Funding was provided by the state, as well as corporate and individual sponsors. Cities, towns, counties, and tribal and federal governments also contributed.

For those who received official status, benefits included the right to use the official Centennial logo, inclusion in the Centennial calendar of events, promotion with other projects through press releases, newsletters and other media, and designation in Oklahoma Tourism and Recreation Department brochures and promotions.

A THOUSAND PROJECTS. A MILLION MEMORIES. What began with just a handful of projects grew quickly as the Centennial gained speed. By the time it was all said and done, and the last firework had shot brilliant bursts of color into the sky, there were more than 1,000 projects and events.

Categories were broad and all-encompassing: art, landmarks, parks, gardens, cultural centers, conference and civic centers, historic restorations, heritage activities, museums, memorials, exhibits, military and veteran sites, festivals, sports, recreation, multimedia, publications, research and commemorative items. And there was no town left behind – almost every city in the state was represented in some way.

In 2001, Centennial Commission Deputy Director Jeanie Edney had created an umbrella theme for the celebration: "Celebrate Oklahoma! A Unique History. An Extraordinary Future." It soon became the tagline that inspired Oklahomans to share a sense of pride in our rich roots and a feeling of accomplishment for the seeds we've sown for the new century to come.

1
PREMIER EVENTS

CONTRACTORS

CONCERT

PRIDE

SCULPTURE

DANCERS ROTUNDA MUSIC

CELEBRATE FIREWORKS MARCHING BANDS

ARCHITECT GAILLARDIA

CROWDS DOME NATIVE AMERICANS

FAVORITE SONS BALLOONS STAINED GLASS

PREVIEW GALA DEDICATION

STARS HEROES

LASERS SEAL GUARDIAN

STATE SEAL

OKLAHOMA

'07

CENTENNIAL

STATE CAPITOL DOME

PRELUDE TO THE CENTENNIAL

In 2002, Oklahoma capped off a project
85 years in the making.
It was the completion of a 1914 dream
and today is a visible symbol of our state's
determination and dedication.
It's truly our crowning glory . . .

THE STATE CAPITOL
DOME

O n July 20, 1914, some 5,000 people witnessed history in the making as Gov. Lee Cruce broke ground on Oklahoma's new State Capitol. The neoclassical architectural plans originally called for a dome, but as the building was nearing completion in 1917, the nation was heading into World War I – a situation that resulted in materials slated for the dome to be diverted to the war effort. This predicament left state officials with no other choice but to select an alternate roof design. Thus, a circular stained glass piece was installed – from the inside, it gave the illusion of the dome. From the outside, the omission was obvious.

Oklahoma's shining new State Capitol was dedicated on June 30, 1917, and was a source of pride statewide. Yet its lack of a dome left many feeling that the building remained unfinished. Throughout the next 80-plus years, several private efforts were initiated to raise funds for the dome construction – ultimately, all fell short.

It wasn't until the mid-1990s, with Gov. Frank Keating at the helm, that renewed efforts to build a dome gained momentum. Gov. Keating's long-awaited announcement came in July 2000: Oklahoma would construct a Capitol dome as part of the state's Centennial celebration.

A SHINING MOMENT *After 95 years of statehood, 85 years of waiting and two years of construction, the magnificent dome lights the night sky at Oklahoma's State Capitol.*

INTERIOR ROTUNDA *The Capitol is brimming with more than 100 works of art. The permanent collection houses murals and paintings by acclaimed artists including* **Wilson Hurley**, **Charles Banks Wilson**, **Thomas Gilbert White**, **Mike Larsen** *and many more. The canopy in the upper dome features a stained glass replica of the Oklahoma state seal.*

THE STATE CAPITOL DOME CONSTRUCTION

BUILDING BEGINS *To ensure that the dome remained true to its original vision, Oklahoma's oldest and largest construction firms —* **Manhattan Construction Company** *and* **Flintco**, *both headquartered in Tulsa — came together to form* **Capitol Dome Builders***. They joined forces with* **Frankfurt-Short-Bruza Associates,** *an Oklahoma-owned architecture, engineering and planning firm, to create a dome that was based on the design intent as drawn up by Layton Wemyss & Smith in 1914.*

JUNE 2001

JUNE 2001

DECEMBER 2001

APRIL 2001

SCULPTURE *"The Guardian" is a bronze statue by former Oklahoma Senator Enoch Kelly Haney.*

LANTERN *Small circular turret that crowns the dome with a colonnade of 16 Corinthian columns.*

OUTER DOME *Curved surface sitting on the drum that has 16 raised ribs.*

PEDIMENT *Triangular gable above the 16 smaller windows that circles the outer dome.*

BUTTRESS *Ornamental scroll that spans the lower to upper portion of dome.*

DRUM *Circular vertical wall supports the dome. Has 16 divided light windows.*

COLONNADE *Series of cylindrical, tapered columns that encircle the drum. There are 16 pairs with decorative Corinthian capitals.*

JUNE 2002

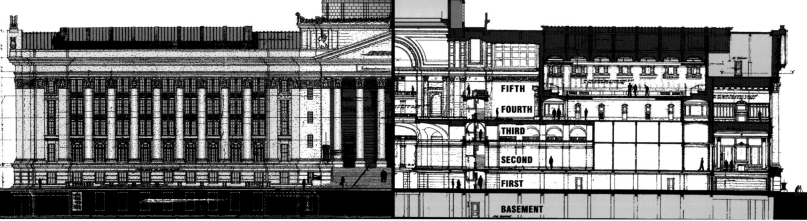

BUILDING BASE *The original design and construction of the Capitol incorporated the necessary foundation to support the dome, even though it wasn't built at the time. A 1998 feasibility study confirmed the building's sound structural qualities.*

FIFTH
FOURTH
THIRD
SECOND
FIRST
BASEMENT

20

JULY 2001

OCTOBER 2001

MARCH 2002

JUNE 2002

JULY 2002

JUNE 7, 2002 *"The Guardian" statue is placed atop the dome.*

AT LONG LAST, A DOME

Construction of Oklahoma's State Capitol dome was completed on Statehood Day, November 16, 2002. Architectural detailing captured the essence of the earlier design, but incorporated modern materials, techniques and applications.

"THE GUARDIAN" *Prior to installation, the 17-foot-tall statue stood on the steps of the Capitol, towering above the Native American color guard.*

ARTIST ENOCH KELLY HANEY
*The bronze statue of a young Indian warrior was sculpted by former Oklahoma State Sen. **Enoch Kelly Haney,** an American Indian of Seminole and Creek descent whose family followed the Trail of Tears to Oklahoma seven generations ago.*

GOV. FRANK KEATING *visits with "The Guardian" artist **Enoch Kelly Haney** as he puts the finishing touches on his sculpture (below).*

DEDICATION AND RAISING *The dedication ceremony was performed by Gov. **Frank Keating** (below at podium) and featured a moving tribute by former Sen. **Enoch Kelly Haney** as the "voice" of "The Guardian" (below). Following the ceremonies, the 6,000-pound statue was airlifted to its permanent home atop the dome.*

" . . . soon, I will be raised to the top of this Capitol building . . .
inside are many guardians of this state.
Our governor, our legislators, our judges; they all are charged
with a very sacred task of being the guardians of Oklahoma . . .
a state that is nearing its first Centennial.
And I will stand guard here, over our great state,
over our majestic land, over our values.
My lance pierces my legging and is planted in the ground.
I will not be moved from my duty,
from my love of Oklahoma and all of its people;
people who came from far and near,
people who have withstood adversities and hardships,
and still stand strong and proud.
I will stand my ground, and I will not be moved.
From this day on, I will stand guard,
I will stand strong and be proud of Oklahoma, our home."

THE OKLAHOMA STATE SEAL *The canopy over the opening in the upper dome (bottom left) features a magnificent stained glass artwork that includes a replication of the Oklahoma state seal in the center. It was produced by* **Triffo's Glass Arts,** *which produced the original, pre-dome stained glass. The piece is backlit to provide a striking view from any angle. Gov.* **Frank Keating** *(above) views the in-progress piece.*

STRUCTURAL DESIGN *The steel framing system was constructed to withstand seismic forces at levels far greater than those required by governing codes and standards. Special procedures involved coring of the basement floor and footings, compressive strength tests of concrete cores and measurement of bearing capacity of the soil and rock materials on which the Capitol is built.*

Courtesy of Frankfurt-Short-Bruza Associates

On the 95th anniversary of statehood,
an estimated 16,000 people gathered
to celebrate the first official Centennial project –
it was a breathtaking display at
the Oklahoma State Capitol.

DOME
DEDICATION

Stars illuminated the sky and stage during the memorable State Capitol Dome Dedication. The 90-minute "Spirit of a New Frontier" show featured an array of Oklahoma celebrities, along with a high-energy light show, dazzling lasers and a shower of fireworks. Country music legend Vince Gill served as emcee for the evening and headed the star-studded cast of performers.

"It reaches for the stars, and so do we," Gov. Frank Keating said as throngs of people crowded into the Capitol's north lawn to dedicate the 155-foot-tall dome. "Today, we know that there are no limits to what Oklahoma and Oklahomans can achieve, and our dome tells that story, too," he said.

Oklahoma's dome was the first to be built on an existing Capitol building in the United States since the nation's Capitol was completed in 1865. The dedication ceremony capped off the 18-month, $21 million dome project. And it kicked off a series of statewide events leading up to Oklahoma's Centennial celebration in 2007.

STATE OF OKLAHOMA · DOME DEDICATION · NOVEMBER 16, 2002

RED, WHITE AND "OOOOH!"

*Gov. **Frank Keating** and First Lady **Cathy Keating** enjoyed the 90-minute star-spangled show, which featured photo projections using the Capitol as a backdrop and ended with a breathtaking laser and fireworks display. The ceremony was made possible thanks to many generous sponsors that included **Chesapeake Energy**, **Kerr-McGee** and **Six Flags**.*

In Appreciation to the Following Sponsors:

Chesapeake Energy
Kerr-McGee
Six Flags

Cox Communications
SBC Southwestern Bell

Ackerman McQueen
Advantage Marketing Systems
American Airlines
Bank of America
Libby & G.T. Blankenship
Blue Cross & Blue Shield of Oklahoma
Boeing
Devon Energy
Jean I. Everest Foundation
FLINTCO
Frankfurt Short Bruza
Fred Jones Companies
Integris Health
Local Oklahoma Bank
Manhattan Construction
Mathis Brothers
McClain's RV
LaDonna & Herman Meinders
Naifco Realty
ONEOK
Presbyterian Health Foundation
Jeannette & Richard Sias

LEONA MITCHELL (above) The Enid native and New York Metropolitan Opera star performed the national anthem.

VINCE GILL AND AMY GRANT (right) These musical giants have won more than 50 awards combined. Gill, whose hometown is Oklahoma City, began his career as the lead singer in the country-rock band Pure Prairie League before going solo. Grant is an honorary Oklahoman and is the best-selling contemporary Christian artist of all time.

STRIKE UP THE BAND! The ceremony featured numerous musical numbers and appearances by marching bands from the **University of Oklahoma** and the cast of The Music Man.

ONE LAND, ONE HEART, ONE NATION (above) The **U.S. Color Guard** presented flags prior to the singing of the national anthem. Joining **Leona Mitchell** in her performance was the **Canterbury Children's Choir**.

JIMMY WEBB (above) A member of the Oklahoma Hall of Fame and Elk City native, Webb performed a medley of songs. To this day, he looks back upon the evening fondly. "I had tears in my eyes that night," Webb recalls. "I was so proud of the occasion, and I thought the results were so beautiful. I loved to see a Native American up on top of the Capitol like that. My great grandmother was Cherokee and it was just a very emotional time for me."

MISS AMERICAS (above) Three of Oklahoma's very own Miss Americas – **Shawntel Smith Wuerch**, **Jane Jayroe Gamble** and **Susan Powell** – welcomed the crowd and opened the show with a musical number.

BASEBALL LEGENDS (below) **Johnny Bench** and **Bobby Murcer** appeared with the **University** of **Oklahoma** and **Oklahoma State University** Cheer squads.

KATRINA ELAM (above) Accompanied by **Kyle Dillingham** and **Jody Teeter**, Elam performed "My Little Lady Who."

BRYAN WHITE (above) Country music's Top New Male Vocalist (1996) star performed "Love Is The Right Place."

AMERICAN SPIRIT DANCERS This talented, 10-member **Oklahoma City University** troupe performed a number under the direction of Professor **Jo Rowan**. They were backed by the **Pride of Oklahoma,** the **University of Oklahoma's** marching band.

JONATHAN BECK REED *(left) Portraying the lead from the "Will Rogers Follies" musical, Reed was joined by other cast members for his number, "Never Met A Man I Didn't Like."*

JET FLYOVER *The ceremony included a flyover by the* **Oklahoma Air National Guard**.

WILL ROGERS FOLLIES *(below) Oklahoma City University's* **American Spirit Dancers** *perform to the tune of "Our Favorite Son" from the Tony Award-winning Broadway musical.*

THE MUSIC MAN *The cast of* The Music Man, *fresh from their national tour of the Broadway revival, performed "Seventy-Six Trombones." Thanks to* **Larry Payton** *of* **Celebrity Attractions** *for his effort in bringing the show to Oklahoma.*

SPORTS HEROES TURN OUT TO SALUTE THE STATE

Baseball superstars **Johnny Bench** *and* **Bobby Murcer** *were just two of many Oklahoma sports celebrities appearing at the dedication ceremony. Others included Olympic gold medalist* **Shannon Miller***; the University of Oklahoma men's gymnastics coach and former Shannon Miller coach* **Steve Nunno***;* **J.W. Mashburn***, Olympic gold medalist in track;* **Bob Kurland***, as the first seven-footer on the basketball scene, he helped Oklahoma State University win back-to-back championships and also played on two U.S. Olympic teams; OU football All-American and two-time national championship winner* **Clendon Thomas***; former lightweight boxing champ* **Sean O'Grady***; former OSU player* **Bob Fenimore***, first two-time All-American in football; 16-time Rodeo World Championship winner* **Jim Shoulders***;* **Eddie Sutton***, former OSU basketball coach and four-time winner of National Coach of the Year; OU women's basketball coach* **Sherri Coale***, who headed the team to its first national championship game appearance; Oklahoma Hall of Fame member* **Jim Hartz***; and* **Barry Switzer***, head coach of three OU national football championships and a Super Bowl win as coach of the Dallas Cowboys.*

THE STATE CAPITOL DOME DEDICATION

LIVE ENTERTAINMENT *Performers at the Preview Gala included two nationally recognized recording artists: classical guitarist **Edgar Cruz** and trumpeter **David B. Hooten**.*

CELEBRATING THE DOME *Two nights of preview parties opened the doors of the newly domed Capitol and rotunda to an enthusiastic public. Special thanks to **The Petroleum Club, Mary Ellen Alexander and Eventures**, and **New Leaf Floral**.*

PREVIEW GALA *A black-tie reception was held in the Capitol rotunda the night before formal dedication ceremonies. Oklahoma dignitaries in attendance included **Lee Allan** and **DeAnn Smith, Dee** and **Beth Ann Sadler**, and friends.*

STATE LEADERS *Special guests (right) at the Preview Gala included First Lady **Cathy Keating** and Gov. **Frank Keating**, **Donna Nigh** and former Gov. **George Nigh**, and Lt. Gov. **Mary Fallin**.*

ENJOYING THE EVENING *Shown left to right are **David Durrett**, Dr. **Gary Massad, Richard Cudjo** and **Paula Root**.*

SOUNDS OF THE NEW CENTURY
*Resounding performances by the **Canterbury Choral Society** (below) and the **Ambassadors' Concert Choir** (right) filled all four levels of the Capitol rotunda.*

THE GUARDIAN *A life-size replica of the sculpture on top of the dome was donated by **Nancy Payne Ellis** and is a permanent addition to the state Capitol rotunda.*

A DAZZLING FINALE

*The ceremony concluded with a magnificent laser and fireworks display staged by **Austin Pyrotechnics**. Special thanks to **Bill Thrash** and **OETA**, **J. Blake Wade, Lee Allan Smith** and **Jennifer Kiersch**, plus **Gary Story** and **Six Flags Productions** – including producer **David Thomas** and director **Steve Dahlem** – for their efforts in presenting such a spectacular show.*

CLOSING NUMBER

*Oklahoma Miss Americas **Susan Powell** (1981), **Shawntel Smith Wuerch** (1996) and **Jane Jayroe Gamble** (1967), along with **Vince Gill** and **Amy Grant,** took the stage to thank the crowds for attending the evening's festivities. They were joined by the **Oklahoma City Philharmonic** under the direction of **Joel Levine**.*

EXTRAVAGANZA
CHOIRS
CONCERT
BENEFIT BOOKS ROCKIN FESTIVALS
LASER SPECIAL
MARATHON PARADE BALLET POWER LUNCH
FIREWORKS FESTIVAL
RIVERFEST ALL-STAR BAND
CELEBRATE
FANTASTIC PARK BLAST SHRINERS
BASH POSTERS SPIRIT POLES
CENTENARIANS
LUNCHEON
SCULPT

OKLAHOMA
'07
CENTENNIAL

TULSA KICKOFF
TO THE CENTENNIAL CELEBRATION

An 11-day commencement to
Oklahoma's statehood celebration featured
concerts, parades, art shows,
fireworks, films and festivals.
It all took place in Tulsa,
the city designated the official host
for Oklahoma's

CENTENNIAL YEAR
KICKOFF

For 11 days in November, Tulsa put on a party that had the entire town rockin'. The "Tulsa Kickoff of the Oklahoma Centennial" consisted of 25 events that included a downtown parade, Kids World, performances by Blue Man Group, Tony Bennett and Carrie Underwood, a Tulsa Ballet world premiere, a youth art show, RiverFest, Best Fest, a film festival, the Route 66 marathon, a classic car parade and several concerts.

The abundance and diversity of activities attracted young and old alike, and the crowds came out in droves. For them, it was a once-in-a-lifetime opportunity to jumpstart the celebration of the century.

Capping off the kickoff festivities was a dazzling three-day fireworks extravaganza that utilized Tulsa's skyline as a stage. As rooftop pyrotechnics showered the sky, hundreds of computer-controlled moving lights and color-changing searchlights created beam effects and projected graphics onto the city's skyscrapers. The show was synchronized to music that was broadcast over a local radio station.

ON THE TOWN *Downtown Tulsa was transformed into an enormous theater on November 18, 2006, when the "Great State of Oklahoma Extravaganza" took center stage. A videotaped message from Gov.* **Brad Henry** *— which was projected on four massive screens, the largest of which measured 104' x 187' — set a tone of state pride for the dazzling 30-minute production that synchronized music, laser lights, fireworks and video images.*

NOT A BAD SEAT IN THE HOUSE *With more than a dozen downtown buildings serving as giant movie screens, every seat offered a spectacular view.*

HIGH NOTES *Toni Estes, a Tulsa native, kicked off the Extravaganza with a thrilling rendition of the national anthem from atop the Bernsen Building. American flags projected onto two giant screens added to the moment.*

A REALLY BIG SHOW *A forest of speakers and a radio simulcast over* **KTSO** *enabled more than 50,000 spectators to experience the Extravaganza outside or from their vehicles, while others at home watched over* **KQCW-TV**. *Behind the scenes, "command center" staff (from left)* **Jimmy Page**, **Walter Meador**, **Al Hornung** *and* **Lawrence Langva**, *produced the show to perfection.*

33

CENTENNIAL YEAR
KICKOFF

SPECIAL THANKS *to the **City of Tulsa** and Mayor **Kathy Taylor**; **American Electric Power-Public Service Company of Oklahoma**; downtown Tulsa building owners, engineers and electricians; **KTSO** radio; **KQCW-TV**; and the hundreds of crew members and volunteers who created the kickoff event of the century.*

APPLAUSE, APPLAUSE *Continuous cheering and thunderous applause accompanied the fast-moving multimedia event which earned national recognition for the Centennial celebration and the producers: Executive Producer **Gary Caimano**, **Celebrate Productions, Inc.**, Carrier, Oklahoma; Associate Producers **Jeff Olsen**, **Omni Lighting, Inc.**, Tulsa; and **Steve Frantz**, **Western Enterprises, Inc.**, also of Carrier.*

THE GOOD, THE BAD AND THE INCREDIBLE *"The Top 46 Events in Oklahoma Political History" was the focus of a "Power Lunch" hosted by* Oklahoma Today *magazine and the Tulsa Press Club in the historic Cain's Ballroom. The 2006 Statehood Day event informed and entertained some 350 guests. Tahlequah-based band* **My-Tea Kind** *–* **Sarah Garde**, **James Townsend**, *and* **Anna** *and* **Bonnie Paine** *– performed before the presentations.*

AND THE TOP 10 ARE ... *(right)* **Chad Smith**, *principal chief of the Cherokee Nation, was one of 12 speakers who presented the top 10 events that shaped Oklahoma. The daunting task of identifying not only the top 46 events, but also the top 10, was accomplished by Dr.* **Bob Blackburn**, **Danney Goble**, **Robert Henry**, **Ed Kelley** *and* **Randy Krehbiel**.

THEN AND NOW

Jenk Jones Jr., former Tulsa Tribune *publisher (far left), and Dr.* **JoAnn Haysbert,** *Langston University president (near left), were among the dozen speakers who used both humor and sensitivity to explain the significance of the selected historical events.*

THE SOONER SAID THE BETTER

Bob Davis, *executive director of Guthrie's Scottish Rite Masonic Center (near right), was dressed in period clothing when he discussed the state's Constitutional Convention. Judge* **Robert Henry** *(far right) provided opening remarks and served as one of the presenters.*

POWERING ON *(far left)*

Historian Dr. **John Wolf** *was among the prestigious speakers that also included Gov.* **Brad Henry,** *First Lady* **Kim Henry,** **Ed Kelley,** *Tulsa Mayor* **Kathy Taylor,** **Mike Turpen, George Watts** *and* **Burns Hargis.** *In closing,* **Louisa McCune-Elmore** *(near left),* Oklahoma Today *editor, urged guests to "power on" into Oklahoma's promising future.*

CENTENNIAL YEAR
KICKOFF

A CENTURY OF MEMORIES *(right) Alfred Adams escorts his parents, Bertha and Roy Adams, both 101 years of age. The Pryor residents, who passed away in spring 2008, were recognized as having the longest marriage in the nation. (bottom right) 101-year-old William Kennedy discusses M.J. Alexander's Centenarian photographs with his daughter Cathryn. (bottom left) Tulsa Historical Society volunteers Carmen Kinsey (left) and Phyllis Logsdon dressed in vintage clothing.*

WISDOM OF THE AGES *Oklahomans born before or during 1907 were honored on Statehood Day 2006 at a reception hosted by the Northeast Active Timers (NEATs) and held at the Tulsa Historical Society. Portraits of many of the honorees, known as Centenarians, graced the walls, and each of the special guests was recognized and shared a few thoughts – some serious, others humorous, all insightful.*

IN STYLE *Linda Greenshields* *(below) brought back memories with her display of period items. Centenarians* **Roy Adams**, **Martha Berryhill** *and* **Arnold Richardson** *(in back) enjoyed the presentation, part of the tribute to those Oklahomans whose longevity exceeded or equaled Oklahoma's.*

OFFICIAL RECOGNITION **Sarah Hawkins**, *a 101-year-old from Tulsa, was among Centenarians congratulated by Gov.* **Brad Henry** *and Tulsa Mayor* **Kathy Taylor** *(in back).*

ENERGETIC *(right)* **Thelma Leone Swisshelm Hopkins**, *100, of Tulsa exemplified the enduring spirit of her fellow Centenarians, many of whom are active members of their communities, churches or families.*

HONORING OUR ELDERS *Rev.* **Richard V. Ziglar** *(above) planned the reception and served as master of ceremonies, sharing information about each Centenarian and placing each in the spotlight. At left, two reception guests admire portraits conveying the dignity and determination of Oklahoma's Centenarians.*

Phyllis Frances Long
Benson Whitchurch
Age 102, Tulsa

Nora Owens Reed Simmons
Age 102, Tulsa

Roy Adams
Age 101, Pryor

Arnold B. Richardson
Age 100, Miami

Rose Agnes "Sudie"
Musgrove Clevenger
Age 99, Tulsa

Bertha Naomi Nalley Adams
Age 101, Pryor

Sarah Harmon Armstrong
Age 103, Okmulgee

Ocie Hughes
Age 101, Sapulpa

Jessie Mae Childs Carter
Age 100, Tulsa

Ellen Moore
Age 100, Bixby

Lula Ball Jennings
Age 102, Tulsa

Greta Cottrell
Woodson Storey
Saye Mill Heslet
Age 100, Tulsa

Martha May Berryhill
Age 106, Okmulgee

Sarah Hawkins
Age 101, Tulsa

Alclair Pleasant
Age 100, Tulsa

Ethel Rose Zamba Brockelbank
Age 100, Tulsa

Roy Elmore Giles
Age 104, Tulsa

Rev. Otis Granville Clark
Age 103, Tulsa

Ora Reed Holland
Age 105, Tulsa

John Howard Council
Age 100, Heavener

Margaret Moran
Age 100, Tulsa

Laura Hawkins
Age 100, Tulsa

Mary Pace
Age 100, Barnsdall

Marian Harrison Weimer
Age 99, Tulsa

Lucille Holman Wooden
Age 101, Tulsa

Elsie Chase Kilpatrick
Age 100, Tulsa

CENTENNIAL YEAR
KICKOFF

"OKIE DOKIE" *(left) Flag collector **Stephen "Okie Dokie" Smith** marched with an original Oklahoma state flag that he obtained from the State Capitol a decade ago. The red flag – displaying a large star with "46" inside, signifying Oklahoma as the 46th state – was replaced by the current flag in 1925.*

I LOVE A PARADE *Spectators lining Tulsa's Riverside Drive were treated to a two-hour parade bursting with Oklahoma pride and spirit. (below) Members of **Tulsa's Veterans of Foreign Wars, Post 577** were greeted with heartfelt cheers.*

PAWNEE BILL *Oklahoma's Centennial marked the 17th year that **Wayne Spears** has portrayed the legendary Wild West showman. Since his first appearance as Pawnee Bill in 1990, the now 70-year-old Spears has worn his hair to his shoulders and the familiar handlebar mustache. He's shown riding his beautiful horse, "Y."*

MISS TULSA 2007
Simone Mullinax smiles at the crowd during the parade.

STRIKE UP THE BAND (below) The 150-member **Oklahoma All★Star Centennial Band** made its public debut at the Tulsa Kickoff parade, the first of the band's dozen appearances across the state. The 45-entry parade was organized by Tulsa volunteer **Pat Kroblin** of **PK Promotions**.

HAPPY FACES (Clockwise from top) The beautiful costumes and vibrant music of the **Gypsy Fire Belly Dance of Tulsa** entertained Oklahoma families who bundled up for the brisk November weather. **Jim Dunne** was one of the **AKDAR Shriners of Tulsa** whose miniature motorcycle and car hijinks brought additional smiles to already happy faces.

CITY OF TULSA PIPES AND DRUMS The bagpipe music reflected Oklahoma's Celtic heritage. Musicians included Drum Major **Kenneth Smith** along with (background, left to right) **Bruce Mitchell**, **David Marshall** and **Max Tankersley**.

OKLAHOMA CENTENARIAN Rev. **Otis Clark**, 103, waves to the crowd lining Riverside Drive. Clark has served as an international evangelist for 80 years and he was one of 11 Centenarians who served as parade grand marshal.

(PONY) EXPRESS MAIL *With the kickoff drawing to a close, a rider readied to gallop off with a proclamation handing over the Centennial commemoration to the rest of the state. The kickoff set the stage for the most extensive state celebration in the nation's memory.*

SO MANY CHOICES *(right) Thanks to the careful planning of the Tulsa Kickoff Committee, the 11-day roster of events and activities offered something for Oklahomans of all ages and interests. Free or affordable admission ensured that everyone had an opportunity to participate.*

OKLAHOMA SPIRIT *Soaring some 20 feet, the multi-colored Oklahoma Centennial Spirit Poles – designed by Tulsan **Kerry Walsh** – symbolize the state's Native American heritage, leadership in energy and aerospace, and passion for the arts, all of which inspire the Oklahoma spirit of achievement and optimism.*

Tulsa Kick-off
of the Oklahoma Centennial

Don't miss this celebration of Oklahoma's first 100 years!

November 9-19, 2006

NOVEMBER 9TH – 12TH *Circle Cinema and Riverwalk*
Oklahoma Centennial Film Festival
NOVEMBER 9TH – 12TH *Expo Square*
Kids' World
NOVEMBER 9TH *Blank Slate*
TYPros Centennial Concert
NOVEMBER 10TH *Mabee Center*
Blue Man Group
NOVEMBER 10TH & 11TH *Tulsa Historical Society*
State of the Art:
Tulsa Artists Salute Oklahoma
NOVEMBER 10TH *Downtown Tulsa*
Veteran's Day Parade
NOVEMBER 11TH *Downtown Tulsa & Veteran's Park*
Tulsa Run
NOVEMBER 10TH – 12TH *Performing Arts Center*
Celebrate Oklahoma! Tulsa Ballet
NOVEMBER 12TH *Hispanic Resource Center at Martin Regional Library*
¡Latinos Presentes!
An Oklahoma Hispanic History Project
NOVEMBER 12TH *Boston Avenue Methodist Church*
We Sing Thy Praise
NOVEMBER 14TH *All Souls Unitarian Church*
Hyechka Club's Spirit of Oklahoma Winners' Concert
NOVEMBER 16TH *Greenwood Cultural Center*
Statehood Day Interfaith Prayer Breakfast
NOVEMBER 16TH *Tulsa Historical Society*
NEATs Centenarian Celebration
NOVEMBER 16TH *Cain's Ballroom*
Power Lunch:
The Top 46 Moments in Oklahoma Politics
NOVEMBER 16TH *96th Street Bridge*
"Welcome to Our Centennial" Fireworks
NOVEMBER 16TH *Renaissance Center*
Oklahoma Heritage Association Hall of Fame
NOVEMBER 16TH *Tulsa Air and Space Museum*
Centennial Youth Art Show
NOVEMBER 17TH *Riverfield Country Day School*
Red Dirt Rangers Salute Oklahoma Musicians
NOVEMBER 17TH-19TH *East & West Banks of the Arkansas River*
Oklahoma Best Fest and RiverFest
NOVEMBER 17TH *21st Street Bridge*
"Tulsa Tribute" Fireworks QT
NOVEMBER 17TH *Brady Theater*
Air Supply Concert
NOVEMBER 18TH *Riverside Drive – 45th to 21st*
The Parade of a Century!
NOVEMBER 18TH *Downtown Tulsa*
"The Great State of Oklahoma Extravaganza"
Light Show, Fireworks and Centennial Gala
NOVEMBER 19TH *Mabee Center*
Tony Bennett's Birthday Salute to Oklahoma
NOVEMBER 19TH *Route 66*
Tulsa World Route 66 Marathon
and Classic Car Parade

Tulsa Spirit.
OKLAHOMA
'07
CENTENNIAL

For more information
visit our website at
oklahomacentennialtulsa.com
Or contact our office at (918) 619-6098

TALENT TO SHARE *(left) A four-day film festival featured more than 20 films by, about or starring Oklahomans. Lectures and discussions by producers, directors and actors such as Tulsa native* **Tim Blake Nelson** *(right) added insight.* **Clark Wiens** *(left) of Circle Cinema hosted the festival, which was organized by* **Barbara VanHanken***.*

THE SOUND OF MUSIC

(left) A birthday salute to Oklahoma featured one of the legends of jazz and popular music, **Tony Bennett***. Preceding him on stage were nearly 100 members of the* **Tulsa Children's Chorus***, who sang several selections. The Bennett concert was one of eight musical events located throughout the city. A concert series arranged by volunteer* **Tony Winters***, manager of the Mabee Center, also included a sold-out performance by the internationally acclaimed* **Blue Man Group***.*

CENTENNIAL LEADERS

(right) Tulsa Oklahoma Centennial Director **Paula Hale** *(left) and chairs* **Sharon King Davis** *and* **Don Walker** *oversaw a myriad of Tulsa Centennial projects, including the kickoff.*

OKLAHOMA IMAGES *Students with winning images of Oklahoma received congratulations from Gov.* **Brad Henry** *and Tulsa Mayor* **Kathy Taylor** *at the Youth Art Show ceremony: Top, left to right:* **John Powell***,* **David Wassall***,* **Oscar Rodriquez***,* **Michelle Solomon** *and* **Elizabeth Lee***. Bottom, left to right:* **Melissa Oxford***,* **Gary Arauz***,* **LeeAnn Downey***,* **Jennifer Randolph***,* **Rebecca Brown***, Gov. Henry,* **Kristen Nevels***, Mayor Taylor,* **Raiyan Naytah** *and* **Zia Bowles***. Volunteer* **Barbara Smallwood** *organized the competition.*

By Jessica Shenoi

By Gary Arauz

By LeeAnn Downey

By Michelle Solomon (Best of Show)

CENTENNIAL YEAR
KICKOFF

IN GOOD FAITH *(left to right)* ***George Calvin McCutchen Jr.***, *Rev.* ***Victor Orta II***, *Pastor* ***Mouzon Biggs Jr.*** *and* ***Don Walker*** *were among the more than 350 people who gathered in the Greenwood Cultural Center on Statehood morning 2006 for an interfaith prayer breakfast sponsored by the Oklahoma Conference for Community and Justice.*

FELLOWSHIP *Chaired by* ***Nancy Day***, *the event brought together faith communities from throughout Oklahoma.* ***Clayton Vaughn***, *former newscaster (at left), served as master of ceremonies. (from left) Rev.* ***Victor Orta II***, *Rev.* ***Martin Lavanhar***, *Dr.* ***Sandra Kaye Rana*** *and former Tulsa Public Schools Director of Indian Education* ***Archie Mason*** *offered prayers for Oklahoma's new century.*

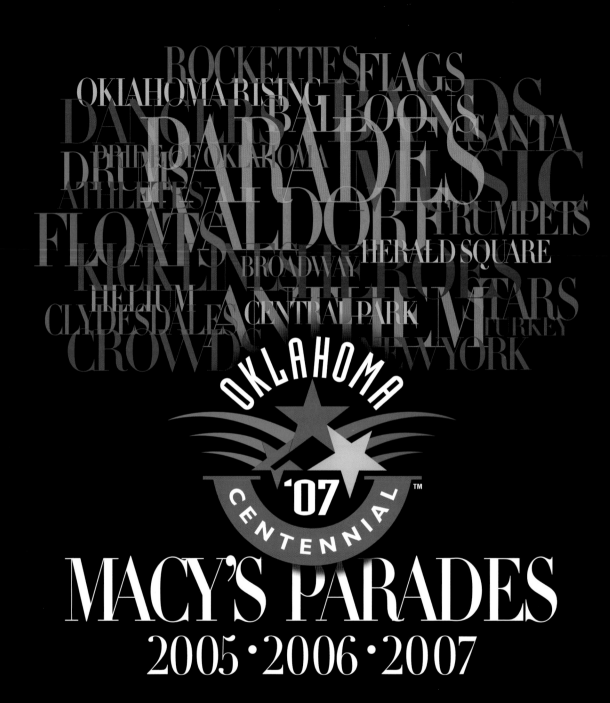

MACY'S PARADES
2005 · 2006 · 2007

For three consecutive years,
the state of Oklahoma has proudly marched down
New York's famed Broadway, passing Central Park
through Times Square, in the legendary

MACY'S
THANKSGIVING DAY
PARADES

KRISTIN CHENOWETH *This Oklahoma City University graduate and Tony Award-winning actress sang "Oklahoma!" and was one of the many celebrities and dignitaries aboard the "Oklahoma Rising" float.*

HERALD SQUARE *The Macy's Parade marches down Broadway and turns west on 34th Street, just past Herald Square. Forming the intersection of Broadway, Sixth Avenue and 34th, Herald Square is named for the **New York Herald**, a newspaper originally headquartered there. Today, it's a retail hub whose most notable attraction is the Macy's flagship department store, the largest in the United States.*

It's as much a Thanksgiving Day tradition as the turkey itself. Since 1924, the Macy's Parade has taken to the streets of New York, delighting first-time visitors and regulars alike with a spectacular annual showing on Thanksgiving morning.

Oklahoma's first appearance in the Macy's Parade in 2005 was history-making: it debuted the first float to ever represent an entire state. "Oklahoma Rising" commemorated the upcoming Centennial and featured celebrities riding in a covered wagon pulled by eight Express Clydesdale horses.

For 2006, the state made its second of three appearances. Multi-Grammy Award-winner Sandi Patty performed the new Oklahoma Centennial anthem, "Oklahoma Rising." Other renowned musical artists and athletes from the state joined in the celebration. The final year, 2007, featured the Pride of Oklahoma, University of Oklahoma's marching band performing under the direction of Brian Britt.

ONE WAY

W 35th St
Herald Square

HERALD SQ
West 35th St

HOMETOWN SUPPORT *Many Oklahoma officials and citizens made the trek to New York City in support of the state's parade appearance. Shown here are* **Donna Wade, J. Blake Wade,** *executive director of the Oklahoma Centennial Commission, and* **Scotty Kramer.**

THE MAN WHO MADE IT HAPPEN *Lee Allan Smith, shown here with his wife* **DeAnn,** *was the chairman of projects and events for the Oklahoma Centennial Commission. It was Smith's original vision that led to the state's participation in this prestigious parade.*

"OKLAHOMA RISING" *The state's official Centennial float debuts in the 2005 Macy's Parade. Shown turning the corner at Herald Square, the 55-foot-long float was pulled by the* **Express Clydesdales,** *an eight-horse team that traveled from their stable in Yukon.*

THANKSGIVING DAY
MACY'S PARADE
2005

ALL ABOARD! *Getting ready to ride on "Oklahoma Rising" were (top photo)* **Gena Howard** *and* **Shannon Miller,** *(middle)* **Leona Mitchell** *and* **Bobby Murcer,** *and* **Johnny Bench** *(bottom).*

OKLAHOMA ON BROADWAY *Displaying a large Centennial logo, the Oklahoma float honored the state's contributions to aerospace, arts, medicine, science and sports. An oversized sun represented the Centennial year theme, Oklahoma Rising. Preceding the float was a covered wagon filled with Oklahoma personalities (left to right):* **Gena Howard,** *director of the American Indian Cultural Center and Museum,* **Laura Savini Webb** *(wife of Jimmy Webb),* **Bobby Murcer** *and* **Barry Switzer**. *The two drivers are Macy's parade officials.*

THE EXPRESS CLYDESDALES *This locally owned team of Clydesdales pulled the Oklahoma caravan. The horses are owned by* **Express Personnel Services** *founder and CEO* **Bob Funk** *and managed by* **Josh Minshull***. The team makes more than 80 appearances each year and was named the Eight-Horse Hitch World Champions at the 2007 World Clydesdale Show, with Minshull taking home best driver honors.*

GREETING A YANKEE GREAT *One of New York's finest meets one of the New York Yankees' finest.* **Bobby Murcer,** *an Oklahoma native who became one of the most beloved Yankees of all time, takes a moment during the parade to say hello to a New York City policeman and baseball fan.*

A FAN FAVORITE *With his long and successful career – including a stint at one of America's most popular teams –* **Barry Switzer** *is a crowd pleaser wherever he goes. Here, the former Dallas Cowboys and University of Oklahoma football coach waves to the parade-goers.*

MACY'S VOLUNTEERS
Horse handlers are shown here with the **Express Clydesdales'** *traveling hitch. More than 40 rare black-and-white Clydesdales are housed at* **Express Ranches** *in Yukon.*

THANKSGIVING DAY
MACY'S PARADE
2005

GREETINGS FROM NYC *Oklahoma residents (below, left to right)* **Homer** *and* **Ramona Paul** *and* **Gerald** *and* **Jane Jayroe Gamble** *enjoy their home state's historic moment in the parade. Shown at right:* **Jeannette Sias***.*

CENTENNIAL SPONSORS *Major sponsors of the Oklahoma Centennial included the* **Williams family:** **Jim***,* **Jill** *and their daughter,* **Alexandria***.*

JIMMY WEBB *Many Oklahoma supporters stayed at the Waldorf Astoria, a New York City landmark. Providing entertainment during the post-parade brunch was none other than Oklahoma native Webb.*

MORE LOCAL SUPPORT *The Oklahoma contingent also included* **Becky Switzer,** *who was in attendance with her husband,* **Barry**.

THANKSGIVING BRUNCH *Attendees included (top photo) The* Oklahoman *publisher* **David Thompson** *and* **Jennifer Kiersch** *of OK Events, (above)* **Laura Savini Webb, Jimmy Webb, Jane Jayroe Gamble** *and* **Gerald Gamble,** *(far left)* **Mary Lou Casper,** *and (left)* **Kristin Chenoweth** *and* **Lee Allan Smith**.

THANKSGIVING DAY
MACY'S PARADE
2006

A TRIUMPHANT RETURN *The rains of 2006 couldn't keep the state of Oklahoma away. Nor could it dampen the spirit and enthusiasm of those participating, including* **Sandi Patty** *(in pink), who debuted a moving rendition of the new Oklahoma Centennial anthem, "Oklahoma Rising."*

THE CLYDESDALES ARE COMING *The Oklahoma float was once again pulled by the* **Express Clydesdales**. *They're stabled at* **Bob Funk's Express Ranches** – *an internationally recognized working ranch with one of the most extensive purebred operations in North America.*

TELEVISED LIVE *(right) More than 44 million people watch the Macy's Parade on television each year. Since 1955, NBC has been the official broadcaster of the event — the 2006 telecast was hosted by* **Meredith Vieira, Matt Lauer** *and* **Al Roker** *(not shown).*

SANDI PATTY *(above) Known simply as "The Voice," Patty is one of the biggest stars in Christian contemporary music. She earned three platinum albums, five gold albums, 33 Dove Awards and five Grammys over a 15-year period. Born in Oklahoma City, Patty made her performing debut singing "Jesus Loves Me" in church at the age of two.*

BART CONNER AND NADIA COMANECI *(left) Riding along on the Oklahoma float were Olympic gold medal-winning gymnasts, the husband-and-wife team of Conner and Comaneci.*

TURKEY FLOAT *(right) What's Thanksgiving without the turkey? This traditional float ushers in and celebrates the November holiday.*

JOHN SMITH *(above) A successful college wrestler who currently coaches wrestling at his alma mater, Oklahoma State University, Smith was joined by Macy's volunteers (riding in back) and other noted Oklahoma athletes including BMX rider* **Mat Hoffman** *and baseball legend* **Joe Carter** *(not shown).*

THANKSGIVING DAY
MACY'S PARADE
2007

THE PRIDE OF OKLAHOMA
*The 2007 Macy's Thanksgiving Day Parade featured the University of Oklahoma marching band, the **Pride of Oklahoma**. The band arrived in New York on Monday, early enough to allow plenty of practice and sightseeing time before Thursday's main event.*

MARCHING IN THE RAIN *Under the supervision of OU band director **Brian Britt** (in far left of photo), drum major **Chauvin Aaron** (on ladder and in photos at left) lead band members in one final, damp practice.*

A FINAL DRESS REHEARSAL *The night before the parade, the band tuned up one last time at Herald Square. It was a full dress rehearsal used for perfecting formations, marching and timing.*

HEADING FOR THE SUBWAY
The band finally called it a night and entered the subway to take a short ride back to their hotel. Next up: the Macy's Thanksgiving Day Parade!

THANKSGIVING DAY
MACY'S PARADE
2007

DRUMROLL PLEASE *Pride members freshman **Ryan Martin**, sophomore **Jeff Garza**, senior **Paige Bannecker** and junior **Andrew Boes** (front row, front to back) get ready to march the two-and-a-half mile route.*

GO BIG RED *As a highlight of their Macy's appearance, **the Pride of Oklahoma** debuted new all-red uniform coats, shown left on senior **Josh Johnson**. (The previous red coats were retired seven years ago after band director **Gene Thrailkill's** retirement in 2000.) The new coats feature an interlocking "OU" logo on the front in white parquet, with "OKLAHOMA" on the sleeves in white embroidery.*

IT'S SHOWTIME! *Almost two hours into the parade and the University of Oklahoma marching band's big moment was finally at hand. They played the school fight song in Times Square while avid Sooner fans celebrated their school's first appearance in the famed parade.*

FLAG CORPS *Carrying flags for the Pride are (above, left to right) sophomore **Maile Naone**, senior **Beth Powell**, junior **Alyssa Krase**, senior **Lacey Taylor** and sophomore **Gina Hooper**. The baton twirler is **Meredith Sigler**, a senior.*

THANKSGIVING DAY
MACY'S PARADE
2007

BOOMER SOONER *More than 300 university marching band members represented the state and the Centennial in 2007. They alternately performed "Oklahoma!" and "Boomer Sooner" and on this day were truly, the Pride of Oklahoma.*

OKLAHOMA RISING

ANTHEM

As the curtain rose in the Civic Center,
the crowd waited in anticipation
for the debut of the song that was created
solely for the Centennial.

"OKLAHOMA RISING" ANTHEM PREMIERE

A SMASH DEBUT *The 2,500 in attendance at the Civic Center were treated to the first public performance of "Oklahoma Rising."*

The crowd gathered at Oklahoma City's Civic Center Music Hall to witness history: the introduction of Oklahoma's Centennial anthem. Created as a complement to Rodgers and Hammerstein's *Oklahoma!*, it marked the first collaboration between Grammy Award winner Jimmy Webb and Country Music Hall of Fame legend Vince Gill.

"The song is a tribute to Oklahoma's history," said Gill, an Oklahoma City native. He wrote the music while Elk City native Webb wrote the lyrics. The song starts off with Native Amercian flutes and chants from Bill Miller, a Mohican Indian, and goes on to paint a portrait of a state hitting its stride as it enters its second century.

Gill and Webb performed the song accompanied by the Oklahoma City Philharmonic. The evening also featured special appearances by Sandi Patty, Reverend Joseph Bias, the Canterbury Choral Society and the Ambassadors' Concert Choir.

"Oklahoma Rising" became part of a limited edition two-disc, 46-track commemorative Centennial compilation.

CENTENNIAL SUITE *Jimmy Webb also debuted a 16-minute musical composition, "Oklahoma Rising: The Centennial Suite." He was accompanied by the **Oklahoma City Philharmonic** under the direction of Maestro **Joel Levine** (shaking hands with Webb at right). A 30-foot screen above the stage displayed rotating images of Oklahoma, past and present, courtesy of **CorporateMagic**.*

"OKLAHOMA RISING"
Although they had known each other for years, the Centennial anthem marked the first collaboration between Oklahoma natives Jimmy Webb and Vince Gill. The song embodies the pride that so many Oklahomans feel for their state.

THE ROUSING FINALE *"Oklahoma Rising" was greeted with an enthusiastic response from the standing-room-only audience. It was an electrifying end to a memorable evening.*

SPECIAL GUESTS *The evening featured an appearance by Sandi Patty (near left), one of the most recognizable and distinctive voices in Christian music. She returned to her hometown of Oklahoma City for the evening and sang "I Hear a Song," "America the Beautiful" and "God Bless America." Also making an appearance was Reverend Joseph Bias (far left) of the First United Methodist Church in Tulsa.*

FACES IN THE CROWD *(above) In attendance were prominent Oklahoma City residents including Lisa Cornett, Mayor Mick Cornett, Nancy Leonard, Tim Leonard, Clark Nye, Polly Nichols, Suzanne Spradling, Scott Spradling, Jackie Cooper, Barbara Cooper, Jeaneen Naifeh, Bob Naifeh, Stan Hupfeld and Mary Cole.*

"OKLAHOMA RISING" ANTHEM

JIMMY WEBB *(below) Tapped to write the lyrics for Oklahoma's new anthem, this son of an Elk City Baptist minister made his first public appearance as a performer playing the organ at church. In an early sign of things to come, he improvised, rearranged and re-harmonized the hymns.*

VINCE GILL *(left) Serving as the evening's emcee, Gill was no stranger to the task, having hosted the nationally televised CMA Awards numerous times. Thanks to his quick wit and affable demeanor, the singer, songwriter, producer and musician has become the unofficial ambassador of country music – and quite possibly of Oklahoma, as well.*

BILL MILLER *(below) Presenting flute accompaniment to both the Centennial Suite and "Oklahoma Rising" was Miller, a longtime friend of* **Vince Gill** *and a member of the Mohican tribe.*

ENCORE! ENCORE! *(above) Accepting well-deserved applause are (left to right)* **Bill Miller** *(behind Gill),* **Vince Gill, Joel Levine, Benny Garcia** *(behind Patty),* **Sandi Patty,** *Reverend* **Joseph Bias, Jimmy Webb, Dawn Sears,** *the* **Oklahoma City Philharmonic** *and the* **Canterbury Choral Society.**

THE AFTER PARTY *(left) Joining together for post-concert festivities were* **Blake** *and* **Donna Wade, Lee Allan Smith, Jennifer Kiersch, DeAnn Smith** *and* **Vince Gill.**

We're Oklahoma Risin',
brighter than a star –
Stand up and sing about her,
let the world know who we are

From a rugged territory
to the Oklahoma Run,
We've made our dreams come true,
just look at what we've done
We're the Heartland of America,
our heart is in the race
We've sailed our prairie schooners
right into outer space
We are young and we are strong,
we are comin' with a roar
Sooner than later
we'll be knockin' on your door
Say hello to the future,
gonna shake the future's hand
and build a better world
upon this sacred, ancient land

CHORUS
We're Oklahoma Risin', brighter than a star
Stand up and sing about her
let the world know who we are
We're the sons and the daughters,
children of the West
We're Oklahoma Risin',
risin' up to be the best!

Guts and grace and mercy,
we have shown them in our turn
When the fields had turned to dust
and the skies began to burn
When the storm shook our souls
and the mighty buildings fell
Through fires and desperation
our faith has served us well
I choke back the emotion,
I'm an Okie and I'm proud
So when you call me Okie, man,
you better say it loud
Now we look into the heavens
at the eagle climbing free
It's the spirit of our people
on the wing, can you see?

REPEAT CHORUS

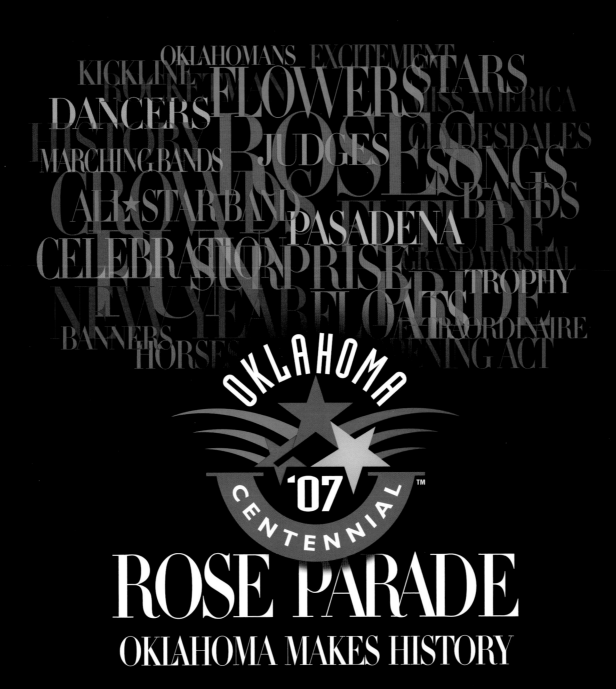

OKLAHOMANS EXCITEMENT
KICKLINE FLOWERS STARS
DANCERS MISS AMERICA
HISTORY ROSES JUDGES CLYDESDALES
MARCHING BANDS SONGS
CROWD ALL★STAR BAND BANDS
CELEBRATION PASADENA
SURPRISE GRAND MARSHAL
NEW YEAR FLOATS TROPHY
BANNERS EXTRAORDINAIRE
HORSES OPENING ACT

ROSE PARADE

OKLAHOMA MAKES HISTORY

OKLAHOMA
'07
CENTENNIAL™

Just a few hours into its Centennial year celebration,
Oklahoma was already making national headlines
with a show-starting – and show-*stopping* – performance
in the 118th edition of the famed

TOURNAMENT OF
ROSES
PARADE

Televised live from Pasadena to millions of viewers worldwide, the New Year's Day Rose Parade was Oklahoma's Centennial coming-out party. As the state took center stage in the nation's grandest parade, it became the first entity ever in the storied tradition to present more than one float.

The spectacular opening number featured Oklahomans past and present, and included the Oklahoma All★Star Centennial Band, the only band in the history of the Rose Parade to perform in the opening ceremonies. Oklahoma's two floats soon followed. "A Unique History" came sweeping down Colorado Boulevard led by an eight-horse team of black-and-white Express Clydesdales who pulled the "surrey with the fringe on top." The float featured iconic Oklahoma images including an American Indian headdress, flowing waters, a lasso twirling Will Rogers, an American bison, an oil well, cowboy boots, a grove of redbuds and the Centennial logo.

Next up, "Oklahoma Rising" honored the state's contributions to aerospace, arts, medicine, science and sports. Adorning this second float were animated stars, a rotating birthday cake (hiding a special surprise), a spinning sun kaleidoscope and the state name spelled out in 5- to 10-foot-tall letters made of mainly roses.

THE BUILDING PROCESS *Like all the Rose Parade floats, Oklahoma's two entries were designed and constructed by professional builders. Taking up to a year to create, they were built in large warehouses using a wide variety of materials and construction techniques.*

FIRST INSPECTION *On hand to view the early proceedings were **David** and **Jane Thompson** and **Lee Allan** and **DeAnn Smith**.*

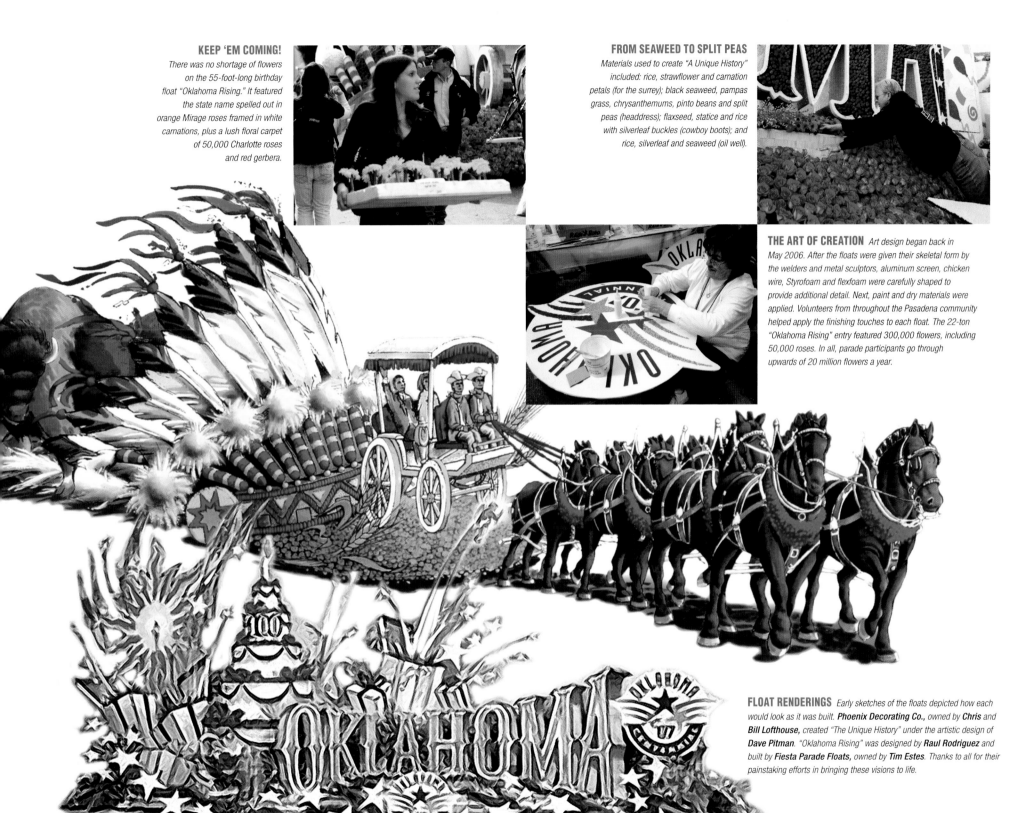

KEEP 'EM COMING!
There was no shortage of flowers on the 55-foot-long birthday float "Oklahoma Rising." It featured the state name spelled out in orange Mirage roses framed in white carnations, plus a lush floral carpet of 50,000 Charlotte roses and red gerbera.

FROM SEAWEED TO SPLIT PEAS
Materials used to create "A Unique History" included: rice, strawflower and carnation petals (for the surrey); black seaweed, pampas grass, chrysanthemums, pinto beans and split peas (headdress); flaxseed, statice and rice with silverleaf buckles (cowboy boots); and rice, silverleaf and seaweed (oil well).

THE ART OF CREATION Art design began back in May 2006. After the floats were given their skeletal form by the welders and metal sculptors, aluminum screen, chicken wire, Styrofoam and flexfoam were carefully shaped to provide additional detail. Next, paint and dry materials were applied. Volunteers from throughout the Pasadena community helped apply the finishing touches to each float. The 22-ton "Oklahoma Rising" entry featured 300,000 flowers, including 50,000 roses. In all, parade participants go through upwards of 20 million flowers a year.

FLOAT RENDERINGS Early sketches of the floats depicted how each would look as it was built. **Phoenix Decorating Co.,** owned by **Chris** and **Bill Lofthouse,** created "The Unique History" under the artistic design of **Dave Pitman**. "Oklahoma Rising" was designed by **Raul Rodriguez** and built by **Fiesta Parade Floats,** owned by **Tim Estes**. Thanks to all for their painstaking efforts in bringing these visions to life.

ROSE PARADE

EXPRESS CLYDESDALES *Standing 17 hands high and weighing more than a ton each, this national award-winning hitch team led Oklahoma's "A Unique History" float. The team is part of a 40-horse herd owned by* **Bob Funk,** *the founder and CEO of Oklahoma-based* **Express Personnel Services.**

LET THE JUDGING BEGIN

A three-member panel evaluated the floats within a range of classifications. Criteria included floral craftsmanship, artistic merit, computerized animation and dramatic impact. Two judging sessions took place during the decorating stages and the results were released immediately prior to the start of the parade. Twenty-four entries in the 2007 Rose Parade – including Oklahoma – received official honors.

OFFICIAL FLOAT PINS *It's a long-standing Rose Parade tradition to have a custom lapel pin made for each entry that appears in the festivities. To commemorate its appearance, Oklahoma created four different pin designs.*

UP CLOSE AND PERSONAL
(below) **Hardy Watkins,** *executive director of Oklahoma Tourism and Recreation Department, his wife* **Kari,** *executive director of the Oklahoma City National Memorial, along with their children,* **Caroline** *and* **Ford,** *examine the craftsmanship of 20-foot-tall cowboy boots.*

THE GRAND MARSHAL
(right) "Star Wars" creator **George Lucas** *served as grand marshal of the 2007 parade. He was joined here by opera star* **Leona Mitchell,** *Miss America 1981* **Susan Powell** *and Miss America 1967* **Jane Jayroe Gamble**.

NEW YEAR'S DAY 2007
ROSE PARADE

A ROSE PARADE WELCOME *(right) The reigning Miss America,* **Jennifer Berry,** *rode alongside* **Paul Holman,** *2007 Tournament of Roses president. After being introduced by Oklahoma native* **James Garner,** *Berry wished the crowd a Happy New Year and spoke of her appreciation in having her home state kick off the parade festivities.*

AMERICAN SPIRIT DANCE COMPANY *This nationally acclaimed troupe from* **Oklahoma City University** *joined the* **Oklahoma All★Star Centennial Band** *for the parade's opening number, which featured OCU graduate* **Kristin Chenoweth.** *A total of 34 dancers participated under the direction of* **Jo Rowan,** *chair of the OCU dance department, and performed choreography by* **Suzie Lalone** *of Orlando and staging by* **Chase Senge,** *both formerly with Walt Disney World in Orlando.*

KRISTIN CHENOWETH *This Broken Arrow native and Tony Award-winning Broadway star performed "Our Good Nature" in the two-minute opening ceremony. The original score was penned for the parade's 2007 theme, and was the first-ever theme composition in the parade's 118-year history.*

OKLAHOMA SUPPORTERS
*Special guests who rode in the balloon with **Chenoweth** were **Alexandria Williams** and **Megan Szymanski.***

OPENING OF THE PARADE *The Rose Parade's opening performance was produced by **Michael Davis** and **Charles Jones II**. Davis was a former conductor of the Walt Disney World Band and Orchestra, and he directed the **Oklahoma All★Star Centennial Band**. Jones was a live entertainment production consultant to the Walt Disney World theme park division.*

ROSE PARADE

THE OKLAHOMA ALL★STAR CENTENNIAL BAND

A marching unit created solely for Oklahoma's Centennial, this band was comprised of 150 high school musicians from across the state – one drum major, 96 brass, 21 percussion, 30 woodwinds and two banner carriers. Serving as the lead band for the Rose Parade, they marched along the streets of Pasadena for six miles.

GLOBAL EXPOSURE

An estimated one million spectators lined the Pasadena parade route. Watching at home was a U.S. television audience comprised of nearly 40 million viewers. The parade was broadcast to 150 international territories.

EXPERIENCED LEADERSHIP

*The **Oklahoma All★Star Centennial Band** was led by veteran talents including Director **Michael Davis** (right) and Assistant Director **Robyn Hilger** (next to band, on left). Not shown: Associate Director **Gary E. Smith**.*

PRAISE FROM THE PRESIDENT

*"One of the best bands I've ever heard."
That was 2007 Tournament of Roses
President **Paul Holman's** declaration
after hearing the **Oklahoma All★Star
Centennial Band** perform.*

OKLAHOMA'S AMBASSADORS
The *Oklahoma All★Star Centennial Band* served as musical ambassadors for the state during Oklahoma's Centennial celebration. Their journey lasted nearly a year, and the Rose Parade was their second official performance.

CHARLES JONES II *The Oklahoma All★Star Centennial Band* producer is a native Oklahoman and was the founder of the State Fair of Oklahoma High School Honor Band. He went on to work at the Walt Disney Company before forming his own company, Fresh Ideas Entertainment, which is responsible for the video production of all Magic Music Days entertainment at Walt Disney World and Disneyland.

NEW YEAR'S DAY 2007
ROSE PARADE

FAVORITE SONS AND DAUGHTERS
*(left) Oklahoma celebrities riding aboard the "A Unique History" float included **Barry Switzer**, **Patti Page** and **James Garner**. Shown below (left to right) are Miss America 1981 **Susan Powell**, baseball great **Johnny Bench** and gymnasts **Nadia Comaneci**, **Bart Conner** and **Shannon Miller**.*

HOMETOWN SUPPORT *(above) A contingency of 500-plus Oklahomans traveled to Pasadena to cheer on their home state's participation in the parade. On hand were Centennial sponsors (left to right) **Sally Saunders**, **Cathy Freede**, **Bill Shdeed**, **Jose Freede** and **Pam Shdeed**.*

THE PAST ON PARADE *Oklahoma's rich American Indian, western and oil heritages were represented in the form of an Indian headdress, an oil derrick and a lasso-twirling cowboy in the likeness of Will Rogers.*

ALONG FOR THE RIDE *(right) Enjoying the crowds were Miss America 1981* **Susan Powell** *and Metropolitan Opera soprano* **Leona Mitchell**.

MISS AMERICA AND MORE *Still others riding aboard "A Unique History" included Miss America 1967* **Jane Jayroe Gamble** *(below), plus baseball Hall of Famer* **Johnny Bench**; *Olympic Gold Medalists* **Nadia Comaneci, Bart Conner** *and* **Shannon Miller**; *Emmy Award-winning actor* **James Garner**; *Pro Rodeo Hall of Famer* **Clem McSpadden**; *legendary music artist* **Patti Page**; *former Dallas Cowboys and three-time NCAA Championship University of Oklahoma head coach* **Barry Switzer**; **Jack and Bill Thorpe,** *sons of America's greatest overall athlete Jim Thorpe; and multi-Grammy Award-winning composer* **Jimmy Webb**.

OKLAHOMA: EXTRAORDINAIRE! *Led by the* **Express Clydesdales,** *the state's "A Unique History" float received the prestigious Extraordinaire Trophy, an award that is recognized as one of the Rose Parade's top honors.*

NEW YEAR'S DAY 2007
ROSE PARADE

REPRESENTING THEIR HOME STATE *(below) Waving to the crowd are (left to right) "Desperate Housewives" creator* **Marc Cherry,** *columnist* **Argus Hamilton,** *Hollywood producer* **Hunt Lowry** *and casting agent* **Junie Lowry-Johnson.**

THE STARS COME OUT *(above) Oklahoma's first Rose Parade appearance brought out a host of celebrities including Miss America 2006* **Jennifer Berry** *(far left); Gov. and Mrs.* **Brad Henry** *and their daughters* **Laynie, Baylee** *and* **Leah;** *and astronaut* **John Herrington.**

THE FLAMING LIPS *Acclaimed for their elaborate concerts which feature costumes, balloons and confetti, The Flaming Lips appearance at the Rose Parade was a natural fit. Shown above are two of the band members,* **Michael Ivins** *and* **Wayne Coyne.**

HAPPY BIRTHDAY, OKLAHOMA!
No birthday celebration is complete without a cake and gifts, and this Centennial float presents those in larger-than-life form.

HOMETOWN PRIDE *(left) Oklahoma representatives included Miss America 2006* **Jennifer Berry,** *Gov.* **Brad Henry,** *First Lady* **Kim Henry** *and* **Marc Cherry.**

A ROSE PARADE FIRST *No float had ever before stopped in the Rose Bowl parade – but "Oklahoma Rising" did just that, allowing* **Dan Schlund** *to emerge from one of the gift boxes via hydraulic lift. From there, a jet pack powered* **"Rocketman"** *up over the parade route for 100 yards, where he landed smoothly and pulled out an Oklahoma Centennial flag to wave to the crowd. This surprise performance was a real crowd-pleaser and the hit of the 2007 parade.*

NEW YEAR'S DAY 2007
ROSE PARADE

ENJOYING THE EVENING *(right, top photo)* **Clem McSpadden** and **Patti Page**. *(second from top)* **Donna Nigh, Denise Bode, Leona Mitchell, Elmer Bush** and **John Bode**. *(third from top)* **Lisa Cornett,** *Oklahoma City Mayor* **Mick Cornett, Jim Williams** *(in back),* **Carol Hansen** and **Vera Taylor**.

NEW YEAR'S GALA *A group of approximately 500 Oklahomans – including sponsors, members of the media, event staffs and government officials – traveled to Pasadena for the Tournament of Roses festivities. Many attended the float judging the morning prior to the parade, and a New Year's Eve party was held later that evening. The first day of 2007 brought the 118th edition of the Rose Parade, followed by a post-parade brunch and, later in the evening, a watch party for the Fiesta Bowl, featuring a matchup between the* **University of Oklahoma** *and Boise State.*

The New Year's Eve gala featured **The Oak Ridge Boys** *(above) and* **The Larry "T-Byrd" Gordon Band** *(below).*

SPECIAL THANKS *to* **New Leaf Floral, Eventures** *and* **Toucan Lighting**.

HAPPY NEW YEAR! *(left, third photo from bottom)* **Nancy deCordova,** *Lt. Gov.* **Jari Askins, Tom McDaniel, Jane Jayroe Gamble, Bob Naifeh** *and* **Art Cotton** *(in back). (left, second from bottom)* **Jim Brewer, Barry Switzer, Bill Saxon** *and former Gov.* **George Nigh**. *(left, bottom)* **Jeaneen Naifeh, Leona Mitchell, Elmer Bush, Bob Naifeh, DeLee Smith, Juli Lyles** *and* **DeAnn Smith**. *(right)* **Nadia Comaneci** *and* **Bart Conner**.

THE CENTENNIAL PARADE

CELEBRATING 100 YEARS

They came from all 77 counties and every corner of the state.
Bands, performance groups, spirit squads,
Native American dancers, rodeo queens, square dancers, athletes,
musicians, Miss Americas, celebrities and politicians –
all gathered together for one momentous occasion,
one memorable celebration.

THE CENTENNIAL
PARADE

More than 175,000 spectators lined the downtown Oklahoma City streets of Hudson, Sheridan, Northwest 8th and Broadway. Another 25,000 looked on from buildings, hotels and parking garages. One hundred and seventy thousand more had their TV sets tuned to the live coverage on OETA.

What they saw was the largest parade in Oklahoma history. One-and-a-half miles and two hours that showcased more than 3,400 participants from all areas of the state. Included were 11 floats, 13 giant, helium-filled balloons, a dozen marching bands, seven animal groups, vintage cars and wagons, plus confetti, music and dancing.

From a dazzling opening production number featuring Oklahoma's five living Miss Americas to the Rocketman's spectacular 30-second airborne finale, this grand event gloriously celebrated all aspects of Oklahoma's first 100 years of statehood.

HERE THEY COME, MISS AMERICAS
(left) The Centennial Parade kicked off with a flourish of fanfare that brought all of the Oklahoma Miss America royalty – along with the **Oklahoma City University American Spirit Dance** troupe – together in an introductory number.

GRAND MARSHAL JAMES GARNER
(right) Oklahoma's favorite Hollywood son returned home to join in this historic celebration, serving as a Grand Marshal of the Centennial Parade. Flanking Garner are a parade volunteer and **Lisa Speer**.

SHOW-STOPPERS *Oklahoma Miss Americas (left to right)* **Susan Powell, Jennifer Berry Gooden** *and* **Shawntel Smith Wuerch** *— backed by high school pom squads — helped get the parade underway.*

THE OKLAHOMA ALL*STAR CENTENNIAL BAND *Produced by* **Charles Jones II** *and under the direction of* **Mike Davis, Gary Smith** *and* **Robyn Hilger,** *the All*Star Band led the parade.*

STATEWIDE SQUADS
Cheerleaders and pom squads came from across the state to participate in Oklahoma's grandest parade.

81

THE CENTENNIAL PARADE

FANS OF ALL AGES
Parade-lovers young and old lined the streets for the state's history-making day.

THE CROWDS CAME OUT An estimated crowd of more than 175,000 packed the parade route. Enjoying the festivities from rows of bleachers that were set up near the starting line were *Sugar Smith, DeAnn* and *Lee Allan Smith, Jennifer* and *Fritz Kiersch, Libby Blankenship, Lt. Gov. Jari Askins, Juli Lyles, DeLee Smith, David Durrett, Lucinda Pennington, Gay Reed, Geraldine Raupe, Carla* and *Dick Ellis, Brett Willison* and *Devon Willison,* among others.

STEALTH BOMBER *As the thunderous sound rumbled through downtown, the crowd gazed up to catch sight of a* **B-2 Stealth Bomber** *roaring through the skies in this dramatic fly-by, coordinated by Retired Air Force Lt. General* **Richard Burpee**.

DANCING KITES *Look closely and you'll spot Oklahoma state symbols flying high in the sky – a beautiful array of flowers, lizards, birds, fish, buffalo, raccoons, bees and butterflies. Kites are presented by dancers from the* **Pointe Performing Arts Center** *in Oklahoma City.*

CENTOONIALS *These lovable characters served as state ambassadors in carrying the Centennial message to Oklahoma's youth. The four CenTOONials were named by the state's schoolchildren:* **Lizzy the Mountain Boomer Lizard, Scissy the Scissor-Tailed Flycatcher, Buckley the Buffalo** *and* **Rascal the Raccoon**.

BROADCAST LIVE ON OETA *The parade was televised live on OETA and hosted by baseball legend* **Johnny Bench** *with Miss Americas* **Jane Jayroe Gamble** *and* **Susan Powell**. *Thanks to* **Bill Thrash, Mickie Smith** *and* **Price Wooldridge** *of* **OETA,** *and to* **New Leaf Floral,** *who provided all of the floral arrangements.*

HIGH SCHOOL PRIDE *Marching bands from five Oklahoma high schools performed in the parade: **Altus, Wilburton, Konawa, Antlers** and **Broken Arrow**.*

SCOTTISH BAGPIPES *(right) Oklahoma Centennial Massed Pipes and Drums is a cooperative effort of all the state's bagpipe and drum bands, and it was the largest bagpipe unit ever to march in Oklahoma.*

"A SOONER CENTURY" *Miss America 2007 **Lauren Nelson** served as one of the grand marshals of the parade and rode aboard the first float of the day. She was introduced to the crowd by baseball legend **Johnny Bench**.*

UNIVERSITY MARCHING BANDS *Oklahoma's higher education institutions were well-represented — marching bands from* **Oklahoma State University, The University of Oklahoma** *and* **Langston University** *each performed.*

U.S. MARINE DRUM & BUGLE CORPS *Known as a premier musical marching unit worldwide, the* **Marine "D&BC"** *is comprised of more than 80 musicians. They were dressed in their ceremonial red-and-white uniforms.*

KEEPING THE BEAT
Big marching bands were a big hit with little ones, who clapped along every step of the way.

85

THE CENTENNIAL
PARADE

GIANT INFLATABLES *Never before have there been 60-foot-long floats and 45-foot-tall helium balloons in Oklahoma City. Thanks to native Oklahomans **Greg Sadler** and **Charlie Trimble** of **Big Events, Inc.**, out of Oceanside, California, who provided these spectacular balloons.*

BALD EAGLE *This 33-foot American Bald Eagle was handled by the **United States District Court for the Western District of Oklahoma**. Volunteers included survivors of the Murrah Building bombing, who represented the "can-do" spirit of the Sooner State.*

Farmers Insurance presents
HORTON

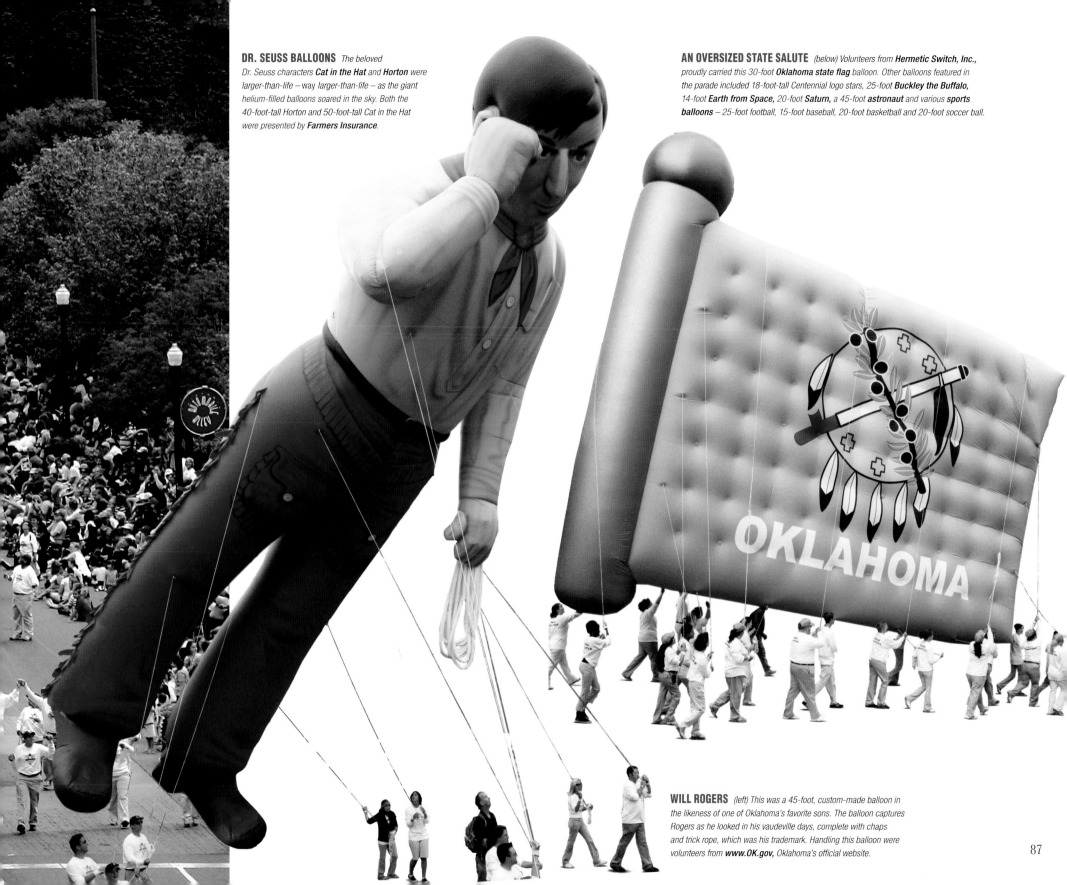

DR. SEUSS BALLOONS *The beloved Dr. Seuss characters* **Cat in the Hat** *and* **Horton** *were larger-than-life – way larger-than-life – as the giant helium-filled balloons soared in the sky. Both the 40-foot-tall Horton and 50-foot-tall Cat in the Hat were presented by* **Farmers Insurance**.

AN OVERSIZED STATE SALUTE *(below) Volunteers from* **Hermetic Switch, Inc.,** *proudly carried this 30-foot* **Oklahoma state flag** *balloon. Other balloons featured in the parade included 18-foot-tall Centennial logo stars, 25-foot* **Buckley the Buffalo,** *14-foot* **Earth from Space,** *20-foot* **Saturn,** *a 45-foot* **astronaut** *and various* **sports balloons** *– 25-foot football, 15-foot baseball, 20-foot basketball and 20-foot soccer ball.*

WILL ROGERS *(left) This was a 45-foot, custom-made balloon in the likeness of one of Oklahoma's favorite sons. The balloon captures Rogers as he looked in his vaudeville days, complete with chaps and trick rope, which was his trademark. Handling this balloon were volunteers from* **www.OK.gov,** *Oklahoma's official website.*

87

FANCIFUL FLOATS

*All floats were made by **Expo Design** – special thanks to **Scott Vankirk** and **Kathleen McGuire**.*

HOME OF THE CHAMPIONS

This float celebrated our state's pride and passion for sports of all sorts – including baseball, football, basketball, golf and tennis.

SOONER EXPRESS

***SandRidge Energy** sponsored the Sooner Express, which focused on three of Oklahoma's major agricultural exports: corn, wheat and cotton. A secondary theme was the railway in Oklahoma. **The Byron Berline Band** headlined the Sooner Express.*

STATE OF THE ARTS

This colorful float showcased all things artful – from theater and visual arts to film and TV – and the Oklahomans who make them great.

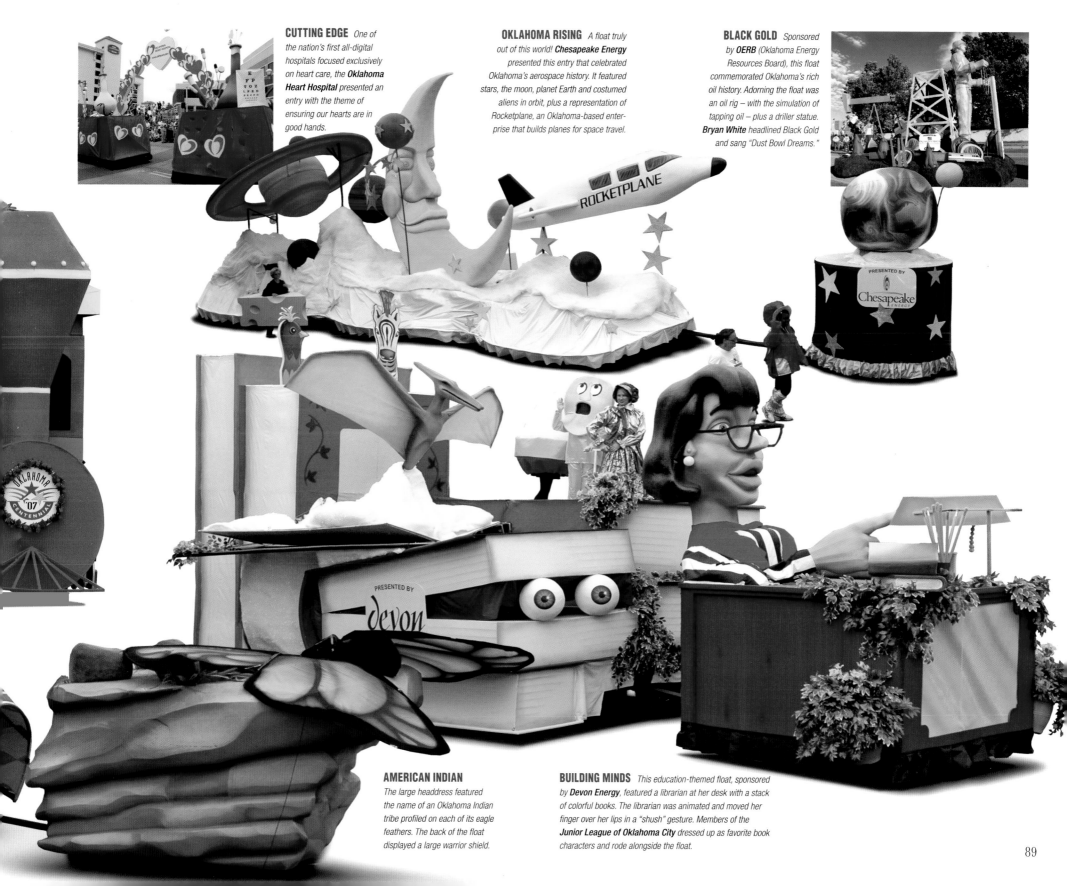

CUTTING EDGE One of the nation's first all-digital hospitals focused exclusively on heart care, the **Oklahoma Heart Hospital** presented an entry with the theme of ensuring our hearts are in good hands.

OKLAHOMA RISING A float truly out of this world! **Chesapeake Energy** presented this entry that celebrated Oklahoma's aerospace history. It featured stars, the moon, planet Earth and costumed aliens in orbit, plus a representation of Rocketplane, an Oklahoma-based enterprise that builds planes for space travel.

BLACK GOLD Sponsored by **OERB** (Oklahoma Energy Resources Board), this float commemorated Oklahoma's rich oil history. Adorning the float was an oil rig – with the simulation of tapping oil – plus a driller statue. **Bryan White** headlined Black Gold and sang "Dust Bowl Dreams."

AMERICAN INDIAN The large headdress featured the name of an Oklahoma Indian tribe profiled on each of its eagle feathers. The back of the float displayed a large warrior shield.

BUILDING MINDS This education-themed float, sponsored by **Devon Energy**, featured a librarian at her desk with a stack of colorful books. The librarian was animated and moved her finger over her lips in a "shush" gesture. Members of the **Junior League of Oklahoma City** dressed up as favorite book characters and rode alongside the float.

THE CENTENNIAL
PARADE

COUNTRY MUSIC CAPITAL
Country superstar **Ty England** joined
this float that included dancers from
the **Victory School of the Arts**
in Oklahoma City. This entry was
presented by **The Oklahoman.**

TY ENGLAND *Raised in Oklahoma, England
was the touring guitarist for **Garth Brooks** during the
height of his stardom. England struck out for a solo
career in 1995 and has had success with the singles
"Should've Asked Her Faster" and "Smoke in Her Eyes."
During the parade, he performed "Redneck Son."*

PRESENTED BY
THE OKLAHOMAN

MISS OKLAHOMA RODEO
*Lauren Holt was chosen Miss Oklahoma
Rodeo for 2007 by the **Oklahoma Rodeo
Pageants Council.***

RODEO QUEENS *This group rode
through the parade on horesback decked
out in full rodeo attire. They carried flags
representing our nation, state, the
Centennial and their organization.*

SQUARE DANCERS *Who knew that
square dancing was the official folk dance
of Oklahoma? Performing it in the parade
were dancers from the **Central District
Square Dance Association,** which has 22
clubs in the Oklahoma City metro area.*

OKLAHOMA! *Young performers from **Lyric Theatre's Thelma Gaylord Academy** wore costumes depicting characters from Oklahoma!, the beloved Rodgers and Hammerstein musical.*

FANCY DANCERS *Wearing Southern Plains American Indian dress, the **Eagle Sky Dancers** performed the "Oklahoma-style" Fancy Dance. Shown above is a member of the **Norahua Mexican Folkloric Group,** who performed traditional Mexican folk dances. Norahua is part of the touring group for the Oklahoma State Arts Council.*

THE CENTENNIAL PARADE

WEIRD SCIENCE *The **Shawnee Academy of Ballet** – garbed in scrubs, lab coats and with stethoscopes – demonstrated Oklahoma's achievements in the medical arts through the art of dance.*

DANCING SCARECROWS *Students from the **Shannon Crites School of Dance** in Ardmore brought the scarecrow to life in a fun and entertaining presentation.*

FLYING HIGH *No need to look to the skies to see planes in this parade – these plane props were escorted by volunteers from the **Section 9 Royal Rangers,** an international mentoring group.*

OUTER SPACED OUT *The dancers from **Dove Dance School** in Oklahoma City and Tulsa celebrate the aerospace industry by dancing … as aliens! The Dove Dance School has 400+ students, many of whom perform in professional venues as well.*

4-H CLUB *When Oklahoma was only two years old, the 4-H program was taking root in rural communities in the form of tomato clubs for girls and corn clubs for boys. By 1909, the first 4-H club was established in Tishomingo. Today, 4-H serves more than 150,000 boys and girls across Oklahoma.*

OU VIPs *This trio of Heisman Trophy winners represents University of Oklahoma sporting excellence. (shown left in backseat)* **Steve Owens**, **Billy Sims** *and* **Jason White** *earned their coveted awards in 1969, 1978 and 2003, respectively.*

THOMAS STAFFORD *(above) This former astronaut and Air Force lieutenant general is one of fewer than 30 men to have flown to the moon. Stafford is a Weatherford native.*

OSU VIPs *Oklahoma State University coaches* **Eddie Sutton** *(left) and* **John Smith** *have led their respective squads to much success. Sutton's basketball teams reached the postseason 14 times in his 17 years; Smith's wrestling teams have won five national titles.*

OLYMPIC AND BASEBALL GREATS *Shannon Miller is the most decorated gymnast, male or female, in U.S. history – having won seven Olympic medals and nine World Championship medals.* **Bobby Murcer** *played professional baseball for 17 seasons, the majority with the New York Yankees. He was a five-time All-Star selection and a Gold Glove winner. Murcer was inducted into the Oklahoma Sports Hall of Fame in 1993 and the Oklahoma Hall of Fame in 2005.*

LLAMA ASSOCIATION *Llamas were adorned in a variety of costumes representing Oklahoma's oil industry – they included tin man, flying red horse, dinosaur and more.*

TINKER AIR FORCE BASE
More than 50 military members marched in support of Oklahoma's Centennial and the 60th anniversary of the Air Force. Tinker AFB is the largest single-site employer in the state with 27,000 military and civilian employees.

93

HOCKEY AND HORSES
The **Express Clydesdales** pulling members of the **Oklahoma City Blazers** minor league hockey team. The black-and-white horses are owned by **Bob A. Funk** of Yukon, Oklahoma. The Blazers of the Central Hockey League have been entertaining hockey fans in Oklahoma City since 1992.

RIDE 'EM, COWBOY
Steers "Pistol" and "Pete" pulled a covered wagon sponsored by the **Oklahoma State University Rodeo Association**.

BUDWEISER CLYDESDALES

(above) The legendary team of horses owned by **Anheuser-Busch** joined in the parade. August A. Busch Jr. acquired the horses in 1933 to celebrate the end of Prohibition. The Clydesdales transported the first case of post-Prohibition beer from the brewery in St. Louis.

LAWTON RANGERS (left) The official
riding club of the Centennial Commission, the Rangers served as the parade's mounted color guard. The Rangers have been holding rodeos near Lawton since 1945.

WELLS FARGO WAGON (below) As a tribute to their long
history in Oklahoma, **Wells Fargo** was proud to have their wagon
participate in the parade. Oklahoma native and country singer
Katrina Elam rode in the coach and performed "No End In Sight."

MICK CORNETT (below)
Oklahoma City's mayor
enjoyed a ride in this
old-fashioned automobile.

FORT SILL FIELD ARTILLERY HALF SECTION
(above) The United States Army's last horse-drawn
artillery unit is an authentic representation of a
horse-drawn artillery section as used in World War I.
The uniforms are replicas of those worn by artillery
units from 1918 into the 1930s.

PAWNEE BILL (right) The
legendary Wild West showman,
played by **Wayne Spears**, waves to
spectators from atop his horse, "Y."
The centennial year marked the
17th year that Spears has been
delighting audiences with his
portrayal of Pawnee Bill.

THANKS TO THE CITY
of **Oklahoma City**, the **Oklahoma
City Police Department** and the
Oklahoma City Manager for their
efforts in clearing the way, moving
stoplights, relocating wires and
doing whatever it took to put
on this successful parade!

95

A SOARING FINALE *"Rocketman"*
Dan Schlund took flight during the parade,
flying 100 yards before returning to land
in a crowd-pleasing stunt that generated
enthusiastic waves of approval.

YOU'RE DOIN' FINE, OKLAHOMA! *Standing high atop the giant birthday
cake was* **Regina Dowling** *– Los Angeles actress and native Oklahoman –
who sang the Centennial anthem "Oklahoma Rising" in a spectacular closing
production number. Dowling is flanked by* **Brittany Carradine,** *Miss Black
Oklahoma USA 2007, and* **Makenna Smith,** *Miss Oklahoma 2007.*

AFRICAN-AMERICAN
FLOATS CAPITAL TRAIN
BANDS WEDDING
CENTENNIAL
CELEBRATIONS BALL
GOVERNOR
PROCLAMATION WAGONS
GUTHRIE
ALL★STAR BAND TERRITORIAL
SUNSET CEREMONY
HISTORIC PARADE HERITAGE
CAVALRY
REENACTORS TRIBES
NATIVE AMERICANS HORSES
EXCURSION LEGISLATURE

OKLAHOMA '07 CENTENNIAL™

GUTHRIE

THE FIRST CAPITAL

It was the city that started it all.
The territorial capital and later,
the state's first capital.
So it was only fitting that a celebration
of the first 100 years would
wind up here.

GUTHRIE
STATEHOOD WEEK

O n November 16, 1907, Dr. Hugh Scott, secretary to Territorial Gov. Frank Frantz, ran from the telegraph office in Guthrie and fired a pistol at 9:16 a.m., declaring that Oklahoma had officially become a state. Exactly 100 years to the day later, the secretary's great-grandson, Hugh Scott, reenacted that same event.

It was all part of Guthrie's Statehood Week activities, which included a re-creation of the actual ceremonies from 1907, featuring a reading of the statehood proclamation, appointment of the state's U.S. senators and the inauguration of Charles Haskell as Oklahoma's first governor. On November 15, 2007, a special legislative ceremonial session was held in the First Legislative Hall. It was the first time legislators had met in Guthrie since 1910. Officials arrived in town aboard the Centennial Express train.

Capping off the week was a re-creation of another event: the original statehood ball. The Scottish Rite Masonic Center hosted present-day festivities, which featured a champagne reception and introduction of honored guests, followed by dinner, dancing and an auction.

ALL ABOARD! *(right) Gov.* **Brad Henry** *and his family arrive at the train station to board the Centennial Express train.*

PERIOD DRESS *(below) State Rep.* **Phil Richardson** *and his wife,* **Janalee,** *clad in 1907 attire, await the arrival of the Centennial Express.*

MAKING TRACKS TO GUTHRIE *(above) Sitting in the front row (right) is U.S. Senior District Judge* **Tim Leonard.** *He's joined by Sen.* **Glenn Coffee** *(row behind), co-president pro tempore of the Oklahoma State Senate. Sitting adjacent to Coffee is* **John Richard,** *director of the Oklahoma Department of Central Services.*

THE CENTENNIAL EXPRESS *(right) The train transported some 400 Oklahoma legislators, state officials and dignitaries from Oklahoma City to Guthrie for the special legislative ceremonial session. A waiting crowd of nearly 500 was on hand to greet the train's arrival.*

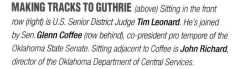

COMMEMORATIVE MEDALLIONS *(left) Displaying their Centennial medallions are* **Gwen Faulconer Lippert** *and Oklahoma State Rep.* **Charlie Joyner**, *who joined the legislators aboard the train bound for Guthrie.*

GUTHRIE MAYOR *(left) Following the arrival of the Centennial Express, Guthrie Mayor* **Chuck Burtcher** *addressed the crowd at the welcome ceremony.*

TRAVELING BACK IN TIME *(right)* **Mickey Kalman** *of Guthrie was one of many meeting the Centennial train. Wearing 1907 attire, he was dressed appropriately for the occasion and also arrived with proper transportation — an antique brakeless bicycle, dubbed a "bone-shaker."*

A ROUSING WELCOME *(above) Crowds gathered at the Santa Fe Depot for the Centennial Express Welcome Ceremony, which was hosted by the* **Guthrie Lions Club**.

ARRIVING IN STYLE *(left to right) Oklahoma State Rep.* **Jabar Shumate**, *Sen.* **Judy Easton McIntyre** *and the senator's mother,* **Jeanne Phillips**, *attended the round of events.*

HORSE & BUGGIES *(above) State dignitaries were taken from the Santa Fe Depot to Granny Had One restaurant in the heart of Guthrie's historic district. The buggies were provided by Guthrie's* **"Love is Carriages"** *team, a group led by* **Steve Bowers**.

A DAY IN HISTORY *(above) Displaying collector's edition newspapers are Gov.* **Brad Henry** *and one of the many children who participated in the historic Statehood Week activities.*

STATEHOOD WEEK
GUTHRIE

THE GOVERNOR IS ANNOUNCED *(left)*
Senate Sergeant-at-Arms **Bob Craig** announces
the arrival of Gov. and Mrs. **Brad Henry**.

HEADING TO SESSION *Legislators and state officials make their way into the Scottish Rite Masonic Center, the site of Oklahoma's First Legislative Hall.*

HOUSE MEMBERS *(left to right) State Reps.*
Larry Glenn *and* ***Wade Rousselot*** *are pictured with their wives,* ***Janet*** *and* ***Margie***.

SPECIAL THANKS *to the Heartland Flyer Coalition,* **BSNF Railroad,** **Amtrak,** **Oklahoma Department of Transportation,** **Guthrie Rotary and Lions Clubs,** **Bob Davis** *of the* **Masonic Center,** *former Reps.* **Frank Davis** *and* **Dale DePue,** **Brewer Enterprises,** **Oklahoma Farm Bureau** *and Secretary of State* **Susan Savage.**

GOV. BRAD HENRY

SPECIAL LEGISLATIVE SESSION *(left)*

Gov. **Brad Henry** *hugs Lt. Gov.* **Jari Askins** *during the session as he comes to the podium to speak. Held at the Scottish Rite Masonic Center in honor of the gathering 100 years ago, the session featured presentations by key history experts including Dr.* **Bob Blackburn,** *who gave a narrative of actual events relating to the state seal and Guthrie. The special session was open to the public.*

JOSH H. HENRY
Student, Shawnee

JEFF W. RABON
Oklahoma State Senate

MIKE MORGAN
President Pro Tempore Oklahoma State Senate

PAYING RESPECT (right) Oklahoma Indian tribal communities paid homage to the past 100 years with anticipation of the next 100. At the podium is Oklahoma State Rep. **Shane Jett**. Seated next to him are (left to right) **Me-Way-Seh Greenwood**, Otoe Missouria-Ponca-Chickasaw, and **Terry Tsotigh**, Kiowa.

TRADITIONAL CEDAR BLESSING (right) Conducting the blessing ceremony is **Stuart Owings**, Wichita (center). He's flanked by **Blas Preciado**, Kiowa, and **Harvey Pratt**, Cheyenne.

SUNSET CEREMONY Tribal people including **Jim Anquoe Sr.**, Kiowa (above), gathered from across the state to participate in three distinct ceremonies: "Remembrance," represented by tribal elders, "Rebirth," by Native American adults and "Ceremony of Hope for the Future," for the **Chahta vlla vlheha Choctaw Children's Choir**.

A NATIVE CELEBRATION *The American Indian Sunset Ceremony was organized by the American Indian Cultural Center and Museum in Oklahoma City. Shown at left surrounded by a crowd is* **Jimmy Reeder***.*

GENA TIMBERMAN *(above) The executive director of the Native American Cultural and Education Authority and a Choctaw Indian, Timberman served as event chair and master of ceremonies. Guthrie volunteer* **Richard Hendricks** *was co-chair.*

MUSICAL TRIBUTE *(above)* **Me-Way-Seh Greenwood** *and* **Terry Tsotigh** *played traditional flute music as the sun set. Tsotigh plays drums and harmonica in the Blues Nation Band, based out of Anadarko.*

SOAKING IT UP *(left)* **Sandra Medrano***, Thlopthlocco Tribal Town-Muscogee (Creek) Nation, holds her granddaughter,* **Tvske Billy***, Thlopthlocco Tribal Town-Muscogee (Creek) Nation and Thlopthlocco Tribal Town-Muscogee (Creek) Nation-Kiowa-Comanche-Choctaw-Alabama Quassarte Tribal Town, while the two take in the ceremony.*

STUART OWINGS *Prior to conducting the traditional cedar blessing, Owings explains the significance of the ceremony.*

103

STATEHOOD WEEK
GUTHRIE

THE INAUGURATION *(Shown right and far right)* **Edward S. Haskell**, *descendant of Oklahoma's first governor* **Charles Haskell**, *is sworn in by Guthrie State Rep.* **Jason Murphey** *during a reenactment of the first inauguration.*

CHILDREN CHIME IN *(right)*
Following the wedding, music director **Chris DiGiovanni** *led a chorus of second- and third-graders from Fogarty Centennial Honor Choir in singing "Oklahoma!."*

"I NOW PRONOUNCE YOU … " *The couple is announced by* **Reverend Dale DePue**. *Shown at right, next to the couple, is* **Maggie Haskell Potter**, *the great-granddaughter of Oklahoma's first governor,* **Charles Haskell**.

SYMBOLIC WEDDING *In a re-creation of the 1907 ceremony,* **Ashlee Choudoin** *portrayed* **Anna Bennett**, *"Miss Indian Territory," and* **Jay Hannah** *portrayed* **Charles C. Jones**, *"Mr. Oklahoma Territory." The wedding represented the joining of the twin territories.*

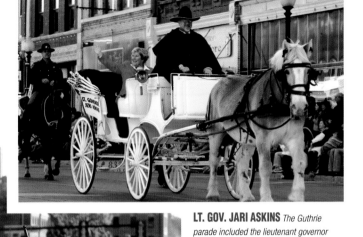

STATEHOOD IS DECLARED! *(left)*
Just as his grandfather had done 100 years before him, **Hugh Scott** *fired a pistol into the air, announcing that Oklahoma had officially joined the union.*

LT. GOV. JARI ASKINS *The Guthrie parade included the lieutenant governor riding in a horse-drawn carriage provided by Guthrie's* **Steve Bowers**.

A HISTORIC VIEW
(above) Executive director of the Oklahoma Historical Society, Dr. **Bob Blackburn** *served as narrator of the Statehood Day inauguration reenactment. The ceremonies were scripted by* **Valerie Haynes**.

A 21-GUN SALUTE *(above) The* **Oklahoma 4th Cavalry Militia** *honored the occasion with an official gun salute. They then led a processional through downtown Guthrie to the Carnegie Library.*

46-STAR FLAG
Guthrie volunteers **Skye** *and* **April Thoms** *carry a 46-star flag, leading the Proclamation Parade. It was Oklahoma's original state flag and the "46" symbolized Oklahoma as the nation's 46th state.*

LAWTON RANGERS *Joining in the festivities is Oklahoma's official centennial riding club, a group that formed in 1941.*

STATEHOOD WEEK
GUTHRIE

STATEWIDE PARTICIPATION *Communities from across the state were represented by high school marching bands and parade floats. Volunteers **Dennis Ochs** and **Rose Williams** chaired the parade committee. Woodward's entry is shown at left.*

DOWNTOWN PARADE *Nearly 85,000 people descended on downtown to take in the historic parade. Some 250 entries included 14 different marching bands that ranged from **Guthrie High School** (right) to **Oklahoma State University** (above) to the **Oklahoma All★Star Centennial Band** (below).*

NON-STOP ENTERTAINMENT *(left) The more than 5,000 parade participants included marching bands from across the state: (left, top to bottom)* **University of Oklahoma**, **145th Army**, **Perkins-Tryon High School** *and* **University of Central Oklahoma**.

VINTAGE WHEELS *(above) The antique tractors and automobiles parading through downtown signified life at the time of Oklahoma's statehood. Shown at right are the* **CenTOONials**, *four mascots representing various Oklahoma symbols.*

107

STATEHOOD WEEK
GUTHRIE
CENTENNIAL DAY PARADE

DRESSING THE PART *Among the parade participants were several reenactors portraying Oklahoma's original citizens. Shown below are actors from* New Chance Cities, *a play depicting African-American experiences during early Oklahoma statehood. It was written for the Centennial by* **Sharon Fisher**. *The bottom photo features members of the* **Oklahoma Heritage Equestrian Riders**.

A PARADE FOR THE AGES *Crowds gathered all along the parade route, which began at the Scottish Rite Masonic Center and proceeded through downtown before winding up at Mineral Wells Park.*

A CENTURY OF MEMORIES *(clockwise from top left)*
The **Centennial Riders***, the* **Two Belgian Horse Team***,*
a stagecoach from **Pawnee Bill's Wild West Show***,*
participants dressed in period costumes, and **Girl Scout**
troops from across Oklahoma all joined in the fun.

STATEHOOD WEEK
GUTHRIE
CENTENNIAL DAY
PARADE

FLAGS ON PARADE *The Riverside Indian School* from Anadarko and other Indian youth carried tribal flags representing Indian nations in Oklahoma.

COLOR GUARD *(below) Students from the Riverside Indian School ROTC present the flags.*

A PROUD HERITAGE *(above) With the float theme "Bridging the Past to the Future," Native Americans of all ages participated in the parade.*

ALL SMILES *(above) Caitlin Baker from the Muscogee (Creek) Nation enjoys the parade.*

FULL REGALIA *Elizabeth Rey Guy* of the Caddo Nation proudly rides in the parade.

CELEBRATING WITH SONG *The* **Chahta vlla vlheha** *(top), a children's choir from the Choctaw Nation, entertained with their traditional spoken language and hymn singing. Joining them in the parade were Cheyenne and Arapaho Peace Chiefs (middle) and native community elders (bottom).*

STATEHOOD WEEK
GUTHRIE
CENTENNIAL BALL

STATEHOOD INAUGURAL BALL *This was a re-creation of the 1907 statehood ball. Held at the Scottish Rite Masonic Center, guests enjoyed a champagne reception and introduction of honored guests, followed by dinner, dancing and an auction.* **Kathy Montgomery** *chaired the event. With appreciation to* **George Watts** *of the Guthrie Centennial Committee, the City of Guthrie, City Manager* **Melody Kellogg**, *Guthrie Chamber Director* **Kathy Montgomery**, *the 20 Guthrie Centennial subcommittees and 500 volunteers for a week of memorable events.*

DALE *and* **LISA SORRELL**, *Guthrie*

DREW EDMONDSON *The Oklahoma Attorney General attended with his wife,* **Linda**.

DAN *and* **JOY NEWTON**, *Guthrie*

RICK *and* **STACY STATON**, *Guthrie*

MAGGIE HASKELL POTTER *and* **BILL SCHMIDT**
Potter is wearing the gown her great-grandmother wore to the 1907 inaugural ball.

EDWARD S. HASKELL *(below) The great-grandson of Oklahoma's first governor, Charles Haskell, delivers a toast.*

BETTE *and* **STEVE HASKELL** *(above) Steve Haskell is a descendant of Oklahoma's first governor,* **Charles Haskell**, *and traveled from Harwinton, Connecticut, for this special Statehood Day celebration.*

MARY JO *and* **CHUCK ALLEN** *(below), Wellston*

GOV. AND MRS. BRAD HENRY *There were more than 1,000 people in attendance at Gov. Charles Haskell's inaugural ball. Guests at the 2007 event included Gov. Brad Henry, shown here dancing with his wife, Kim.*

THE SPECTACULAR

It was an event that had been
100 years in the making.
Our night of nights, our stars aligned,
our state on stage.

OKLAHOMA CENTENNIAL SPECTACULAR

Oklahoma's 100th birthday celebration culminated with the Centennial Spectacular – a celebrity-filled Statehood Day salute that featured an unprecedented gathering of Oklahoma's most famous sons and daughters. It was a night of paying tribute to all who paved the way over the first 100 years, and to honor their efforts, endeavors and achievements.

A sold-out crowd packed into downtown Oklahoma City's Ford Center to catch this once-in-a-century performance. Additional seating was available at the nearby Bricktown Ballpark, where the event was simulcast live. Viewers there were also treated to a post-Spectacular concert and fireworks display.

The show's lineup was a veritable Who's Who of Oklahoma superstars and included appearances by Vince Gill, Reba McEntire, Carrie Underwood, Toby Keith and Garth Brooks. In all, hundreds of stars – entertainers, actors musicians, athletes, even Miss Americas – graced the stage.

The Centennial Spectacular aired live on OETA on the night of the show and it has been rebroadcast several times since. To all who have watched, it's clear that the show more than lived up to its billing. Indeed, it truly was … *spectacular.*

GOV. BRAD HENRY *The governor addressed the crowd in a speech that not only reflected his pride and passion for the state, but also shared in the optimism for Oklahoma's second century and the exciting times that are sure to lie ahead.*

VINCE GILL AND REBA McENTIRE *(left) Two of Oklahoma's favorite country musicians, Gill and McEntire sang a duet on "Oklahoma Swing." During their performance, dozens of colorfully clad square dancers – the **Central District Square Dancers** – sashayed down the aisles and filled the perimeter stages.*

OPENING NUMBER *Kelli O'Hara began the show with "Nowhere Else But Oklahoma," an energetic production number that included the* **Oklahoma City University American Spirit Dance Company** *(top right), the* **Oklahoma All★Star Centennial Band** *(left) and various pom squads.*

OKLAHOMA CENTENNIAL SPECTACULAR

VITALY TOMANOV *(right) This eagle-costumed acrobat ascended and descended on two red silk ropes as he gracefully depicted the life cycle of an eagle, from first flight to the return to the spirit world. Below him on stage are Native American drummers. (left to right)* **Many Goats**, *Navajo;* **Homer Wassanna**, *Cheyenne-Arapaho;* **Jim Anquoe Jr.**, *Kiowa-Cheyenne-Arapaho;* **Jim Anquoe Sr.**, *Kiowa;* **Eric Anquoe**, *Kiowa-Cheyenne-Arapaho; and* **Terry Tsotigh**, *Kiowa.*

THE RED STONE SINGERS AND DANCERS
(below) One of the few fancy dance-only troupes left in today's pow-wows, this group – including **George Alexander**, *from the Otoe-Missouria tribe, shown below – performed a beautiful rendition of the Eagle Dance.*

N. SCOTT MOMADAY *(right)*
The Centennial poet laureate of Oklahoma, Momaday is a Kiowa and a member of the renowned Kiowa Gourd Dance Society. This poet, novelist, playwright, storyteller, artist, Pulitzer Prize winner, and professor of English and American literature is a native of Lawton.

SHAYNA STEELE This world-class vocalist sang as **Tomanov** "the flyer" performed his artful dance. Steele lived in Enid early in her life while her father was stationed at Vance Air Force Base; she later went on to success on Broadway and on the New York City music scene.

CHALLENGER THE EAGLE Challenger soared high above the stage and crowd before returning to his handler **Al Cecere's** hand. Named in honor of the space shuttle crew, Challenger was blown from a wild nest as a baby during a storm and was hand-raised by the people who rescued him. As a result, he's unable to survive on his own in the wild and is cared for by the American Eagle Foundation.

BILL MILLER A Mohican Indian, Miller provided flute accompaniment on "Oklahoma Rising." An award-winning recording artist, performer and songwriter, Miller has long been one of the most admired figures in the Native Amercian music arena.

OKLAHOMA CENTENNIAL SPECTACULAR

ARGUS HAMILTON *(below)* Ardmore native Hamilton presented a funny and touching tribute to **Will Rogers**. Hamilton's grandfather was a lifelong friend of Rogers, so Hamilton considered it quite a compliment to have been dubbed by Robin Williams as "the Will Rogers of the Baby Boom." Hamilton's daily column of irreverent and humorous commentary on current events is syndicated in more than 100 U.S. newspapers.

JOHNNY BENCH *(above)* Binger hometown hero Bench introduced another Oklahoma legend, **Patti Page**. Bench played for the Cincinnati Reds for 17 seasons and was inducted into the Baseball Hall of Fame in 1989. He's a member of both the Oklahoma Hall of Fame and Oklahoma Sports Hall of Fame.

RANCE HOWARD *(below)* A native Oklahoman from Duncan, Howard graduated from the University of Oklahoma. He has appeared in more than 100 films and is known for his TV roles in "Gentle Ben" and "Babylon 5." Howard is the father of director **Ron Howard** and actor Clint Howard – he introduced a video clip of his son Ron.

MEGAN MULLALLY *(above)* Mullally's videotaped salute to her home state offered her Happy Birthday greetings. Mullally got her start with the Ballet Oklahoma troupe in Oklahoma City, and has since gone on to appear in theater, films and TV, including an Emmy Award-winning role as Karen Walker on "Will & Grace."

MELVIN WELCH *(below)* A Helena resident, 101-year-old Welch nearly stole the show with his performance of the original Oklahoma state song, "Oklahoma, a Toast." When asked how he thought he did when singing the song, the one-time farmer and teacher replied, "Well, they did give me a standing ovation and after I left the stage they tried to get me to come back up and do an encore, but I just didn't want to climb back up those steps and figured folks had heard enough." Welch is a 1928 Oklahoma A&M graduate who helped establish a Civilian Conservation Corps camp in Geary and worked for the USDA Soil Conservation Service for many years before retiring back to the farm in Oklahoma.

BOBBY MURCER *(below)* A five-time All-Star Major League baseball player, Murcer is a member of the Oklahoma Sports Hall of Fame and Oklahoma Hall of Fame. In 1983, he traded his glove and bat for a microphone and began broadcasting Yankees baseball. On this evening, he introduced one of America's leading sopranos, **Leona Mitchell**.

WILLARD SCOTT *(above)* A great advocate of honoring Centenarians, Scott offers twice-a-week birthday greetings on NBC's TODAY show to 100-year-olds across the nation. At the Spectacular, Willard spoke on behalf of Oklahoma's Centenarians and introduced 101-year-old **Melvin Welch**.

RON HOWARD *(above)* Introduced by his dad, Howard praised his Oklahoma heritage in a videotaped greeting. Now an Academy Award-winning film director and producer, Howard is still well-known for his roles on sitcoms, movies and television – millions remembering him as Opie in "The Andy Griffith Show" (debuted in 1960) and, later, as Richie Cunningham on "Happy Days" (1974).

BART CONNER AND NADIA COMANECI *This husband-and-wife team are gymnastics royalty – he's America's most decorated male gymnast and she scored the first perfect 10 in summer Olympic history. Residents of Norman, they introduced an equally decorated musical artist: multi-Grammy, Dove and Christian Contemporary Music Award winner* **Amy Grant**.

BARRY SWITZER *(above) A College Football Hall of Famer, a Jim Thorpe Lifetime Achievement Award recipient, winner of three national collegiate championships and one Super Bowl, Switzer is known as none other than "The King" throughout Oklahoma. He resides in Norman and is one of the state's finest ambassadors. Switzer introduced the multi-Grammy Award-winning band,* **The Flaming Lips**.

THE FLAMING LIPS *(above and right) Formed in Oklahoma City in 1983, "The Lips" have earned international cult status with their outrageous use of video, costuming and unusual onstage props. Shown performing "Do You Realize" are* **Steven Drozd**, **Wayne Coyne** *and* **Michael Ivins**.

119

OKLAHOMA CENTENNIAL
SPECTACULAR

SHIRLEY JONES *(left) Oklahoma officially adopted Jones in 1955 after her enchanting screen debut in the film classic* Oklahoma!. *Younger audiences may know her as the musical matriarch of the hit '70s TV show, "The Partridge Family." Jones performed two hits from the Broadway musical: "Oh, What a Beautiful Morning" and "People Will Say We're in Love."*

KELLI O'HARA *(above) Broadway leading lady and Elk City native, O'Hara opened the evening with a production number titled "Nowhere Else But Oklahoma" – the audience was invited to join in and O'Hara was soon joined by the* **Oklahoma All•Star Centennial Band**. *Later in the show, O'Hara reappeared to present a tribute to the* Oklahoma! *movie.*

OKLAHOMA CITY UNIVERSITY DANCERS
As **Kelli O'Hara** *sang "Out Of My Dreams" from the movie* Oklahoma!, **Jenny Rice** *and* **Todd Walker** *of the* **OCU American Spirit Dance Company** *performed on the stage below O'Hara.*

AMY GRANT *Grant is the best-selling contemporary Christian music singer to date, and had the first Christian album ever to go platinum. She performed "Every Heartbeat" backed by husband* **Vince Gill**'s *band.*

LEONA MITCHELL *(right) A graduate of Oklahoma City University, Mitchell began singing at an early age in the choir of the Antioch Oklahoma Baptist Church. From those stalwart beginnings, she is now known as one the greatest opera sopranos worldwide and has performed with the most prestigious international opera companies. Mitchell performed "Simple Gifts" and "Make Our Garden Grow" with the men's chorus of the **Canterbury Choral Society**.*

CARRIE UNDERWOOD *(below) She won "American Idol" in 2005 and from there went on to country music super-stardom. Underwood has won a host of music awards including Best New Artist, Best Female Country Vocal Performance, Song of the Year and Best Country Performance. She was also named Oklahoman of the Year 2006 by* Oklahoma *magazine. Hailing from Checotah, Underwood sang "I Ain't in Checotah Anymore."*

REBA McENTIRE *The "Queen of Country Music" joined* **Vince Gill** *on "Oklahoma Swing" and later sang "If I Had Only Known." She also introduced* **Carrie Underwood**. *From McEntire's early days in McAlester to a highly successful, two decade-plus career as a country artist and actress, she has sold more than 50 million records and earned honors including 15 American Music Awards, 12 Academy of Country Music awards, seven Country Music Association awards, two Grammy Awards and Drama Desk and Outer Critics awards for her Broadway run in* Annie Get Your Gun.

PATTI PAGE *(above) Born in Claremore and with more than 100 number-one hits in her singing arsenal, "The Singing Rage, Miss Patti Page" performed the "Tennessee Waltz" and "Get Your Kicks on Route 66." Page was the best-selling female artist of the 1950s and was among the first to cross over from country music to pop.*

OKLAHOMA CENTENNIAL
SPECTACULAR

VINCE GILL *There's not much in country music that Gill hasn't accomplished: sales in excess of 22 million, induction into the Grand Ole Opry and Country Music Hall of Fame, 18 Grammy Awards, 17 Country Music Association Awards and many more honors. He's also a member of the Oklahoma Hall of Fame and one of Oklahoma's favorite native sons, so it was only natural that he be asked to join in the composition of a song befitting of the state's 100th celebration. "Oklahoma Rising" was the result and Gill performed it in the Spectacular along with* **Jimmy Webb**, **Bill Miller**, *the* **Canterbury Choral Society** *and the* **Oklahoma City Philharmonic**.

"OKLAHOMA RISING" *(right) At the conclusion of the Centennial anthem, a giant state flag was unfurled to a thunderous standing ovation from the crowd.*

JIMMY WEBB *(left) Born in Elk City and raised in Laverne, Webb's accomplishments over 35 years as a writer, composer, arranger and producer have been unparalleled. He has earned widespread acclaim and received numerous awards and honors, including being the only artist to ever receive Grammy Awards for music, lyrics and orchestration. Webb wrote the lyrics for the Centennial anthem, "Oklahoma Rising," and joined* **Vince Gill** *in performing it during the finale. Webb also sang "By The Time I Get To Phoenix," one of the many mega-hits he has written.*

BLAKE SHELTON *(above) The Ada native and country music artist sang "Wichita Lineman" – he was accompanied by* **Jimmy Webb**, *the song's composer. Shelton's 1997 debut single "Austin" stayed at number one on Billboard's singles chart for five weeks, tying Billy Ray Cyrus' record for a debut single. He also reached number one for three weeks with "The Baby" in 2003.*

GARTH BROOKS *(right) He's a country music legend. The fastest-selling solo artist in music history, Brooks sold in excess of 100 million albums in just 10 years. He's the only solo artist in the Recording Industry Association of America history to have four albums top the 10 million mark. At the Spectacular, Brooks presented a moving and heartfelt segment on the Murrah Federal Building bombing and honored those Oklahomans who were so untimely taken.*

MISS AMERICAS *All of Oklahoma's living title-holders were present (left to right):* **Shawntel Smith Wuerch** *(Miss America 1996) from Muldrow,* **Jane Jayroe Gamble** *(1967) from Laverne,* **Lauren Nelson** *(2007) from Lawton,* **Susan Powell** *(1981) from Elk City and* **Jennifer Berry Gooden** *(2006) from Tulsa. The five ladies presented a salute to the armed forces and introduced* **Toby Keith**.

LAURA BUSH *The First Lady of the United States appeared in a videotaped greeting where she expressed congratulations to Oklahomans on the historic occasion. On behalf of President Bush, she saluted the state on 100 years of accomplishments and wished Oklahomans the very best as they entered the next century.*

AMERICAN HEROES *The brave soldiers from the **Army National Guard at Fort Sill** – each of whom served in either Operation Iraqi Freedom or Operation Enduring Freedom – were honored and saluted for their courageous efforts in battle.*

ALL-AMERICAN REJECTS *2007 Grammy Award winners, the Rejects performed "Move Along." Band members **Chris Gaylor, Mike Kennerty, Tyson Ritter** and **Nick Wheeler** are from Edmond and Stillwater.*

TOBY KEITH *This multi-platinum singer and songwriter has traveled to Iraq, Afghanistan, Kuwait, Germany, Bosnia, Kosovo, Macedonia, Italy, Guantanamo Bay (Cuba) and Belgium and has performed more than 60 shows during his annual trips to play for troops around the world. Keith has produced five number-one albums in his career. A native Oklahoman, he makes his home in Norman.*

MILITARY SALUTE *As **Toby Keith** performed the unofficial military anthem "American Soldier," Oklahoma soldiers took the stage and the crowd raised their glow sticks in support.*

OKLAHOMA CENTENNIAL SPECTACULAR

THE GRAND FINALE *Following the performance of "Oklahoma Rising," the entire cast took the stage for a rousing rendition of "Oklahoma!." More than 150 dancers from Oklahoma City University's American Spirit Dance Company lined the aisles as the cheering crowd sang along and a blizzard of confetti filled the air.*

OKLAHOMA CENTENNIAL SPECTACULAR

BRYAN WHITE *(right) Born in Lawton, White is a country music singer whose debut album in 1994 produced back-to-back number-one singles. To date, he's charted 17 singles on the Billboard charts, and four have reached number one. White performed with drummer* **Jimmy Butler** *at the AT&T Bricktown Ballpark.*

DESTAN OWENS *Singing at the Ballpark, Owens is an Oklahoma City University graduate who has appeared on Broadway in* Rent *and* Chicago, *in movies such as "Get Rich or Die Tryin'" and on TV shows including "30 Rock."*

LIGHTING UP THE SKY *Capping off the ceremonies was a magnificent fireworks display in honor of the state's 100th birthday.*

LIVE SIMULCAST *(above) A celebration this big knew no boundaries. The evening's festivities were televised live via simulcast at the AT&T Bricktown Ballpark, where crowds also enjoyed live music and spectacular fireworks.*

SWEET ADELINES *The Oklahoma City chorus Sweet Adelines is one of the top performing groups in Oklahoma. Their four-part a cappella harmony has garnered rave reviews over the past 50 years, and they brought their 90-voice performance chorus to the Ballpark.*

HORSESHOE ROAD *This Oklahoma band has an extensive range and style of music that they call Oklahoma heartland acoustic. Shown at the Ballpark are fiddler* **Kyle Dillingham** *and guitarist* **Brad Benge.**

OKLAHOMA CENTENNIAL RODEO OPRY *(left) Joining the list of performers at the Ballpark was a music group that included* **Mike Price**, *keyboards;* **Gary Bryan**, *drums;* **Kenny Anderson**, *guitar; and* **Susan McGee**, *fiddle. Appreciative fans (above) cheered on all of the evening's musicians.*

PRESS CONFERENCE *A pre-event gathering brought together nearly all of the personalities appearing in the Spectacular.*
Top row, left to right: **Bill Miller, Blake Shelton, Bobby Murcer, Byron Berline, Argus Hamilton, Willard Scott, Bart Conner, Amy Grant, Nadia Comaneci, Vince Gill, Lauren Nelson, Shawntel Smith Wuerch, Jimmy Webb, Susan Powell, Jennifer Berry Gooden, Garth Brooks, Jane Jayroe Gamble, Wayne Coyne** *and his wife,* **Michelle,** *and* **J. Blake Wade.** *Bottom row, left to right:* **Barry Switzer, Carrie Underwood, Lee Allan Smith, Patti Page, Shirley Jones, Leona Mitchell** *and* **Johnny Bench.** *Not pictured:* **Kelli O'Hara, Reba McEntire, Toby Keith** *and* **Rance Howard,** *all of whom were rehearsing.*

CARRIE UNDERWOOD

VINCE GILL

LAUREN NELSON

GARTH BROOKS

WAYNE COYNE

JIMMY WEBB

2
NOTABLE
PROJECTS

OKLAHOMA ALL★STAR CENTENNIAL BAND

This group of musical ambassadors
was formed solely for the
purpose of the state's Centennial Celebration.
They came from 75 different schools
across the state to create the

OKLAHOMA ALL★STAR CENTENNIAL BAND

No celebration is complete without music. But what to do if the celebration is a commemoration of 100 years? Music befitting of such a momentous occasion is a *must*. Which is why the Oklahoma Centennial Commission did more than pull together a playlist – they pulled together an entire *band*.

The Oklahoma All★Star Centennial Band was comprised of 150 of the state's most talented high school students – selected from more than 400 who auditioned. With the assistance of Sandy Garrett, state superintendent of public instruction, the students were able to come together to form the most prestigious high school band in the country and performed in a dozen events related to Oklahoma's Statehood celebration. The Oklahoma All★Star Centennial Band was the lead band for the 2007 Tournament of Roses Parade and was the only band in the history of the parade to perform in the opening ceremonies.

Leading the musicians were Director Michael Davis, former band and orchestra director for Walt Disney World® Resort; Producer Charles Jones II, a native Oklahoman who now is responsible for the video production of all Magic Music Days entertainment at Walt Disney World and Disneyland; Associate Director Gary Smith; and Assistant Director Robyn Hilger.

THE OKLAHOMA ALL★STAR CENTENNIAL BAND (middle picture) The band poses in front of the Oklahoma State Capitol. Shown at top and above are students auditioning from across the state. Top row: **Avery Johnson** and **Andrew Miner**. Above: **Jared Wingo** and **Kyle Jolliff**. Playing the clarinet at left is **Jessica Pasquini**.

OKLAHOMA ALL★STAR CENTENNIAL BAND

Band Directors
Charles Jones, Producer
Mike Davis, Head Director
Gary Smith, Associate Director
Robyn Hilger, Assistant Director
Jo Ellen Brown
John Davis
Lynne Davis
Jack Francis
Travis Hathcote
David Hilger
Harvey Price
Marsha Shaffer
Grant Thompson
Jennifer Thompson
Kay Merrill
Joe Wilhelm
Patsy Wilhelm
Sally Wojciechowski

BAND AUDITIONS *More than 400 high school students from across the state tried out in April 2006 for a spot in the special one-time band. The panel of judges (right) included (left to right)* **Jo Ellen Brown**, **Gary Brown** *and* **Gary Smith**.

A BAND HOPEFUL *(below) Snare drummer* **Cody O'Hara** *performs during his audition. He was one of 150 students to be notified in May 2006 of their selection to the band.*

GARY SMITH *(left)*
Judges evaluated the students' performances for tone quality and technical ability.

OKLAHOMA ALL★STAR CENTENNIAL BAND

Band Members

Deanna Acree, Jenks
Rhyan Adams, Oklahoma City
Derek Akers, Sulphur
Jordan Anderson, Tahlequah
Shelby Atkinson, Wilburton
Joshua Attaway, Oklahoma City
Robert Barnes, Bartlesville
Sean Bender, Edmond
Terri Bernard, Norman
Mark Billy, Finley
Josh Blankenship, Skiatook
Melissa Broaddus, Jenks
Cody Bryant, Idabel
Ryan Buggs, Oklahoma City
Emily Buller, Ringwood
Tyler Burkhart (Brewer), Oklahoma City
Andrew Cao, Yukon
Kendal Chevalier, Skiatook
Megan Coatney, Yukon
Lynleigh Cooper, Oklahoma City
Shayna Cowan, Salina
Evan Crabtree, Edmond

Kyle Critchnau, Owasso
Casey Cunningham, Miami
Anderson Daniel, Tahlequah
Josh Davis, Midwest City
Andrew Dawson, Guymon
Daniel Dew, Tahlequah
Lauren Diehl, Tulsa
Clint Dismore, Fairland
Robert Dodson, Miami
Sarah Donica, Noble
Levi Duethman, Broken Arrow
Andrew Enis, Wilburton
Jamie Estep, Ardmore
Zachary Evans, Wellston
Evan Everett, Tahlequah
Justin Fernan, Muskogee
Bruce Franklin, Spencer
Meagen Fry, Shawnee
Trevor Galvin, Edmond
Sonny Galyon, Midwest City
Darryl Gellenbeck, Guthrie
Garrison Gillham, Broken Arrow
Tanner Golden, Shawnee
Stephanie Gonzales, Choctaw
Alex Haar, Owasso
Erica Hamm, Okmulgee

Kristie Harris, Chester
Jacob Heck, Washington
Ronald Hernandez, Oklahoma City
William Herndon, Moore
Valarie Holly, Sapulpa
Brittney Housley, Oklahoma City
Sy Huffer, Fort Gibson
Alisha Humphrey, Del City
Mallory Irwinsky, Oklahoma City
Tabitha Jackson, Tahlequah
Kaitlyn Jennings, Duncan
Avery Johnson, Yukon
Britny Johnson, Sapulpa
Cory Johnson, Mustang
Mallory Johnson, Yukon
Tyler Johnson, Miami
Kyle Jolliff, Lone Grove
Samuel Kelley, Pocola
Jeremiah Kelly, Wilburton
Chris King, Purcell
Brian Kriegh, Mustang
Katherine Large, Guthrie
Ben Lewis, Noble
Maureen Lewis, El Reno
Saxon Lewis, Collinsville
Cindy Lin, Tulsa

Rebecca Little, Tuskahoma
Nick Livingston, Broken Arrow
Cameron Mabury, Miami
Emily Mapes, Skiatook
Emily Martin, Bethany
Hannah Martin, Yukon
Taylor Martin, Maysville
Jessica McDow, Woodward
Jackie McGuire, Sapulpa
Sean McKinney, Broken Arrow
Nikita Miles, Tulsa
Andrew Miner, Muskogee
Shaelynn Morefield, Edmond
Susan Moring, Tecumseh
Victor Mortson, Duncan
Jonathan Murrah, Edmond
Tyler Neighbors, Skiatook
Shane Nichols, Coalgate
Cody O'Hara, Tuttle
Gabe Osborn, Broken Arrow
Michael Osborn, Broken Arrow
Jessica Pasquini, Edmond
Heather Peden, Tulsa
Savanna Petricek, Oklahoma City
Kyle Price, Oklahoma City
Paige Quinn, Sand Springs

Erin Raiber, Norman
Ettore Rastelli, Miami
Nathan Reed, Edmond
Kyle Richardson, Edmond
Amy Ridgeway, Newalla
Nikki Robbins, Ponca City
Riley Robertson, Norman
Tim Robinson, Oklahoma City
Ari Rooker, Oklahoma City
Brittany Russell, Lexington
Taylor Schmidt, Elmore City
Killian Schroeder, Crawford
Blake Shadid, Edmond
Ethan Shaffer, Hartshorne
Elaine Shan, Broken Arrow
Mandy Sharp, Wilburton
J. Will Shaw, Edmond
Levi Sherman, Lexington
Wendy Slater, Guymon
Jeremy Smith, Edmond
Sophie Smith, Grove
Kylie Snow, Grove
Matthew Spinks, McAlester
Trey Stach, Fort Gibson
Matt Stephens, Moore
Kyle Stoltz, Midwest City

Patrick Storm, Edmond
Oliver Stout, Miami
Blanche Sumner, Tahlequah
Stephanie Thompson, Yukon
Nathan Tostenson, Midwest City
Barak Tschirhart, Tahlequah
Brian Tschirhart, Tahlequah
Marc Wade, Tahlequah
Eric Warren, Tahlequah
Steven Watson, Blanchard
Lauren Westbrook, Oklahoma City
Jonathan Wiegner, Midwest City
Jordan Wilhelm, Grove
Joseph Wilhelm, Grove
Steele Willison, Warr Acres
William Windle, Miami
Jared Wingo, Elmore City
Daniel Wojciechowski, Oklahoma City
Aaron Wright, Edmond

OKLAHOMA ALL★STAR
CENTENNIAL BAND

NEW EQUIPMENT *The Yamaha Corporation generously donated new musical instruments for every member of the Oklahoma All★Star Centennial Band. Shown below are* **Steven Watson**, **Taylor Martin** *and* **Kyle Price**.

GROUP BONDING
(left) It was during this first week that students like **Kendal Chevalier** *were transformed from individual musicians into one unified group.*

THE FIRST SHOW *(below right)*
In September 2006, the band performed together for the first time at **Oklahoma City University's Freede Center***. In attendance was* **Paul Holman***, president of the Tournament of Roses Parade. "These kids are all at the top of their game," Holman said. "They're as good as it gets."*

BAND CAMP *The new band members attended a week-long camp in July 2006 at the* **University of Oklahoma***. Shown at left is* **Shelby Atkinson***. At right are* **Ari Rooker** *and* **Ryan Buggs***.*

EARLY PLANS *Chase Senge displays and discusses diagrams of marching band formations and the incorporation of the **American Spirit Dancers**.*

ROSE PARADE PRESIDENT *(left) Tournament of Roses Parade President **Paul Holman** discusses with Oklahoma All★Star Centennial Band Producer **Charles Jones** the possibility of the band leading off the New Year's Day parade.*

IN THE CROWD *(below) Enjoying the preview performance of the band were **Lee Allan Smith**, Oklahoma Centennial Commission chairman of projects and events, Oklahoma City University president **Tom McDaniel** and his wife, **Brenda**.*

OKLAHOMA CITY UNIVERSITY DANCERS *The 32 dancers selected to perform with the Oklahoma All★Star Centennial Band were among the best dancers in the **American Spirit Dance Company**, OCU's dance troupe.*

A STUDY IN CONCENTRATION *Shown warming up in her All★Star cap and shirt is **Riley Robertson**.*

OKLAHOMA ALL★STAR CENTENNIAL BAND

MARCHING ON *The Oklahoma All★Star Centennial Band made its official debut at the Tulsa Kickoff Parade in November 2006. The band's next performance was the Tournament of Roses Parade in January 2007 (right), where it became the only band in the history of the parade to perform in the opening ceremonies. The band marched for more than six miles in the parade, playing its musical repertoire 56 times.*

A ROSY DEMEANOR
Elaine Shan, Emily Martin and Deanna Acree were all smiles as they prepared for their history-making day.

AMERICAN SPIRIT TROUPE *The Oklahoma City University dancers frequently performed with the band. At the Tournament of Roses Parade, the group performed a routine custom-designed around the 2007 theme "Our Good Nature."*

HEROES
HISTORY LEGENDARY
FUTURE MILESTONE
ANCESTRY ENDURING
STATEHOOD TIMELESS
PERSPECTIVE 100 CENTURY
PIONEER PRIDE
VISION LIFETIME
REMARKABLE GRACE DEDICATION
HERITAGE STEADFAST INSIGHT
ESTEEMED HONOR

OKLAHOMA
'07
CENTENNIAL ™

OKLAHOMA CENTENARIANS

They are defined as those
who are 100 years old or older.
So as Oklahoma celebrated its first century,
it was only fitting that they, too,
shared in the honor.

OKLAHOMA
CENTENARIANS

Some were born in Indian Territory, some in Oklahoma Territory, some came here later in life. Together, they form the heart and soul of Oklahoma. They're the dreamers, the believers, the achievers. And they've been around for every day of this state's life.

It's no wonder then that Oklahoma's Centenarians played a prominent role in Centennial festivities. It began during Tulsa kickoff week with a "Celebration of Centenarians" on November 16, 2006 – a unique project that brought together the thoughts, memories, advice and images of 29 individuals from all over the state and all walks of life.

The state's treasured Centenarians were feted at a breakfast at the Oklahoma History Center on Statehood Day, November 16, 2007, and later participated in the Centennial Spectacular at the Ford Center. TV personality Willard Scott introduced 25 Centenarians, who included 101-year-old Melvin Welch. The former teacher brought the crowd to its feet with his rendition of the original state song, "Oklahoma, a Toast."

SALT OF THE RED EARTH *M.J. Alexander's book* Salt of the Red Earth: A Century of Wit and Wisdom from Oklahoma's Elders *(right) is a collection of portraits and stories of Oklahomans born in or before 1907, the year Oklahoma gained statehood. These men and women express their joys and memories of childhood years, their love of each other and their journey to the age of 100. It's a touching, poignant glimpse into the lives of those who formed the foundation of this state.*

O.K. CAMPBELL *Age 100, Commerce*

PHYLLIS FRANCES LONG BENSON WHITCHURCH
Age 102, Tulsa

Salt of the Red Earth

A CENTURY OF WIT AND WISDOM FROM OKLAHOMA'S ELDERS
M.J. Alexander

RAYMOND LEE FISH *Age 102, Oklahoma City*

DEWITT FRANK BLACKARD AND HIS SISTER EUNICE LUCILLE BLACKARD RAIFORD
Ages 103 and 101, both of Valliant

JAMES P. OWENS
Age 101, Okemah

REV. PHILIP BAIER WAHL
Age 100, Duncan

"THE CENTENARIANS" EXHIBIT
On display at the Oklahoma Heritage
Center from October 29, 2007, to
January 6, 2008, "The Centenarians"
is a photographic collection representing
an estimated 400 of the state's residents.
Photographer **M.J. Alexander** said
that the featured portraits depicted
100 different ways to be 100.

THOMAS J. BROWN
Age 100, Okmulgee

MILLARD WESLEY GADDIE
Age 104, Bethany

**SISTERS RUBY LOIS OWENS SANDERS AND
MILDRED MAGGIE OWENS DEVINS DAVIS**
Ages 101 and 103, both of Madill

DAISY HAWLEY BLACKBIRD
Age 103, Oklahoma City

MARIAN HARRISON WEIMER
Age 98, Tulsa

OKLAHOMA CENTENARIANS

WILLARD SCOTT *The television personality served as host at a breakfast honoring the state's Centenarians held on Statehood Day 2007 at the* **Oklahoma History Center***. Scott retired as the TODAY show's full-time weatherman, but occasionally appears on the show to wish Centenarians Happy Birthday. "This really is inspiring because I get to meet some of these folks that I talked about on TV," said Scott. "But I've never seen so many of you under one roof. I want to congratulate all of you. It is a great accomplishment."*

MILDRED HURT *Age 100, Yukon*

CENTENARIAN BREAKFAST *Oklahoma City Mayor* **Mick Cornett** *spoke to the crowd during the morning gathering of Centenarians at the Oklahoma History Center. To the right of the podium are* **Lee Allan Smith** *and* **J. Blake Wade***.*

IDA MAE WILSON *Age 99, Oklahoma City*

MARGUERITE TAYLOR *Age 100*

RUBY LEE PERKINS
Age 100, Oklahoma City

THE SPECTACULAR *During the evening's festivities, **Willard Scott** paid tribute to Oklahoma's Centenarians. As he mentioned individuals by name, their photos appeared on the screen behind him.*

BEULA MARIAN GREEN PASCHALL *Age 100*

OKLAHOMA CENTENARIANS

TULSA PARADE *Oklahoma Centenarians were feted during Tulsa Kickoff activities, which included a parade and reception. Shown below are parade participants* **Arnold Richardson** *of Miami,* **Ellen Moore** *of Tulsa and* **Phyllis Frances Long Benson Whitchurch** *of Tulsa.*

RECEPTION & LUNCHEON *This event was held at the* **Tulsa Historical Society** *on Statehood Day 2006. It honored Centenarians including Tulsa residents (right)* **Mary Pace** *and (below, left to right)* **Ora Reed Holland**, **Lucille Holman Wooden**, **Nora Owens Reed Simmons** *and* **Greta Cottrell Woodson Storey Saye Mill Heslet**.

Centenarian
Arnold Richardson
Miami, 100
Born June 29

Centenarian
Ellen Moore

Centenarian
Phyllis Whitchu

OCIE HUGHES *Age 101, Sapulpa*

OKLAHOMA
CENTENNIAL
'07 ™

LAND RUN MONUMENT

In April 1889, a shot rang out in Indian Territory
that sent homesteaders racing across
the newly opened lands to stake their claims.
They came on foot and by horses, wagons and trains
— with family, possessions and animals in tow.
A century later, that historic occasion
is forever remembered.

LAND RUN
MONUMENT

The rush is on in Bricktown – the Land Rush, that is. On the banks of this historic district's canal stand some prominent – and permanent – new guests. Very *large* guests at that: horses weighing 2,800 pounds and wagons stretching out as far as 35 feet long.

It's an epic salute to the Land Run of 1889: a series of sculptures that will eventually form one of the largest bronze monuments in the world. Created by renowned Oklahoma sculptor Paul Moore, the pieces depict scenes including early settlers, horses, wagons and animals.

The first bronze was unveiled in April 2003 at a dedication ceremony attended by Gov. Brad Henry, Lt. Gov. Mary Fallin and Oklahoma City Mayor Kirk Humphreys. New sculptures are being added each year and will total 46 pieces when complete. It's a massive tribute to a monumental event – the world's first land run and Oklahoma's first step toward statehood.

ARTIST PAUL MOORE *A native Oklahoman, Moore has gained international recognition with his sculptures. He has been working on this land run commemoration for the last few years – a project especially near to Moore's heart, as his great-grandfather was a land run participant.*

INTRICATE DETAILS *In the early stages of larger pieces, Moore creates a foam model of the statue. After the model has been encased in clay, details are sculpted into the clay covering.*

"THE PINNACLE OF SUCCESS"
Oklahoma artist Moore spoke of the land run project being his crowning achievement. He's sculpted more than 100 commissions to date – over half have been installed in his home state, including the nine-foot figure of Johnny Bench at the Bricktown Ballpark. Moore is a fellow and board member of the National Sculpture Society.

MULTI-TASKING *At any given time, Moore works on three to four pieces of the monument at a time – each in a different stage of the process. He works out of his studio in Norman and also serves as the University of Oklahoma sculptor-in-residence.*

PIECE BY PIECE *Moore uses separate molds for the head, legs, torso and other body parts. For the larger statues, such as the wagons, more than 100 molds may be made.*

147

OKLAHOMA CENTENNIAL
LAND RUN
MONUMENT

A TRIBUTE IN BRONZE *"This monument is about hope and opportunity,"* said U.S. Rep. **Ernest Istook** *during the dedication of the first installment. The close attention to detail seen in each piece reflects the same spirit and determination shown by Oklahoma's land run settlers.*

BUILT TO LAST
Each of the sculptures is covered with clear-coat wax to prevent oxidation and protect the pieces. Internal stainless steel supports are also built into each of the horses and wagons.

A MONUMENTAL UNDERTAKING

Once complete, the monument will be an impressive display of 46 separate sculptures featuring men and women, horses, wagons, a buggy, dog, rabbit and cannon.

CROSSING THE CANAL *Wagons and cowboys on horseback are placed in an "S" shape across the east and west sides of the Bricktown Canal. They will eventually cover more than 360 feet – a span longer than a football field.*

A GRAND-SCALE DESIGN

With dimensions reaching 15 feet tall and 35 feet long, the sculptures are an awe-inspiring one-and-a-half times life size.

OKLAHOMA CENTENNIAL
LAND RUN
MONUMENT

GROWING TOURIST ATTRACTION

Not even half complete, the monument has already become a major draw for visitors – one that spurs added interest with each new installment. Many city leaders envision that it will eventually become Oklahoma City's signature attraction.

SCENIC CIRCLE

A spectator area just south of the Bricktown Canal offers the perfect location for viewing the various pieces of the Land Run Monument.

GENEROUS CONTRIBUTORS

*Early significant contributions from **Edward L. Gaylord**, **Kerr-McGee Corp.**, and **LaDonna** and **Herman Meinders** provided funding to begin the project. In addition, the city, state and federal government, along with Oklahoma City Centennial sponsors, contributed to create this massive monument commemorating Oklahoma's land run.*

MAJOR LEAGUE BASEBALL

EXHIBITION GAMES

Ah, the smell of spring. The crack of the bat.
The roar of the crowd.
Throw in a hot dog and bag of peanuts
and it can mean only one thing:
baseball season.

MAJOR LEAGUE
BASEBALL
EXHIBITION GAMES

For two days in the spring of 2005, the SBC Bricktown Ballpark was host to two of Major League Baseball's finest teams – the St. Louis Cardinals and Baltimore Orioles. The Cards, fresh from their National League Championship season, took on another storied franchise in the American League's Orioles.

These major league exhibitions were early-on Centennial events and crowd pleasers at that. Both games welcomed sold-out crowds as fans turned out to cheer on their team and enjoy America's favorite pasttime. Some of the notables in attendance included former Oklahoma City Mayor Kirk Humphreys, Lt. Gov. Mary Fallin, Barry Switzer, Joe Castiglione, Joe Carter Sr., Merlyn Mantle (Mickey Mantle's widow), John Smith and Mickey Tettleton.

Brought to Oklahoma City to celebrate the great history of baseball in the state, the games were presented by Integrated Medical Delivery, Kerr-McGee and *The Oklahoman*. Sponsors were American Airlines, BancFirst, Cox Cable and KWTV Channel 9.

PLAY BALL! *The first Major League Baseball games in Oklahoma City since 1993, the Cardinals-Orioles series featured 14 current and former all-stars.*

AUTOGRAPH SIGNING
Before the games began, players took to the stands to meet fans and sign autographs.

GAMES FOR THE AGES
Visitor interest was high as an estimated 24,580 fans turned out for the two-game series.

Commemorative Issue of the Oklahoma Centennial
Major League Baseball Games
March 31 & April 1, 2005
SBC Bricktown Ballpark
Oklahoma City, Oklahoma

Orioles VS. Cardinals

JANET WILBURN *Accompanied by the University of Oklahoma band, Wilburn, from Ada, sang the national anthem at the March 31 game.*

LEONA MITCHELL *The nationally renowned soprano and Enid native sang "God Bless America" during the seventh-inning stretch of the April 1 game. The soldiers behind her are from the 45th Infantry Brigade and had just returned from serving in combat in Iraq.*

LEE GREENWOOD
During the seventh-inning stretch of the opener, Greenwood sang his hit, "God Bless the U.S.A." He was surrounded by U.S. soldiers who had returned from Iraq.

NATIONAL ANTHEM *As Cardinal players looked on, the University of Oklahoma's Pride of Oklahoma marching band – under the direction of **Brian Britt** – played "The Star Spangled Banner" prior to the first game in the series.*

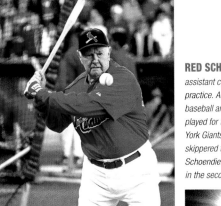

RED SCHOENDIENST *The Cardinals assistant coach led a pre-game fielding practice. A 63-year veteran of professional baseball and a Hall of Famer, Schoendienst played for teams including the Cardinals, New York Giants and Milwaukee Braves. He also skippered the Cardinals team from 1965-1976. Schoendienst threw out a ceremonial first pitch in the second game of the series.*

CHRIS CARPENTER *The Cardinals pitcher started the March 31 game. It turned out to be the beginning of a successful season for Carpenter as he went on to start in the 2005 All-Star Game.*

ONE ROWDY FAN *Oklahoma's minor league baseball team loaned out their mascot Rowdy the RedHawk to help entertain the crowds.*

SAMMY SOSA *One of baseball's most feared sluggers, Sosa played his first season for the Orioles in 2005 after more than a decade-long stint with the Chicago Cubs. Sosa played for the Oklahoma City 89ers for 10 games in 1989.*

OKLAHOMA
CARE
GENEROSITY
TRIBUTE FORD CENTER
DUETS
MUSIC PIANO DRUMS
HEROES
FAMILIES
MEMORIAL
OPRY SURVIVORS
STARS REMEMBER HOPE
FUTURE GRATITUDE
RESCUE WORKERS FIDDLE
HONOR HEART HARMONY
SPIRIT

OKLAHOMA
'07
CENTENNIAL

MEMORIAL CONCERT

Special ceremonies commemorating
the 10th anniversary of the
Alfred P. Murrah Federal Building bombing
took place starting the week of Sunday, April 17.
Friday's event was music to the ears.

OKLAHOMA CITY NATIONAL
MEMORIAL CONCERT

E ach day of the week held a special significance. From Sunday's "Day of Faith" to the following Sunday's "Run to Remember," activities were designed to honor "those who were killed, those who survived and those changed forever" by the 1995 bombing. The Memorial Thank You Concert was held on Friday, the "Day of Caring," and showing just how much they cared were some of Oklahoma's favorite sons and daughters.

Performers at the Ford Center included Vince Gill, Toby Keith, Ty England, Katrina Elam, Jimmy Webb, Byron Berline and Joe Diffie. Musicians from the Centennial Rodeo Opry also took to the stage in front of a packed house. It was a moving, memorable evening that was Oklahoma's way of saying "thank you" to the rescue workers, survivors and family members.

The all-star concert was presented by the Oklahoma City Centennial sponsors and produced by Oklahoma Events. "The concert is a way for the memorial to thank the people of Oklahoma who've worked so hard to support us with their generosity and giving spirit," said Kari Watkins, executive director of the Oklahoma City National Memorial.

SPECIAL APPEARANCES
Addressing the crowd were representatives from Oklahoma City's KWTV-9: Chief Meteorologist **Gary England** (left) and News Anchor **Kelly Ogle**.

PHILIP BAUER The singer joined some of his Rodeo Opry band mates (shown at bottom) on stage for a musical set.

TY ENGLAND The country music star took to the stage, performing with **Shawna Russell**.

SOLD-OUT CROWD Enthusiastic fans packed the Ford Center to witness a star-studded night of entertainment and to say "thank you" to the volunteers and rescue workers of the 1995 bombing.

VINCE GILL (left) Born in Norman, Gill enjoyed acclaim in the bluegrass and pop worlds before actively pursuing a career in mainstream country during the '80s. He went on to achieve commercial success as a frontman in a band and, later, as a solo artist. To date, Gill has sold more than 26 million albums and charted more than 40 singles on U.S. Billboard Hot Country Songs.

CENTENNIAL RODEO OPRY MUSICIANS
Concert attendees enjoyed selections by **Tammy Lee** (left), **Kyle Earhart** (center), and **Pat Payne** and **Kyle Dillingham** (right), performers who frequently appear at the Rodeo Opry.

OKC MEMORIAL CONCERT

MACI WAINWRIGHT
Shown performing at
the Thank You Concert,
vocalist Wainwright
sings at the Centennial
Rodeo Opry.

TOBY KEITH (right)
The "Big Dog Daddy"
entertained the crowd
with some of his
biggest hits, including
"Beer for My Horses."

JIMMY WEBB Webb's
accomplishments as a composer are
legendary and lengthy: he's a member
of the National Academy of Popular
Music Songwriters Hall of Fame,
the Nashville Songwriters Hall of
Fame and, according to BMI, his
"By The Time I Get To Phoenix" has
been the third most performed song in
the last 50 years. In 1999, Webb
was inducted into the Oklahoma Hall
of Fame and, in early 2000, he was
inducted onto the Board of Directors
for The Songwriters Hall of Fame.

JOSH ROBERTS
Roberts is another per-
former who often appears
at the Rodeo Opry.

MEGAN GLYCKHER
Rodeo Opry favorite Glyckher was honored to be part of the tribute.

THE BYRON BERLINE BAND
(below) This group performs traditional bluegrass and western swing and includes (left to right) **Richard Sharp**, **John Hickman**, **Barry Patton** *and* **Byron Berline**. *Shown at right, Berline is a three-time national fiddle champion.*

JOE DIFFIE *This Tulsa native blasted onto the country scene in 1990 with his debut single, the #1 smash "Home." Diffie claimed another 13 top-10 hits for the next decade, five of which went all the way to #1.*

KATRINA ELAM *(right) Her first single, "No End in Sight," was released in 2004 and reached #29 on the Billboard Hot Country Songs chart. Since then, Elam has gone on to tour with Keith Urban and Rascal Flatts.*

NATIVE OKLAHOMANS *Musicians (left to right)* **Kirsten Scott**, **Perry Miears**, **Lara Singletary** *and* **Derek McCarver** *have all made appearances at Oklahoma City's Opry.*

OKC MEMORIAL CONCERT

LAURA GOSSETT *Rodeo Opry star Gossett went on to qualify for "American Idol" and then on to Hollywood.*

STAR-STUDDED SALUTE *The concert ended with all of the evening's performers on stage singing a medley of "America the Beautiful," "God Bless America" and "Oklahoma!."*

KRYSTAL KEITH *Taking the stage at the Oklahoma City Memorial Concert, Keith was introduced by her dad, **Toby Keith**.*

DUSTIN JONES *(above) The guitarist from Horseshoe Road, Jones grew up in Yukon and is one of Oklahoma's leading music producers.*

CONCERT PERFORMERS *(left to right) **Cody Vignal** and **Chance Vignal** of country duo Cody & Chance and **Jarrid Matlock** perform at the Ford Center.*

OKLAHOMA HISTORY CENTER

It was a decade in the making
for a building that would house a century in the telling.
Finally, Oklahoma's rich and colorful heritage
had a new home.

THE OKLAHOMA
HISTORY CENTER
GRAND OPENING GALAS

The Oklahoma Centennial Commission and the Oklahoma Historical Society hosted two galas celebrating the grand opening of Oklahoma's newest architectural masterpiece. More than 1,500 business, government and community leaders from across the state attended two nights of festivities.

All came together for a special preview of the new 18-acre, 215,000-square-foot Oklahoma History Center. The center's Smithsonian-quality exhibits explore the state's rich and diverse history in geology, transportation, commerce, culture, aviation and heritage – bringing to life the voices and visions of Oklahoma. More than 50 topics and 2,000 artifacts reflect the young state's inspiring and adventurous past.

Guests at the galas were greeted by historical reenactors, Indian fancy dancers, a trick roper and a living bronze statue, and were treated to entertainment that included the Al Good Orchestra, the Ambassadors' Concert Choir, Edgar Cruz, Amos Cunningham, David B. Hooten, the Oklahoma City University Choir and the Irv Wagner Choir. Also appearing was opera star Leona Mitchell, who performed rousing renditions of "Oklahoma!" and "God Bless America" as fireworks lit up the sky throughout the evening.

HALLS OF HISTORY (far right) During the final stages of construction, Executive Director Dr. **Bob Blackburn** (left) and Deputy Director **Robert Thomas** enjoy the view of the Oklahoma State Capitol from the Devon Great Hall. Operated by the Oklahoma Historical Society, the History Center opened to the public on November 19, 2005.

FROM DREAM TO REALITY *Oklahoma Gov. Brad Henry (right) speaks to the guests assembled on the first night of the galas. The governor thanked the Historical Society, former Gov. Frank Keating – shown below with his wife, Cathy, and Dr. Bob Blackburn – the legislature and the more than 4,000 generous donors who made the museum's opening possible.*

AMBASSADORS' CONCERT CHOIR *Led by Maestro Kenneth Kilgore, the choir performed at the museum's opening ceremonies.*

LIVING BRONZE COWBOY STATUE *Oklahoma resident Troy Scott is a professional artist and performer who appears across the state and nation as a living statue. He poses on a podium as a statue, then surprises and entertains viewers through movement and improvisation.*

HISTORY MAKERS *The gala is in full swing in Devon Great Hall, as seen from above the replica of the Winnie Mae. At right, American Indian dancers shared their timeless traditions.*

163

PHILLIP HAOZOUS *The son of Oklahoma artist Allan Houser, Haozous stands by a miniature of "Unconquered." The original heroic-sized piece was created by Houser and stands outside the history center. It was during the grand opening that the announcement was made of the gift of the sculpture to the center.*

A NEW RELIC *A fresh piece of Oklahoma history is found in the Centennial saddle, on display in the museum. Embossed with the Centennial logo, the saddle was created by **John Rule** of National Saddlery and generously donated by **Jose Freede**. From left: **J. Blake Wade**, Gov. **Brad Henry**, **Jose Freede**, **Lee Allan Smith**, **Cathy Freede**, First Lady **Kim Henry** and Dr. **Bob Blackburn**.*

A NIGHT TO REMEMBER *(top center) The Capitol provided a dramatic backdrop for an impressive fireworks display. (above) Visitors explored the center's five galleries and more than 200 hands-on exhibits and also enjoyed the quickness and agility of trick roper **John Harrison** (above right). A native of Soper, Harrison is the grandson of the late world champion bull rider, Freckles Brown.*

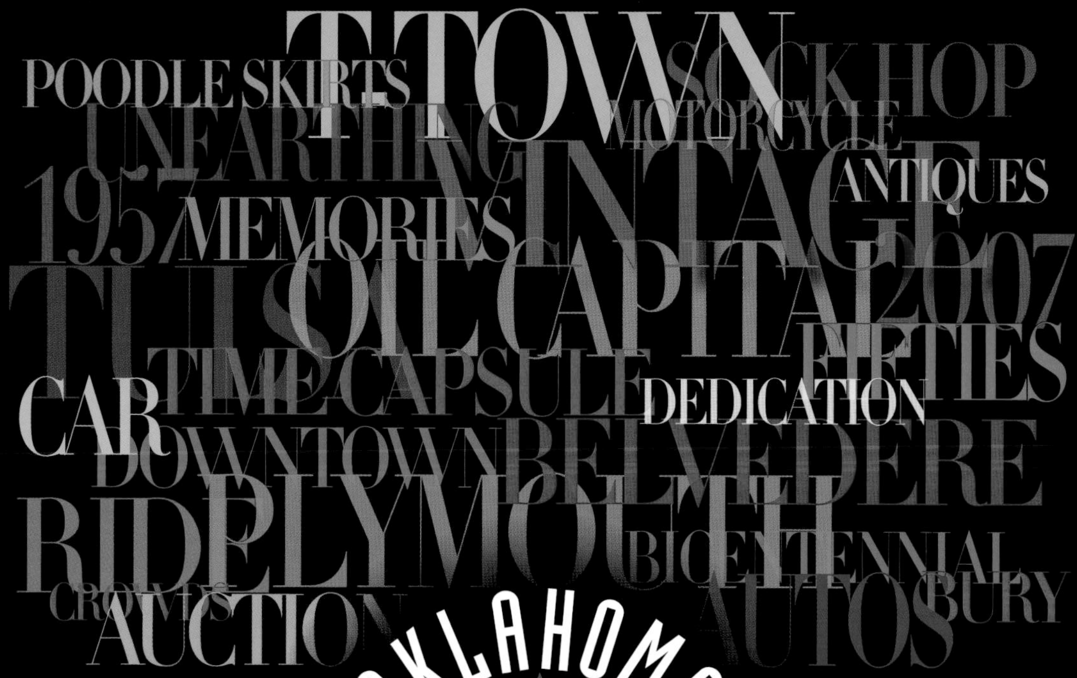
T TOWN
POODLE SKIRTS
SOCK HOP
UNEARTHING
MOTORCYCLE
VINTAGE
ANTIQUES
1957
MEMORIES
2007
TULSA
OIL CAPITAL
FIFTIES
TIME CAPSULE
CAR
DEDICATION
DOWNTOWN
BELVEDERE
RIDE
PLYMOUTH
BICENTENNIAL
CROWDS
AUCTION
AUTOS
BURY

OKLAHOMA '07 CENTENNIAL™

TULSARAMA!

The year was 1957 and the occasion was
Oklahoma's Golden Jubilee celebration.
And into the freshly dug hole on the courthouse lawn
went a brand new Plymouth Belvedere
(sticker price: $2,324).

TULSARAMA!

Inside the car, the glove compartment had been stocked with the contents of a woman's handbag: bobby pins, a compact, cigarettes and matches, two combs, an unpaid parking ticket, a tube of lipstick, a pack of gum, a plastic rain hat, pocket tissues and $2.73 in bills and coins. It was a one-of-a-kind time capsule not to be opened until the state's Centennial celebration.

Come 2007, with the Tulsarama week-long jubilee in full swing, the time had come to unearth the car. Following international media attention and interest, the two-tone, gold-and-white Plymouth was raised from its resting space to reveal a 50-year-old car that had acquired a little bit of rust, but still retained a lot of personality.

Inside the car was a sealed steel capsule that contained a 48-star American flag, letters from various state and city officials and the passbook for a savings account valued at $100 in 1957, which had appreciated to a little over $1,000 by 2007. The capsule also contained postcards from citizens estimating what the city's population might be in 2007 – the closest-to-actual estimate would win the car and savings account. At 384,743, Raymond Humbertson's 1957 entry wasn't far off from 382,457. Humbertson had passed away in 1979 though, so the car went to his two sisters in Maryland.

GOLDEN JUBILEE CELEBRATION *Cloaked in rust-resistant preservatives and placed inside a colossal concrete box, the mint-condition Plymouth Belvedere was gently lowered into its resting place on the Tulsa courthouse lawn, where it would stay for the next 50 years.*

TULSARAMA!
1957 - 2007
Tulsa's Buried Belvedere

AGED TO PERFECTION *The unveiling of the time capsule drew Oklahomans together, curious to see how time had treated the integrity of the car's once-shiny white-and-gold paint. Rusty and dirt-covered, the nostalgic value of the car far surpassed its blue book value.*

TIME CAPSULE DEDICATION *The brand new Plymouth Belvedere was hoisted onto a crane as it was prepared to be buried during the 1957 time capsule ceremony.*

AS TIME ROLLS ON *Before the Belvedere was buried, several citizens signed one of the tires. Fifty years later, those signatures are barely legible on the decaying white wall tires. This one tire is the only part of the car that didn't go to the winner – instead, it went to the Tulsa Historical Society.*

THE FIRST GLIMPSE *(left) Before the car could be raised up, workers had to cut out the cement the car was buried under. Once that was complete, the still-covered car was lifted from its 50-year resting place by a mammoth 120-ton crane-and-strap setup (below left).*

A RUSTY RIDE *It was unknown to the committee of the 1957 burial project that this specific year of Plymouth was particularly prone to rusting. Concerns of moisture in the cement sarcophagus and traffic vibrations further ignited the curiosity of the crowd and added to the anticipation of the long-awaited unveiling.*

EAGER ANTICIPATION *Crowds gathered outside the courthouse to watch as the canvas-shrouded car was lifted out of its cement vault. On hand for the festivities was **Joe Cappy** of Tulsa (left, in far right of photo), whose 47-year career in the auto industry included positions as the head of American Motors and vice president of Chrysler.*

THE HOOD IS RAISED *One look under the hood and it quickly became apparent that the engine was in the same shape as the rest of the car: rusty and discolored with a film of foul water and greenish algae.*

REMOVING THE SHROUD *The automobile enthusiasts delicately unwrapped the car's cover, peeling the plastic back to reveal the oxidized "Miss Belvedere," which was miraculously still in one piece. Since the vault in which the car laid for a half-century had flooded and the vacuum seal package around the car failed, the car had turned a vibrant auburn.*

HOW DID THEY FARE? *(left) Tulsarama committee chairman **John Erling** (also shown above), **Joshua Peck** of the Tulsa Historical Society and Tulsarama chairwoman **Sharon King Davis** examine items found in the time capsule that was buried with the Belvedere.*

TLC'S BOYD CODDINGTON *Host of TLC's hit series "American Hot Rod" and a world-renowned hot rod crafter, **Boyd Coddington** (far left) and his crew prepared the vehicle for its unveiling. Although Coddington had been commissioned to help start the car's engine, its 50 years in an underground tomb had rendered that feat impossible.*

EMPTYING THE TRUNK ***Nancy Shallner** of the Tulsa Historical Society organizes the items that were retrieved from the Belvedere's trunk.*

OKLAHOMA CENTENNIAL
TULSARAMA!

INVITATIONAL CAR SHOW *In addition to the Belvedere, many classic cars were on display at the Tulsa Convention Center.*

AT THE HOP *After the viewing of "Miss Belvedere," as the car came to be known, Tulsans donned their poodle skirts and saddle shoes for the 1950s-themed sock hop. Among the revelers perfecting the hand jive, cha cha and the bop were* **Mayor Kathy Taylor** *and her family (below). Taylor showed up decked out in a black poodle skirt, white button-up blouse, black-and-white saddle shoes and even a petticoat.*

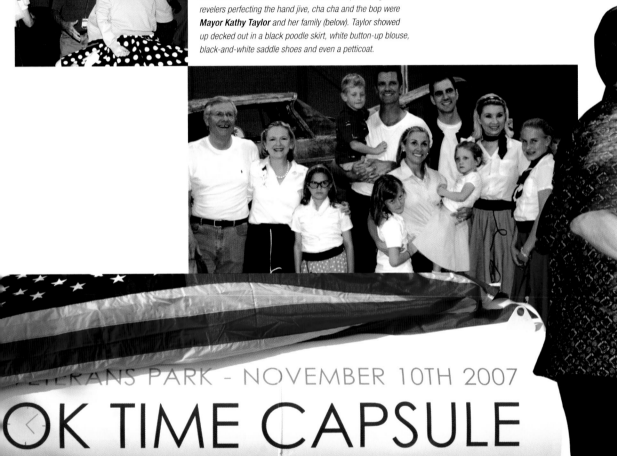

VETERANS PARK - NOVEMBER 10TH 2007

OK TIME CAPSULE

OKLAHOMA CENTENNIAL 1907 - 2007

IN THE SWING *A couple practices their dance moves at the '50s-themed sock hop. Guests twisted to golden oldies from Fabian, Bobby Vee and the Chiffons.*

LOOKING AHEAD *A 2007 Harley-Davidson motorcycle was buried in a cement tube in Veterans Park in Tulsa. This new time capsule will be unearthed in 2057.*

PIONEER BRAND TIMELESS
REMARKABLE COOKOUT
BEANS WAGON HORNS
ROPE
RAWHIDE DROVERS HEARTY
STEAKS WRANGLER
CATTLE
JESSE CHISHOLM HORSES
SADDLE REINS
COWBOYS CALF
RUGGED CAMP SITES
PLAINS HISTORY DEDICATION
LONGHORN MILE MARKERS

OKLAHOMA '07 CENTENNIAL™

CHISHOLM TRAIL

This is where the legend of the American cowboy began.
Rugged cattlemen rounding up longhorns
and driving them north across the plains of Indian Territory.
They were herding steers ... and riding into history.

CHISHOLM TRAIL
CORRIDOR & CATTLE DRIVE

In the latter half of the 19th century, the Chisholm Trail was a dirt trail used as a trade route through Indian Territory. It was established by Scottish-Cherokee cowboy Jesse Chisholm, who opened the way for herds of longhorns to be driven from the prairies of Texas to the railways of Kansas, where they were then sold and shipped eastward.

2007 marked the 140th anniversary of the first cattle drive along the Chisholm Trail. A special Centennial edition drive commemorated the occasion and once again, cattle could be seen moving north through west-central Oklahoma. Drovers pushed the more than 400 head of cattle from Fleetwood, Oklahoma to Caldwell, Kansas, just over the state line.

The month-long drive had rotating foremen for each of the weeks, plus a trail boss who guided the cowboys, horses, wagons and cattle for 12 to 15 miles each day. Several towns planned activities around the cattle drive and many schools brought children out to watch as the drive passed through town.

CHISHOLM TRAIL CORRIDOR
The Oklahoma Centennial Commission funded interpretive sites, monuments and trail crossing signs such as the one shown at left. Bob Klemme of Enid and Chris Jefferies of Duncan headed the Chisholm Trail Corridor initiative.

SETTING OUT *Riders in the Centennial cattle drive, including Scott Williams at right, departed near the Red River. Led by a rotating group of drovers, the herd spent the next month traversing the entire length of the trail across Oklahoma.*

CHISHOLM TRAIL
CENTENNIAL CORRIDOR
TRAIL CROSSING

GRAZING TIME *Counting up his cattle is herder **Roger Shire**. Because the cattle were able to graze in new, ungrazed areas each day, most of them gained weight on the drive.*

RELIVING HISTORY *With the Centennial flag flying high, **Zane Britton** and **Jim Peck** paused for a short break. Their wagon carried the team's bedrolls; cowboys unfurled them at night and slept under the stars – just as was done in the old days.*

CENTENNIAL CATTLE DRIVE

TRAIL BOSS
Ronnie Green

FOREMAN: Fleetwood to Rush Springs
Mike Smith

FOREMEN: Rush Springs to Ft. Reno
Larry Able
Marlene Able

FOREMEN: Ft. Reno to Enid
Floyd Townsend
Gary Townsend

FOREMEN: Enid to Caldwell, KS
Carmen Schultz
Clark Bittle

AN AUTHENTIC DRIVE *In a re-creation of the drives from 100 years ago, **Jack Pollard** led his longhorn cattle north through Oklahoma, up the legendary Chisholm Trail.*

THE HISTORIC
CHISHOLM TRAIL

CHOW TIME *(above)* ***Trammel Rushing*** *checks on his steaks. These modern-day cowboys traveled with two chuck wagons filled with food and cooking supplies.*

A HARD DAY'S NIGHT *Cowboys had precious little time to relax and reflect upon the day before it was time to hit the sack and rest up for another full day of riding.*

FT. RENO BBQ *(below) Guests lined up at the buffet during a sponsors and supporters event held in Ft. Reno on the night the drive camped there.*

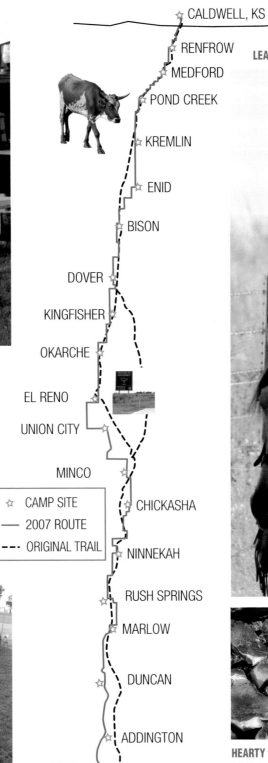

CALDWELL, KS
RENFROW
MEDFORD
POND CREEK
KREMLIN
ENID
BISON
DOVER
KINGFISHER
OKARCHE
EL RENO
UNION CITY
MINCO
CHICKASHA
NINNEKAH
RUSH SPRINGS
MARLOW
DUNCAN
ADDINGTON
RYAN
FLEETWOOD

☆ CAMP SITE
— 2007 ROUTE
- - - ORIGINAL TRAIL

LEADING THE WAY *Freddie Craig drove the herd down U.S. 81 near Duncan.*

HEARTY FARE *There was nothing fancy about meals along the trail. Whatever could be cooked over an open fire is what the trailhands ate – frequently, that meant freshly grilled steak for supper.*

JUST PASSING THROUGH
*As cities have since sprung up along the original cattle drive route, the Centennial drive led to an unusual sight: an entire herd of steers traipsing through town. The cattle were led by **Cituck Anderson**.*

MODERN-DAY HERDERS *The month-long event provided an opportunity for dozens of volunteers to participate. Drovers changed weekly; there were four teams (with approximately 20 per team) for the four weeks of the drive. Shown below is a group from week two. It includes both drovers and drive supporters. Standing in the second row is **Rose Chisholm** (white shirt, blue jeans), the granddaughter of **Jesse Chisholm**.*

ALONG THE TRAIL *Although the Chisholm Trail is now little more than a rut running through the prairie – much of it paved over by roads or railways – the trail's importance will never be forgotten.*

175

THE HISTORIC CHISHOLM TRAIL

"ON THE CHISHOLM TRAIL" *(below) This life-size sculpture of a cattle drive sits outside the Chisholm Trail Heritage Center in Duncan. Commissioned by Oklahoma oilman* **Thomas H. McCasland Jr.**, *and created by the University of Oklahoma's resident sculptor* **Paul Moore***, this bronze is a monument to the American cowboy. "On the Chisholm Trail" stands nearly 15 feet high and stretches 35 feet long – an impressive tribute to the cowboys who molded this land so many years before statehood.*

END OF THE TRAIL *(above) This marker at Duncan's Chisholm Trail Heritage Center was a Centennial project and represents the end of the trail – a welcome sight for the herders who drove five million head of cattle over hundreds of miles of rough and sometimes hostile territory.*

MUSEUM EXHIBIT *The Chisholm Trail Heritage Center in Duncan features exhibits that allow visitors the opportunity to imagine what life was like along the trail in the late 1800s. Items on display include saddles, sculptures, historic photographs and other memorabilia.*

JESSE CHISHOLM SCULPTURE *In Kingfisher,* **John Gooden**'s *heroic-sized bronze statue of Chisholm overlooks Highway 81, which follows the route of the legendary trail. In the latter part of his life, Chisholm made his home in the Creek Nation, near the mouth of the Little River in what is now Hughes County. He had trading posts on the edge of the Great Plains, including one near the site of Lexington (present-day Cleveland County) and one at Council Grove (now Oklahoma City).*

LIFE ON THE TRAIL

WINE DISNEY
SUNSHINE CELEBRATION
FOOD EXHIBITS HERITAGE
FUN WESTERN EPCOT EXCITEMENT
OKLAHOMA TEEPEE
NATIVE
SIGHTS FLORIDA
DEMONSTRATIONS
CONCERTS DANCING
ORLAND ROUTE 66 CUISINE
HISTORY BUFFALO

OKLAHOMA
'07
CENTENNIAL™

EPCOT®

INTERNATIONAL FOOD & WINE FESTIVAL
WALT DISNEY WORLD® RESORT

In honor of the state's Centennial celebration, the **Walt Disney World**® Resort invited Oklahoma to be the first state-dedicated marketplace at the 12th Annual

EPCOT®
INTERNATIONAL FOOD & WINE FESTIVAL

ARTS AND CRAFTS
Visitors to the exhibit browse artwork from Oklahoma. Items on display changed weekly.

Hailed as one of the largest and longest events of its kind in the world, the Epcot Festival features cuisine from around the globe and cooking demonstrations from acclaimed chefs. Oklahoma was honored and pleased to host the first-ever state-themed exhibit.

The backdrop display at The Oklahoma Experience featured "100 Stories of Oklahoma" told through three Walls of Wonder (28' x 16') – each portrayed state trailblazers through photos and narrative. Included in the area were food and beverage kiosks, an authentic chuck wagon, cooking demonstrations, an artisan area, an entertainment stage, children's activities, and an information and gift shop. Artisans such as the Oklahoma Fancy Dancers and trick roper Richard Heinrich performed daily, while craftsmen sold original artwork to festival guests.

State ambassadors were on hand to discuss Oklahoma travel and attractions with guests. Plus, Oklahoma Centennial officials in attendance included Gov. Brad Henry, J. Blake Wade, Georgiana Rymer, Jeanie Edney, Joan Hess and Colin McEwen.

ARTIST'S RENDERING
This early conceptual drawing depicted the size and scope of The Oklahoma Experience.

SMILE! *Oklahoma Department of Commerce General Counsel **Jonna D. Kauger Kirschner** gets into the spirit using the Oklahoma sign as a photo opportunity. The department had a leadership role in planning and staffing the Oklahoma exhibit.*

WHERE'S MICKEY?
Artists from Walt Disney Imagineering decorated a nearly life-size fiberglass buffalo with a luminous Oklahoma landscape containing a cleverly hidden Mickey Mouse design.

THE OKLAHOMA EXPERIENCE The state exhibit featured a teepee that housed children's activities (left), two kiosks offering Oklahoma-style fare and booths featuring state artisans like **Jim VanDeman** (right).

OKLAHOMA GIFTS *The Oklahoma merchandise shop (below center) was modeled after Frank Lloyd Wright's Price Tower, located in Bartlesville. Stopping by to browse the selections was Oklahoma Lt. Gov.* **Jari Askins** *(left, with exhibit worker).*

HOMEGROWN TALENT *Epcot guests were treated to daily performances by Oklahoma musicians including* **Brad Benge** *(above left) and* **Kyle Dillingham** *(above right and also at left) of Horseshoe Road.*

WALLS OF WONDER *The three giant murals featured in the exhibit portrayed historical scenes and current personalities.*

AMERICAN INDIANS *(left) The state's rich Native American heritage was on full display at the exhibit in the form of storytellers such as **Jehnean Washington**, a Cherokee-Yuchi-Seminole, and **Will Hill**, a Muscogee-Cherokee Indian.*

OKLAHOMA AMBASSADORS
*Shown in front of Oklahoma's buffalo sculpture, **Jonna D. Kauger Kirschner** served as one of the state's many ambassadors manning the exhibit. These experts were on hand to answer questions and extend invitations to visit the state.*

LIVE ENTERTAINMENT
A wide variety of acts performed during the six-week run. Much like the artwork, performers and entertainment changed weekly.

THE ART OF STORYTELLING
*Visitors enjoyed storytelling by **Jehnean Washington** of the Oklahoma-based troupe Mahenwahdose, the first to perform at the National Museum of the American Indian in Washington, D.C.*

WELCOME! *Natalie Shirley, Oklahoma Secretary of Commerce and Tourism, and **Gena Timberman**, executive director of the Native American Cultural and Education Authority, greet exhibit visitors.*

OKLAHOMA CENTENNIAL WINE
*Commemorative wines were vented by Joullian Vineyards in California, a winery owned by Oklahoman **Richard Sias**.*

SKILLED ARTISANS
***Jana Jae**, the "first lady of country fiddle," brought her one-of-a-kind style to Epcot where she was joined by her grand-daughter, **Sandra Coleman**.*

PARTY FOR THE SENSES
These palate-pleasing events were a popular ticket. Guests were set in a festival-like atmosphere, where diners savored gourmet foods and sipped fine wines from around the world. The Oklahoma delegation served at both parties.

REGIONAL FEAST *(right)*
***Kurt Fleischfresser**, chef of Oklahoma City's The Coach House restaurant, served as the coordinator for the Regional Feast, where he was joined by chefs from other Oklahoma restaurants. More than 150 people attended the event and enjoyed gourmet Oklahoma dishes accompanied by a Jouillan wine.*

CENTENNIAL RIVER FESTIVALS

Spectators lined the riverbank.
Some sat in bleachers, others were settled in with
a picnic blanket or chair. All were on hand to
witness the fourth annual

CENTENNIAL REGATTA
FESTIVAL

READY TO ROW *Oars are lined up outside the boathouse and lie waiting for the rowers participating in the regatta. The 30-team field corporate challenge attracted Oklahomans from companies across the Oklahoma City metro area.*

The 2007 edition of this four-day festival featured world-class rowing, live entertainment, wine tasting, an arts festival, children's activities and fireworks. The event was held at Regatta Park on the Oklahoma River, just south of downtown and I-40 in Oklahoma City.

Two separate rowing competitions included the Oklahoma City University Head of the Oklahoma for collegiate, high school and master rowers, and the inaugural USA Rowing World Challenge. Traditional powers like Harvard and Stanford competed in the Head of the Oklahoma, along with teams from Duke, UCLA, Texas, Penn, Oklahoma City, Tulsa and Central Florida. The world challenge drew entrants from Canada, Mexico, Australia, New Zealand, Switzerland and the Czech Republic.

"We see this continuing to build as a major community event that people look forward to," said Mike Knopp, Oklahoma City University rowing coach and executive director of the Oklahoma City Boathouse Foundation. "Just coming down, spending an afternoon on the river, watching the racing, enjoying the other activities and making this one of those great events that Oklahoma City is known for."

A DAY AT THE RIVER *The nearly 50,000 in attendance for the four-day event were treated to championship racing from international and collegiate rowers, as well as a lively riverbank filled with music and entertainment, food, arts, demonstrations and even a wine tasting.*

CHESAPEAKE BOATHOUSE *More than 1,000 of the nation's top collegiate and club rowers filtered through the boathouse during the festival. An Oklahoma Centennial project, the Chesapeake Boathouse is a state-of-the-art facility that offers not only rowing, kayaking and dragon boating, but also an event room, fitness center, yoga classes and bicycle rentals.*

RACING ACTION *With the downtown skyline serving as a backdrop, rowers took to the river. The USA Rowing World Challenge featured a 500-meter sprint and a 2,000-meter race, while the Head of the Oklahoma featured 4,000-meter races and the 500-meter OG&E NightSprints, the first sanctioned night rowing event in North America.*

FUN FOR ALL AGES *There was plenty of big fun for little ones, too, with children's activities including face painting, giant inflatables and fishing. Plus, young rowers were able to get some hands-on practice alongside some of the best rowers in the country.*

185

OKLAHOMA CENTENNIAL REGATTA

UNIVERSITY OF OKLAHOMA
(below) Rowers from the local team carry their vessel though the festival grounds. The Sooners have a relatively young crew program, having competed only since 2001, and a varsity Division I women's program began in Fall 2008.

UNIVERSITY OF KANSAS *(below)*
The Jayhawks started their crew program in 1966, and claim over 50 members.

BOTTOMS UP! *J. Blake Wade, executive director of the Oklahoma Centennial Commission, breaks out the bubbly to christen The Centennial, a rowing vessel created in honor of Oklahoma's statehood. Looking on is Tom McDaniel, president of Oklahoma City University.*

KAYAK EXHIBITION *In addition to a canoe/kayak exhibition at the Regatta, Oklahoma City also played host to the U.S. Olympic Trials for Canoe/Kayak in April 2007.*

SOUTHERN METHODIST UNIVERSITY *(above)* *The Dallas-based Mustangs had a successful regatta – eight of their 10 boats finished in the top 10 of their respective races.*

UNIVERSITY OF COLORADO
(above) The Buffaloes started their crew team in 1992, when two transfer students from the University of San Diego wanted to row at a school without a crew program.

GLIDING TO VICTORY
(above) A rower gives an all-out effort on behalf of the Southern Methodist University's rowing team.

OKLAHOMA CITY UNIVERSITY
OCU debuted its new varsity sculling program at the Oklahoma Centennial Regatta.

COLORADO & KANSAS STATE
(above) The two schools battle it out for the lead during the races.

MAKING WAVES *Competitors give it their all as they speed toward the finish.*

BIG-TIME COMPETITION
The regatta drew teams from around the country, including perennial powerhouse Harvard. The Harvard crew team participated in the first intercollegiate athletic competition in America when they raced Yale in 1852.

INNOVATORS IN ROWING
Oklahoma City University was the first school to offer a varsity rowing program in central Oklahoma.

BACK ON DRY LAND *After a long day competing on the river, the Creighton crew unloads their equipment.*

Amid a shower of fireworks
and a sea of festive holiday lights,
Oklahoma City helped launch "Oklahoma's
Second Century of Prosperity."

OKLAHOMA CENTENNIAL
RIVER PARADE

It was a fitting end to the state's official Centennial Weekend celebration. More than 30 brightly decorated boats – showboats, indeed – cruised the Oklahoma River in a special Centennial version of the Holiday River Parade.

As the sun set, the fun began at an event that the year prior had attracted more than 40,000 people. In addition to the parade itself, visitors enjoyed live music, entertainment, food and merchandise booths, and a spectacular fireworks display.

The fourth-annual parade was sponsored by Devon Energy and included prizes for best decorations. Awards were given to Best of Parade, Best Holiday Theme and Best Holiday Spirit, as well as in corporate, individual and nonprofit categories.

NATIVE AMERICAN CELEBRATION *Boat City Prop Shop, owned and operated by **Tom Woods**, and the **Native American Cultural Center** sponsored this salute to the state's Indian heritage. The float was one of the recipients of the Mayor's Award.*

CENTENNIAL LAND RUN *This large float consisted of a horse-drawn wagon pulling the Centennial logo and a giant birthday cake. A live band performed on the back. The entry was provided by **David's Sport Center**, which is owned and operated by **David Ecker**.*

OKLAHOMA'S OIL HERITAGE *Taking second place in the nonprofit category was this brilliantly lit oil rig float sponsored by the **Riverfront Authority**.*

HOLIDAY TRAIN *Riverwind presented this colorful train entry – it earned second place in the corporate category.*

DEVON DISCOVERY *Devon Energy's boat was decorated like a wrapped present to symbolize its status as a gift to Oklahoma City. More than 20,000 lights were used to decorate the boat. The Discovery is now used for public, private and themed cruises on the Oklahoma River.*

NAUTICAL SANTA *(above) A boat decorated as Santa's sleigh was sponsored by **David's Sport Center**.*

MILITARY SALUTE *Retired Rear Admiral **Gregory J. Slavonic** addresses the crowd during the holiday parade.*

EDUCATION DESTINY COURAGE SCIENCE OPTIMISM GROWTH PROMISE DAWN PERSPECTIVE RESEARCH HISTORY INDUSTRY LAKES FUTURE RESOURCES DREAM SUNRISE PRAIRIE TALENT SUNSET SPIRIT FRONTIER RESILIENT CREATIVITY FOUNDATIONS UNIVERSITY OPPORTUNITY PROMISE CHARACTER TECHNOLOGY

OKLAHOMA '07 CENTENNIAL

CENTENNIAL FILM

This piece is a historic document that celebrates the bright promise our state holds for young Oklahomans. It was a key component of the culmination of our Centennial year ...

OKLAHOMA CENTENNIAL FILM

"Oklahoma Rising" is an hour-long film that was designed to inspire ambition and excitement about our state's future and the role young people can play in it. It portrays a "passing of the torch" from the generations of Oklahoma's first century to those who will lead its second century.

As the sun rises on those second hundred years, our Centennial year celebration serves as a lens through which we can set our sights on a truly luminous future. Sections in the film include: Oklahoma's renaissance; community, education and the arts; industry and careers; science, energy and water; our land, cowboys and American Indians; promise, spirit and life; and Oklahoma centenarians. Also featured are Vince Gill and Jimmy Webb performing the Centennial anthem, "Oklahoma Rising."

The first public broadcast of the film was on Sunday, November 11, when it aired on OETA. DVD sets of the film were distributed to all of Oklahoma's 1,875 K-12 schools and 206 libraries. Retail sales of "Oklahoma Rising" benefit the Oklahoma Heritage Association.

DR. BOB BLACKBURN *The executive director of the Oklahoma Historical Society addressed how technology has allowed people to return to rural Oklahoma — and how this blending of rural and urban has created even more possibilities.*

DR. FRANCINE RINGOLD *"There's a genuine hunger for the arts in all of us" was the theme from this former poet laureate for the state of Oklahoma.*

DR. JORDAN TANG *Dr. Tang, J.G. Puterbaugh Chair for Medical Research at the Oklahoma Health Sciences Center, articulated the impact of working in a state where people are pioneers.*

CLIFTON TAULBERT *A best-selling author, Taulbert discussed looking beyond gender and ethnicity, and looking to what is shared in common.*

DAVID L. BOREN *The University of Oklahoma president – and former Oklahoma governor and U.S. senator – describes Oklahomans as those who chase opportunity wholeheartedly, who are unafraid to test their mettle and push forward.*

DR. EARL D. MITCHELL JR. *Expounding on the importance of early childhood education, the professor emeritus of Oklahoma State University notes that these are the young people who will be in our college classes in 15 years, and who will ultimately lead the state over the next 50 years.*

DR. MICHAEL D. ANDERSON *The president of the Presbyterian Health Foundation emphasized that the marketplace for ideas that emerge from the state is not just Oklahoma, not just America – but the entire world.*

GENERAL THOMAS P. STAFFORD *The retired NASA astronaut, a lieutenant general of the U.S. Air Force, commended Oklahoma's inherent pioneering spirit.*

BILL ANOATUBBY *The governor of the Chickasaw Nation stresses the importance of Oklahoma maintaining a high standard of education – not only at the college and university level, but also in elementary and secondary schools.*

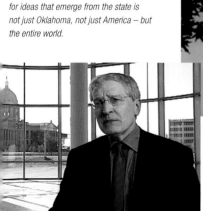

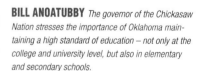

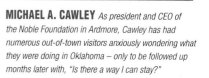

JUDGE ROBERT HENRY *"They are astounded at what they see," reveals the U.S. Court of Appeals Tenth Circuit judge upon meeting people that have come to Oklahoma for the first time.*

LEE ALLAN SMITH *The Centennial leader, vice chairman of Ackerman McQueen and president of Oklahoma Events, issued a reminder that while it's important to celebrate, it's also time to move forward – the future is beginning now.*

MICHAEL A. CAWLEY *As president and CEO of the Noble Foundation in Ardmore, Cawley has had numerous out-of-town visitors anxiously wondering what they were doing in Oklahoma – only to be followed up months later with, "Is there a way I can stay?"*

MICHAEL WALLIS *A noted author of books about the American West, including Route 66, Wallis touches upon the youthfulness of the state and how it plays in our favor.*

NEAL McCALEB *"Oklahoma has a great opportunity in front of it," said the chairman of the board of Chickasaw Nation Industries in reference to the state's abundant energy resources.*

NANCY G. FELDMAN *The former professor at the University of Tulsa discusses how arts provide a welcome change of pace for schoolchildren and ultimately help them learn better and excel on tests.*

ROSS O. SWIMMER *The U.S. Department of Interior's special trustee for American Indians detailed the impact of Indian tribes in Oklahoma and on the future of Oklahoma.*

RAY ACKERMAN *The longtime civic leader discussed Oklahoma's abundant fresh water supply and how it would lead to rapid growth over the next 50 years.*

H.E. "GENE" RAINBOLT *The BancFirst Corp. chairman spoke about the University of Oklahoma's College for Earth Resources and the role that Oklahoma universities will play in developing alternate energy sources.*

PEACE
HONOR WORLD WAR II
CONFLICT
VETERANS HAWAII
MEMORIES MEMORIAL ROOSEVELT
SAILORS
HOPE HOME JAPAN
ALLIANCE
MARTYR PEARL HARBOR BRAVERY
INFAMY SHIPS LIFE
PLANES
SUBMARINES PACIFIC
HEROES
FREEDOM

OKLAHOMA
'07
CENTENNIAL ™

USS OKLAHOMA
MEMORIAL

On December 7, 1941,
a sneak attack by Japanese torpedoes took the lives
of 429 men aboard the USS Oklahoma.
Today, a lasting tribute now stands in their honor.

USS OKLAHOMA
MEMORIAL

Sixty-six years to the day the USS Oklahoma suffered the second-largest loss of life in the 1941 Pearl Harbor attack, a memorial was dedicated to the battleship "Okie."

"It's been too long in coming," said Oklahoma Gov. Brad Henry, who attended the ceremony along with more than 20 survivors and their family members. Prior to this dedication, the USS Oklahoma was the only battleship sunk in the Pearl Harbor attack that didn't have its own memorial. Funding came from the Oklahoma Centennial Commission and private donations raised during the past two decades.

Others present at the dedication included Roland Nee, Oklahoma chairman of the Pearl Harbor Survivors Association, plus representatives from the U.S. Navy, the National Park Service and the USS Oklahoma Memorial Executive Committee. Some of the several hundred Oklahomans in attendance were First Lady Kim Henry, Donna and J. Blake Wade, Jeanie and Bob Edney, Georgiana Rymer, Jennifer Kiersch, DeLee Smith, Juli Lyles, Lou Kerr, Nancy Leonard, Linda English and Gerald Adams.

PEARL HARBOR ATTACKED

The front page of The Daily Oklahoman *reports of the Japanese air attacks that occurred on December 7, 1941.*

THE FALLEN REMEMBERED

Brock Corcoran, a sailor stationed at Oklahoma's Tinker Air Force Base, examines the new memorial.

HUGS AND TEARS

(right) **Joanne Shawver** greets USS Oklahoma survivor **Ray Turpin**. Shawver's uncle, Charles Andrew Montgomery, lost his life aboard the ship.

SURVIVOR GEORGE A. SMITH

(left) USS Oklahoma survivor Smith was just 17 years old when the Japanese attacked Pearl Harbor.

USS OKLAHOMA MEMORIAL

COLOR GUARD *Representatives from Claremore High School Navy Junior ROTC and U.S. Grant High School Marine Junior ROTC of Oklahoma City participated in ceremonies at Pearl Harbor. From left are* **Cody Marts**, **Kati Lortz**, **Jeremy Kirkendall**, **Hilary Keefe**, **Kathrine Carra**, **Kevin Eckols** *and* **Tyler McCaslin**.

MASTER OF CEREMONIES *(center, at podium) Rear Admiral* **Doug McClain** *served as emcee for the day's dedication activities.*

HEARTFELT EMOTION *(left) The ceremony offered a poignant and touching tribute to all of the men present on that fateful day in 1941. At the time of the dedication, 66 years later, the youngest survivor was 83 years old.*

A SOLEMN SALUTE
(above) **George A. Smith** *raises a hand in salute. He was one of 20 survivors to attend the memorial dedication ceremony for the USS Oklahoma.*

IN THEIR HONOR *The names of the 429 USS Oklahoma crew members who lost their lives are carved into white marble. The **Beck Design Group** created the memorial and used marble and granite shipped from Oklahoma City to Pearl Harbor courtesy of the **Swift Transportation Company**.*

TAPS *(above) Staff Sgt. **Hugh Kinsey** played the familiar and moving military bugle call during the dedication ceremony.*

SURVIVOR RAY RICHMOND *(left) During the attack, Richmond swam from the Oklahoma to the USS Maryland, where he climbed aboard and manned an anti-aircraft gun until the threat subsided.*

SURVIVOR GEORGE BROWN *Brown (left, in white cap) bows his head during the dedication service for the USS Oklahoma Memorial. The ship's cook, Brown has been credited with a quotation displayed on the memorial: "That was the most horrible scene that you could ever think of. Shipmates there. You can't save them." To this day, he refuses to talk about what exactly he saw that led him to make this statement.*

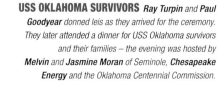

USS OKLAHOMA SURVIVORS *Ray Turpin and **Paul Goodyear** donned leis as they arrived for the ceremony. They later attended a dinner for USS Oklahoma survivors and their families – the evening was hosted by **Melvin** and **Jasmine Moran** of Seminole, **Chesapeake Energy** and the Oklahoma Centennial Commission.*

USS OKLAHOMA
MEMORIAL

WELL DECORATED *Ribbons and medals recognize the honors and achievements of USS Oklahoma survivor **Garlen Eslick**, who was trapped below deck for 28 hours before being rescued.*

SURVIVOR PAUL GOODYEAR *Saluting the flag during the dedication ceremony are USS Oklahoma survivor Goodyear (below left) and National Park Service Ranger **Doug Levin**. Goodyear, 89, was the driving force behind the efforts to establish the memorial. The ceremony ended with a Navy sailor (above) playing "Amazing Grace" on the bagpipes.*

EXCURSION TRAIN
& RAILWAY MUSEUM

All aboard for Oklahoma City!
With some of the top attractions soon tied by train,
navigating between the Bricktown Ballpark
and Softball Hall of Fame or the Land Run Monument
and Oklahoma City Zoo will be easier than ever.

EXCURSION TRAIN
& RAILWAY MUSEUM

Next stop: Bricktown! Oklahoma City's excursion train is already a great way to travel from one entertainment area to another – but coming soon, the locomotive will be escorting passengers between the city's busiest tourist attractions with the Adventure District and Bricktown connection.

Joe Kyle, head of the railway division at the Oklahoma Department of Transportation, has worked with the Oklahoma City Centennial Committee to clear up access to tracks into Bricktown. "It's a really good trip," said Kyle. "It connects a vibrant part of Oklahoma City with another vibrant part of Oklahoma City."

The excursion train operates from its Oakwood base station at the Oklahoma Railway Museum on Grand Boulevard, just off of Northeast 34th Street. A second station – at Northeast 50th Street, east of the Oklahoma State Firefighters Museum and Memorial – was made possible thanks largely to a donation of land by Ben Kates, owner of Midwest Wrecking, and his business partner, David Hamilton.

The Grand-to-50th route runs through Lincoln Park Golf Course and offers passengers easy access to the Adventure District. From there, trolleys take riders to attractions including the National Cowboy & Western Heritage Museum, National Softball Hall of Fame, Oklahoma City Zoo, Oklahoma State Firefighters Museum and Memorial, Remington Park Racing Casino, Cinemark Tinseltown USA and Science Museum Oklahoma.

ALL ABOARD! *The conductor, **Steve Davis**, beckons riders aboard the Excursion Train.*

OKLAHOMA RAILWAY MUSEUM *Situated in a former railroad depot on Grand Boulevard off of Northeast 34th Street in Oklahoma City, the museum operates working diesel locomotives and has a full assortment of railcars. It was begun by the Central Oklahoma Chapter of the National Railway Historical Society – a group of railroad enthusiasts who banded together more than three decades ago. Chapter members worked diligently over the years to raise funds for the museum and, today, it's a non-profit entity staffed and run by volunteers.*

UP AND RUNNING *Efforts to create the excursion train service go back more than 20 years when **Lee Allan Smith**, a longtime civic leader, visited with then-Mayor **Andy Coats** about acquiring old Santa Fe Railway tracks between the Adventure District and downtown.*

ADVENTURE STATION *The train's newest station will be located on Northeast 50th Street, east of the Oklahoma State Firefighters Museum and Memorial.*

O·R·M
OKLAHOMA RAILWAY MUSEUM

OKRX 113

OKLAHOMA CENTENNIAL
EXCURSION TRAIN
& RAILWAY MUSEUM

GENEROUS SPONSORS *The* **Freede Family** *and* **LaDonna** *and* **Herman Meinders** *contributed the* **Oklahoma City University Star Express** *dining car, while the two passenger cars were sponsored by* **Kerr-McGee** *and* **The Oklahoman**.

THE ENGINE *The* **Chickasaw Nation** *provided a charitable contribution for the restoration of the Excursion Train's engine. The engine, built in 1955, was given to the museum – along with many spare parts – by* **Jim Terrell**.

GUARDIAN OF THE GROUNDS *The Oklahoma Centennial Commission donated this wood carving of a train conductor – created by sculptor* **Clayton Coss** *– to watch over the museum grounds. From left,* **J. Blake Wade**, **Jose Freede** *and* **Lee Allan Smith**.

DINING CAR *This 38-seat Santa Fe diner was built in 1942 by the Budd Car Company. It was fully restored by* **Bill Gumerson** *and* **Bill Dinger** *of Gumerson & Associates for Oklahoma's Statehood celebration. Funds for the car were provided by the* **Freede Family**, **LaDonna** *and* **Herman Meinders**, **Kerr-McGee**, **Chickasaw Nation** *and the Oklahoma City Centennial sponsors.*

PASSENGER CAR *Monies also helped purchase a 1929 stainless steel passenger car with a refurbished interior. Shown inside are portraits of famous Oklahomans.*

MUSEUM MURALS *The decorative artwork on a fence at the Oklahoma Railway Museum was made possible by a joint venture between the museum and the Centennial Commission. The artist is* **Huan-Cheng Lin**.

FIRST RUN *Oklahoma City donors and Centennial sponsors climbed aboard one of the newly renovated cars for a ride up to the 50th Street station. Shown at left are (left to right)* **Herman Meinders**, **Tom McDaniel**, **Jim Everest**, **David Thompson** *and* **Lee Allan Smith**.

3
STATEWIDE
ACTIVITIES

ART & LANDMARKS
FINE ART

Dale Chihuly: The Exhibition at Oklahoma City Museum of Art • OKLAHOMA CITY

Originally titled "Dale Chihuly: An Inaugural Exhibition," the Chihuly exhibit was the headlining event at the 2002 opening of the newly-located Oklahoma City Museum of Art. Featuring the 55-foot Eleanor Blake Kirkpatrick Memorial Tower in the museum's atrium, the exhibit included 1,500 pieces of hand-blown glass and various drawings by Dale Chihuly – the most comprehensive collection of Chihuly artwork in the world. With the help of the Oklahoma City Centennial sponsors, in June 2004 the museum purchased the entire collection that has since been renamed "Dale Chihuly: The Exhibition." This extraordinary art continues to enthrall and fascinate locals and tourists from around the world and is the subject of a stunning coffee table-size book, also funded in part by the Oklahoma City Centennial sponsors. Project coordinator: **Oklahoma City Museum of Art**

Centennial Sculpture Garden • ARDMORE

The Centennial Sculpture Garden was completed in October 2007 at the Goddard Art Center to honor individuals who have made significant contributions to the arts and cultural experiences in the state of Oklahoma. Designed by landscape artist **Jane Couch**, this "outdoor gallery" invites visitors to enjoy both traveling exhibits and permanent sculptures. Project coordinator: **Charles B. Goddard Center for Visual and Performing Arts, Inc.**

"Wind Walker" • OKLAHOMA CITY

(left) This dramatic 23-foot-tall sculpture fuses the image of a hawk with the face of a medicine man and graces a large spilling pool on the grounds surrounding the offices of the Oklahoma Attorney General. Created by Oklahoma Native American artist **Bert Seabourn**, the bronze piece was relocated from the Southwestern Bell headquarters to its current location through the generosity of **Marylin Jones Upsher**.

Oklahoma Centennial Suite Paintings • OKLAHOMA CITY

(right) "Oklahoma Suite" by **Wilson Hurley** is featured among the landscapes in the State Capitol rotunda. The series includes four sublime, varying landscapes, each representing a quadrant of the state. Project coordinator: **Oklahoma Arts Council**

Ada Lois Sipuel Fisher Portrait in the Capitol Rotunda
OKLAHOMA CITY

In honor of the first African-American to attend and graduate from the University of Oklahoma College of Law (or any all-white law school), **Mitsuno Reedy**'s *portrait of Ada Lois Sipuel Fisher is also the first portrait of an African-American woman to be placed in the Oklahoma State Capitol. This moving piece reflects the three-year struggle that led to Fisher's triumph over segregation, which would change Oklahoma and the United States forever. Project coordinator:* **Oklahoma Arts Council**

Art for Attorney General's Office Building • *OKLAHOMA CITY The newly renovated state attorney general's office in Oklahoma City features two stunning works that capture conceptual pillars of Oklahoma law enforcement. "Spirit of Justice," a nine-foot bronze sculpture, was created by Oklahoma artist* **Shirley Thomson-Smith** *and depicts a Native American woman participating in a prayer ceremony. "Honor, Serve and Protect" is a three-panel painting created by American Indian artist* **Robert Taylor** *and depicts early Oklahoma lawmen* **Quanah Parker**, *an American Indian;* **Bass Reeves**, *an African-American; and* **Bud Ledbetter**, *a European-American. The paintings were funded by the Oklahoma City Centennial sponsors.*

Theodore Roosevelt Painting/Oklahoma Judicial Center • *OKLAHOMA CITY*

The Theodore Roosevelt painting in the Oklahoma Judicial Center commemorates the president who signed Oklahoma into statehood on November 16, 1907. The work is by Oklahoma artist **Mike Wimmer** *(left) and was made possible by the Oklahoma City Centennial sponsors.*

207

ART & LANDMARKS
HISTORICAL STATUES & MONUMENTS

Legacy Trails • *NORMAN*

*A series of five plazas, each symbolizing a different era in the history of the city of Norman, come together to form the Legacy Trails. The first three plazas feature the city's territorial days, statehood and the early University of Oklahoma. The fourth plaza pays tribute to Norman's vital role in World War II and the final square completes the history of Norman in engraved text. The centerpiece of the installation is a round, granite medallion engraved with a map of Norman. Raised details measuring only a few inches bring the large bronze maps located in the first three plazas to life. The maps were designed by the **Crucible Foundry**, which is located In Norman. Project coordinator: **Norman Park Foundation, Inc.***

Abernathy Boys Sculpture • *FREDERICK*

*Louis and Temple Abernathy of Frederick became national legends in 1910 when, at 10 and six years of age, the two boys rode alone all the way to Washington, D.C., to meet President Taft. After stopping to meet former President Theodore Roosevelt in New York, the boys returned home, driving themselves in a Brush automobile. The new Centennial Square in Frederick pays homage to their extraordinary journey with a life-sized bronze sculpture, by **Gary D. Gardner**, of the two legendary brothers. Project coordinator: **Frederick Arts and Humanities Council***

Sapulpa Centennial Buffalo • *SAPULPA*

*The Centennial buffalo statue, or "Guardian of the Plains," was installed in September 2007, between Route 66 and the Turner Turnpike in Sapulpa. The twice life-sized bronze bison, standing on a 15-foot-tall mound of prairie grass, is 12 feet tall, 18 feet long and weighs 6,000 pounds. It is a symbolic tribute to America's spirit of freedom and Oklahoma's American Indian heritage. **Jim Gilmore** sculpted this prestigious work of art for the community of Sapulpa. Project coordinator: **Sapulpa Area Chamber Foundation***

Stockyards City "Headin' to Market" Sculpture • OKLAHOMA CITY

Oklahoma artist **Harold Holden** honors his state's cattle and stockyards industries with this 12-foot bronze sculpture in Oklahoma City's historic Stockyards City. The dynamic piece depicts a cowboy on horseback driving a steer to market. Project coordinator: **Stockyards City Main Street**

Kentucky Daisy Sculpture
EDMOND

Edmond artist **Mary Lou Gresham** crafted the new "Leaping into History" sculpture located in Edmond Festival Market Place Plaza. The statue depicts '89er Nannita Regina H. Daisy, or "Kentucky Daisy," jumping from a train's cow-catcher to stake her claim in the Land Run of 1889. Project coordinator: **Edmond Parks Foundation**

Quarter Horse Statue at State Fair Park
OKLAHOMA CITY

The Quarter Horse statue at the Oklahoma State Fair Park is a one-and-one-fourth life-sized bronze by Oklahoma artist **Harold Holden** that honors the qualities and beauty of the Quarter Horse breed. Project coordinator: **Oklahoma City Centennial Sponsors**

209

ART & LANDMARKS
CULTURAL STATUES & MONUMENTS

James Garner at the April 2006 dedication ceremony in Norman.

James Garner Plaza • *NORMAN*

Born in Norman, **James Garner** *served in the Merchant Marines and the National Guard, and was awarded two Purple Hearts for his service in the Korean War. Garner, also a popular actor, found much success in his TV roles as Bret Maverick in "Maverick" and Jim Rockford in "The Rockford Files." The James Garner Commemorative Plaza honors Garner's extraordinary life with a beautiful sculpture by Oklahoma artist* **Shan Gray**. *The Oklahoma City Centennial sponsors contributed to this project and partnered with Norman elected and civic leaders on this tribute to a beloved Oklahoman.*

"The Ballerina" at Civic Center Music Hall
OKLAHOMA CITY
Graceful and elegant, "The Ballerina" is an 8'6" statue honoring five Native American ballerinas: **Yvonne Chouteau**, **Rosella Hightower**, **Moscelyne Larkin**, **Maria Tallchief** *and* **Marjorie Tallchief**. *Sculpted by Oklahoma artist* **Mike Larsen**, *it stands in the Civic Center lobby and was a gift from* **Kim** *and* **David Rainbolt** *to their fellow Oklahomans.*

Tinker Tuskegee Airman Memorial

MIDWEST CITY The Tuskegee airmen were the first all-African-American unit in the U.S. Army Air Corps. During World War II, Airman **Charles B. Hall** became the first African-American in U.S. history to shoot down an enemy plane. Following the war, Major Hall served at Oklahoma's Tinker Air Force Base until his death in 1971. The memorial, located on Tinker Air Force Base, honors the legacy of Hall and the Tuskegee airmen. Oklahoma artist **Joel Randell** sculpted the memorial. Project coordinator: **Tinker Air Force Base Heritage Foundation**

"The Maestro" Statue at Civic Center Music Hall

OKLAHOMA CITY
This magnificent bronze statue, sculpted by Oklahoman **Mike Larsen**, pays tribute to the Oklahoma City Philharmonic, its musical director, **Joel Levine**, and Philharmonic conductors from 1937 to 1988. The work was commissioned by **Jeannette** and **Richard Sias**.

THIS STATUE ALSO PAYS TRIBUTE TO THE
PREVIOUS CONDUCTORS OF OKLAHOMA CITY'S ORCHESTRAS
RALPH ROSE 1937-1938
VICTOR ALESSANDRO 1938-1951
GUY FRASER HARRISON 1951-1973
RAY LUKE 1973-1974
AINSLEE COX 1974-1978
LUIS HERRERA de la FUENTE 1978-1988

DEDICATED   ARTIST
MAY 3, 2007   MIKE LARSEN

J. BLAKE WADE EXECUTIVE DIRECTOR, OKLAHOMA CENTENNIAL COMMISSION
LEE ALLAN SMITH CHAIRMAN OF CENTENNIAL PROJECTS AND EVENTS

ART & LANDMARKS
CULTURAL STATUES & MONUMENTS

NOT SHOWN:

Barnsdall Friendship Memory Wall of Honor • BARNSDALL
Over 500 names of individuals who contributed to the community are inscribed on the Wall of Honor located by the 10-acre Bigheart Park. Centennial funds helped to complete the wall, as well as support the installation of a gazebo, park benches, flagpoles, lighting and landscaping. Project coordinator: **Barnsdall Chamber of Commerce**

Pioneer Aviators Sculpture, Vance Air Force Base • ENID
Sculpted by artist **Harold Holden**, "Pioneers Past, Present and Future" features three figures that symbolize the history of Vance Air Force Base and the area: a pioneer of the Cherokee Strip Land Run of 1893, a World War II aviator and an astronaut. The bronze sculpture pays tribute to Lt. Col. **Leon R. Vance Jr.** and Col. **Eileen Collins**, among others, who pioneered American space exploration and aviation. Project coordinator: **City of Enid**

Firefighters Statue, "Courage and Compassion for 100 Years" • TULSA

Designed by local firefighters and sculpted by Tulsa artist **Denise Rinkovsky**, this beautiful bronze statue depicts two courageous firefighters in heroic action. The monument stands at 2nd and Cheyenne in downtown Tulsa, and pays tribute to the teamwork and compassion that is reflected in Tulsa's finest. Project coordinator: **Tulsa Fire Department**

211

ART & LANDMARKS
SPORTS STATUES & MONUMENTS

Heisman Sculpture Park at University of Oklahoma • *NORMAN*

The Heisman Sculpture Park at the University of Oklahoma features four statues honoring OU's Heisman Trophy winners:

Billy Vessels *(1952)*
Steve Owens *(1969)*
Billy Sims *(1978)*
Jason White *(2003)*

Honorees' friends, family members, former teammates and the Oklahoma City Centennial sponsors funded the heroic-sized sculptures.

Clockwise from back left: **Steve Owens**, **Barry Switzer**, **Billy Sims**, **Kate Crowder**, **Susie Vessels** *and* **Jane Vessels**.

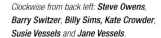

Steve Owens Statue • *NORMAN*

Dedicated in 2006, the sculpture of 1969 Heisman winner Steve Owens was created by **Nick Calcagno**.

Steve and Barbara Owens

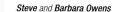

Billy Vessels Statue • *NORMAN*

The Oklahoma Centennial Commission and the University of Oklahoma unveiled this bronze in 2005 commemorating OU's first Heisman Trophy winner. It was designed and sculpted by Oklahoma artist **Shan Gray**. *The Centennial Commission also funded a statue that was placed in Vessels' hometown of Cleveland in 2007.*

University of Oklahoma Athletic Director **Joe Castiglione** *at the Owens dedication.*

Billy Sims Statue • *NORMAN*
*This outstanding running back is forever immortalized in a statue sculpted by **Jim Franklin**. It was unveiled and dedicated in 2007.*

*(right) Former University of Oklahoma head football coach **Barry Switzer** with **Lee Allan Smith**, who helped bring Heisman Park to life.*

*(below) Lt. Gov. **Jari Askins** and University of Oklahoma head football coach **Bob Stoops** were among the many notables in the crowd at the Jason White statue dedication.*

Jason White Statue • *NORMAN*
*He quarterbacked the University of Oklahoma to the 2003 title game and also took home the Heisman Trophy. This statue honoring White was unveiled at the 2007 dedication ceremony. The bronze was sculpted by **Jay O'Meilia**.*

*Fans surround 2003 Heisman winner **White** as he signs autographs.*

*Fans and reporters turned out for the **Billy Sims** statue unveiling and took advantage of the opportunity to ask him about the occasion.*

***Jason White** addresses the crowd during the 2007 dedication ceremony.*

Warren Spahn Statue • *OKLAHOMA CITY* Unveiled in the summer of 2005, this larger-than-life bronze statue depicts the legendary lefty in top form. Sculpted by famed Oklahoma artist **Shan Gray**, the memorial stands outside the AT&T Bricktown Ballpark. Oklahoma City Centennial sponsors funded the sculpture.

Warren Spahn Statue • *GUTHRIE*
This nine-foot bronze version of the Warren Spahn Pitching Award was sculpted by **Shan Gray**. Like the statue at Bricktown, the monument features the legendary lefty in his signature wind-up stance.

Busts of baseball greats line the entrance to the AT&T Bricktown Ballpark in Oklahoma City.

The last of the seven bust sculptures at the AT&T Bricktown Ballpark was dedicated in 2007.

Baseball Busts at AT&T Bricktown Ballpark

*OKLAHOMA CITY These bronze statues depict Oklahoma baseball legends. The busts of Oklahoma City natives **Bobby Murcer** and **Allie Reynolds** were unveiled in the summer of 2005. Four more were revealed in September 2006: Harrah natives **Paul "Big Poison"** and **Lloyd "Little Poison" Waner**, the only brother duo to be elected to the Baseball Hall of Fame; **Carl Hubbell** of Meeker; and **Pepper Martin** of Temple. Oklahoma City's **Joe "Bullet" Rogan**'s bust was dedicated in September 2007. Baseball fans from across the nation appreciate this tribute funded by the Oklahoma City Centennial sponsors.*

Wilber Joe Rogan
"Bullet"
Sculpted by **Joel Randell**

Lloyd James Waner
"Little Poison"
Sculpted by **Jim Franklin**

Allie Pierce Reynolds
Sculpted by **Shan Gray**

Carl Owen Hubbell
Sculpted by **Jay O'Meilia**

Paul Glee Waner
"Big Poison"
Sculpted by **Jim Franklin**

John L.R. Martin
"Pepper"
Sculpted by **Shan Gray**

Bobby Murcer
Sculpted by **John Gooden**

215

ART & LANDMARKS
PUBLIC ART

Western Town Mural • *OKLAHOMA CITY Scenes from an early Oklahoma town provide an attractive cityscape along E.K. Gaylord Boulevard. Created by Dr.* **Bob Palmer** *– University of Central Oklahoma art professor – UCO students and volunteer artists, the scenes incorporate faces of well-known contemporary Oklahomans. Project coordinator:* **Oklahoma City Centennial Sponsors**

Oklahoma! Murals • *OKLAHOMA CITY*
The Oklahoma! murals along E.K. Gaylord Boulevard are colorful depictions of famous scenes from the state's namesake Broadway musical. Scores of artists and University of Central Oklahoma art students painted the block-long work under the direction of UCO Professor of Art Dr. **Bob Palmer**. *Project coordinator:* **Oklahoma City Centennial Sponsors**

Historic Oklahoma Mural, Bricktown (1935-55)
OKLAHOMA CITY This beautiful mural in Bricktown depicts Oklahoma City street scenes from the mid-1900s. Designed by Dr. **Bob Palmer** *and painted by Palmer and his University of Central Oklahoma art students, the mural is an attractive and historically accurate picture of early Oklahoma City. Project coordinator:* **Oklahoma City Centennial Sponsors**

Devon Energy Centennial Mosaic Mural • *OKLAHOMA CITY*
(right) The Devon Energy Centennial Mosaic Mural is an intricate porcelain-tiled mosaic depicting many of the state's official symbols and emblems, and includes red clay tiles listing each of Oklahoma's 77 counties. Crafted by Oklahoma City Community College students and other volunteers under the instruction of artist and professor **Mary Anne Moore**, *the project design incorporates water from the canal. In addition to the* **Devon Energy Corporation**, **Oklahoma City Community College** *and* **Oklahoma City Centennial sponsors** *contributed to the project.*

216

Historical Oklahoma Mural • *OKLAHOMA CITY*

*This mural is painted on the east side of the Santa Fe bridge at the entrance to Bricktown, along E.K. Gaylord Boulevard and Broadway. It offers a historic pictorial of Oklahoma events from 1889 to 2008. Mural sponsors included **Nonna's Restaurant**, **Devon Energy**, **Bricktown Association** and the Oklahoma City Centennial sponsors. The mural was painted by Dr. **Bob Palmer** and art students from the University of Central Oklahoma.*

NOT SHOWN:
Historical Banner Project • *CLAREMORE*
AND ROGERS COUNTY On display throughout Claremore and Rogers County, these canvas banners depict 100 years of Oklahoma history. Project coordinator: **Claremore Main Street**

Rock Town Centennial Mural • *OKLAHOMA CITY*
*(left) The Rock Town Centennial Mural – on a former Oklahoma City grain elevator now used for rock climbing – features a beautiful painting of the Oklahoma state flag. Highly visible from downtown Oklahoma City, it serves as a scenic backdrop for the Land Run Monument. The mural was painted by Dr. **Bob Palmer** and art students from the University of Central Oklahoma. Oklahoma City Centennial sponsors funded the project.*

Centennial Train Mural • *OKLAHOMA CITY Located on the west side of the train tracks at Bricktown's entrance, this mural shows an array of Oklahoma celebrities, city and state leaders, and Centennial officials depicted as train passengers.*

J. Blake Wade

Donna Wade

Eddie Sutton

Tricia Everest and Janell Everest

Jane Jayroe Gamble and Gray Frederickson

Colin, Peter and Mary FitzSimons

Jason White

Joanie and Jack Catlett

Patti Page and Gay Reed

LaDonna Meinders

Herman Meinders

James Pickel

Karen Luke

Dee and Beth Ann Sadler

Troy Aikman

The All-American Rejects

Carolyn Hill

Lauren Nelson

Garth Brooks

Joe Diffie and Megan Mullally

Ray Ackerman and Angus McQueen

Gap Band

Kelly Haney

Kristin Chenoweth

Wendy Smith and Shawntel Smith

Erica Reid and DeLee Smith

Vince Gill

DeAnn Smith

Dave Lopez

Carrie Underwood

Russell Perry

Jimmy Webb and Juli Lyles

David Thompson

Ron Norick and Jim Tolbert

Lee Allan Smith

Ed Martin

Richard and Carla Ellis

John Herrington

Sean O'Grady and Bart Conner

Ron Howard

Susan Powell

Faith Mary and Randy Everest

Leona Mitchell and Sandi Patty

Mat Hoffman

Toby Keith

Burns Hargis

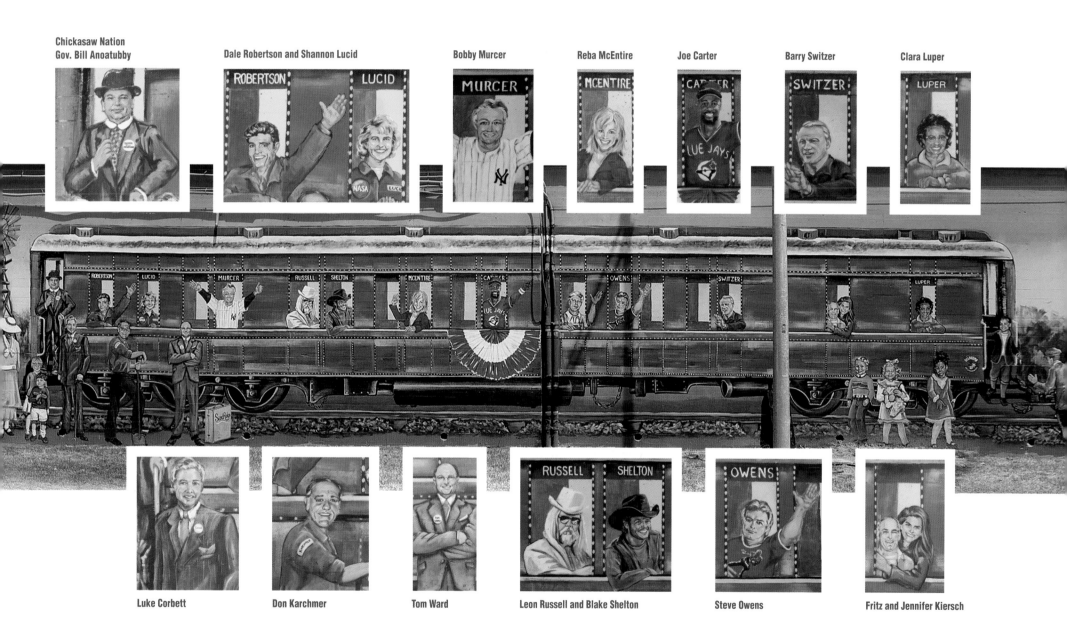

Chickasaw Nation
Gov. Bill Anoatubby

Dale Robertson and Shannon Lucid

Bobby Murcer

Reba McEntire

Joe Carter

Barry Switzer

Clara Luper

Luke Corbett

Don Karchmer

Tom Ward

Leon Russell and Blake Shelton

Steve Owens

Fritz and Jennifer Kiersch

Bob Funk

Shannon Miller and Kelli O'Hara

The Flaming Lips

Wayman Tisdale

James Garner

Jennifer Berry

Roy Clark

Johnny Bench

George Short

B.C. Clark Jr.

Ed and Nancy deCordova

Jeanette and Mick Evenson

Tom Stafford

Molly Boren, Kirk Humphreys, David Boren, Margaret Short and David Rainbolt

Christy Everest

Polly Nichols

J.W. Mashburn

Jim Brewer

Randy Hogan

Argus Hamilton

Richard Sias

Clay Bennett

Jimmy Everest

Aubrey McClendon, Tom McDaniel, Mick Cornett, Larry Nichols and Steve Moore

Kim Rainbolt

Kari Watkins

Jan and Bill Robinson

Jose Freede

ART & LANDMARKS
SPIRIT OF THE BUFFALO

Gov. Brad Henry

Spirit of the Buffalo • *STATEWIDE*

Don't look now, but wild buffalo are roaming. They're everywhere you turn – uptown, downtown, all around the state. Indeed, Oklahoma did experience a stampede, in the form of the Spirit of the Buffalo.

This public art project began in January 2004, when the Nature Conservancy of Oklahoma welcomed the arrival of its first herd. Between January and April, local artists transformed these buffalo into sculptural works of art. Come May, the stampede had begun. Downtown, Bricktown, at the zoo, by the lake, across the metro and all over the state – the colorful, whimsical animals delighted and mesmerized young and old alike.

As the Nature Conservancy display period neared an end, downtown Oklahoma City chose to adopt the project as a result of the tremendous public interest that had been shown. Today, many of the buffalo can still be viewed in their original locations, or at other Oklahoma City sites.

This successful project was a charming celebration of Oklahoma and a unique opportunity to showcase our artists, cities and community spirit. Long may the herd roam!

Clarence and Abuff The Cloud (above)

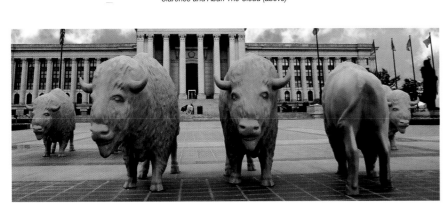

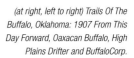

Buffalo Nickel (left)

(at right, left to right) Trails Of The Buffalo, Oklahoma: 1907 From This Day Forward, Oaxacan Buffalo, High Plains Drifter and BuffaloCorp.

Buffalo Bills

Bysontine

Zubee the Zuffalo

Bruce

Blue Suede Hooves

Abuff The Cloud

Oklahoma's Pride

Lady Liberty Comes to the Plains

Father Sky, Endless Cloud

Buffalo Bench

High Plains Drifter

X-Rayed Buffalo

Cupcake

Jules II

PARKS & PLAZAS
OKLAHOMA CENTENNIAL

Centennial Plaza of the Oklahomans • *OKLAHOMA CITY*
(above) Located south of the State Capitol, the plaza is a joint venture between the **Oklahoma Department of Transportation** and the **Department of Central Services**, and is the third phase in a set of improvements to the Capitol complex. The plaza features granite rosettes that commemorate 28 events in Oklahoma history, beginning with 11,000 B.C., when the first Native Americans occupied the land, and ending with the 1995 bombing of the Murrah Building. Sponsored pavers bear the names of current and past Oklahomans.

Beacon of Hope and Founders Plaza • *OKLAHOMA CITY*
(right) Founders Plaza sits in the center of Stiles Park and pays tribute to the five Oklahoma visionaries who established the Oklahoma Health Center: **E.K. Gaylord**, **Stanton L. Young**, **Dean A. McGee**, **Harvey P. Everest** and Dr. **Don O'Donoghue**. The focal point of the plaza is a 100-foot-tall white monolith that shoots a mile-high beam of light into the nighttime sky on a clear night. Funded by the Oklahoma City Centennial sponsors, the site also includes beautiful landscaping, benches and natural carved rocks. Project coordinator: **Oklahoma Health Sciences Center Foundation**

Kiowa County Courthouse Lawn Mosaic Map and Memorial • *HOBART*
(above) The Kiowa County mosaic map – an intricately designed visual model – invites visitors to "walk through" the county's many attractions and historical sites. Surrounding the map are the names, units and ranks of soldiers who died fighting for the U.S., and a wrought iron fence with artwork depicting various military service units encloses the entire area. Project coordinator: **Kiowa County Industrial Development Authority**

Kerr-McGee Trails and Bell Tower
OKLAHOMA CITY (left) Located in Regatta Park, this new half-mile paved trail has been specifically designed for walking, running and biking along the north side of the Oklahoma River; future trails will link to this one in Regatta Park. The tower stands 50 feet tall and chimes every quarter hour. Oklahoma City Centennial sponsors contributed to this project. Project coordinator: **City of Oklahoma City**

Centennial Flag Plaza • *OKLAHOMA CITY Oklahoma Centennial flags fly high alongside Oklahoma and United States flags. The colorful display is located in downtown Oklahoma City's Park Avenue Plaza.*

Centennial Park • *CUSHING (left) Nestled between the exterior walls of downtown buildings, the new Cushing Centennial Park includes a small stage, Centennial benches and several other amenities sponsored by the Centennial Commission. The park provides the community of Cushing with a small area for public performances and a quiet place to reflect or picnic. Project coordinator:* **Downtown Cushing Main Street**

NOT SHOWN:

Centennial Green • *TULSA Stretching half a block, this downtown park features an oval lawn with an unusual and intriguing centerpiece. Known as Gusher Fountain, the 12-foot steel-and-glass work of art is an abstract depiction of an oil derrick that intermittently "erupts." The derrick symbolizes the oil discovery of the 1900s when Tulsa was coined "Oil Capital of the World." In addition to the park, an amphitheater and dining area are being added to create an outdoor environment that the downtown community can enjoy. Project coordinator:* **Tulsa Oklahoma Centennial Committee**

Black Gold Park • *GLENPOOL The new Glenn Pool Oil Field Memorial and Monument recognize the significant role the field played in the creation of the state of Oklahoma in 1907. The memorial consists of a paved courtyard surrounding an illuminated representation of an oil derrick. Standing 28 feet tall, the sculpture sits on a granite base, which is engraved with the story of the 1905 Glenn Pool Oil Field discovery. Project coordinator:* **The Glenpool Commission Foundation**

Oklahoma Territorial Plaza • *PERKINS (right) The Oklahoma Territorial Plaza features 12-foot statues of Frank "Pistol Pete" Eaton and Chief Notchimine, Iowa tribal chief. The plaza also includes an arboretum of native plant life, a paved walking trail, and an outdoor museum depicting the social history of the Iowa Indian tribe and the early settlers of Perkins. Centennial funds supported the restoration of a 1901 log cabin that has been relocated to the plaza. Project coordinator:* **City of Perkins**, **Iowa Tribe of Oklahoma** and **Perkins Community Foundation**

PARKS & PLAZAS
OKLAHOMA CENTENNIAL

Centennial Park • *FORT GIBSON (right) The Fort Gibson Centennial Park is located on the southwest corner of Poplar Avenue and Lee Street. New amenities include a Centennial clock, a gazebo and brick-paved walkways.* Project coordinator: **Town of Fort Gibson**

Centennial Covered Foot Bridge and Working Windmill • *FARGO (below) Centennial park projects include a 40-foot covered foot/bicycle bridge spanning Boggy Creek to join two sections of the Fargo City Park. A working windmill – with a water tank – serves as an old-fashioned pool for children, as well as an irrigation source for the park. These new features complement the existing granite memorial marker commemorating the Great Western Cattle Drive.* Project coordinator: **Fargo Community Association**

Central Park • *NICOMA PARK (above) Nicoma Park's Central Park was renovated with additional picnic tables, park benches and a beautiful gazebo.* Project coordinator: **City of Nicoma Park**

Centennial and Downtown Parks • *CHICKASHA (above)*

The all-new Chickasha Centennial Park spans two-and-a-half acres and includes a multi-level/multi-element wooden playground structure, a pavilion, walking trails, a ball field, tennis/basketball courts, a green belt, restrooms and parking. The Downtown Park, at the corner of 6th Street and Chickasha Avenue, incorporated a Centennial clock and Centennial park benches. Project coordinator: **City of Chickasha**

Youngheim Centennial Plaza

EL RENO (left) A statue of Civil War hero and town namesake Gen. **Jesse Lee Reno** *is the focal point of the Youngheim Centennial Plaza in downtown El Reno. The pocket park includes a trolley stop, benches, sidewalks, water fountains and public restrooms. The plaza is named for* **Stanley Youngheim**, *who donated the land where the plaza is located.* Project coordinators: **El Reno Foundation for Progress, Inc. and Reno Monument and Centennial Society**

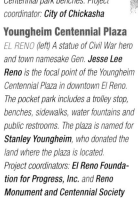

University of Oklahoma Centennial Mums • *NORMAN In celebration of the Oklahoma Centennial, a beautiful array of mums was planted on the campus of the University of Oklahoma in the pattern of Oklahoma state symbols. Under the direction of* **Molly Boren**, *the landscaping was designed by* **Allen King**, *with assistance from* **Kimberly Butler** *and* **Brandon Brooks**.

PARKS & PLAZAS
OKLAHOMA CENTENNIAL

Watonga Main Street Centennial Park • *WATONGA*
(right) The Watonga Main Street Centennial Park now includes a sidewalk of history, a new stage area and restrooms. Project coordinator: **Watonga Main Street, Inc.**

Centennial Corn Maze
HYDRO (left) In 2006, a seven-acre maze in the shape of the Oklahoma Centennial logo provided Oklahomans with hours of fun at PBar Farms along Interstate 40 between Hydro and Weatherford. The seven-foot-high puzzle, made of more than 300,000 corn stalks, contained scores of decision points. Maze-goers who provided the right answer to a question about Oklahoma were given the correct direction to the next decision point and eventually the exit. Project coordinator: **PBar Farms**

Oklahoma Centennial Iris • *STATEWIDE*
Gene and **Jeannine Rainbolt** of Oklahoma City spearheaded the effort to create a unique flower specifically for the state's Centennial – they selected the iris, a wonderful garden plant that comes in many colors. Oklahoma's Centennial iris is a tall-bearded purple that was introduced in 2006.

NOT SHOWN:

Landscaping and Playground • *ANADARKO* New playground equipment, Centennial park benches and landscaping were added to Anadarko City Park. Project coordinator: **City of Anadarko**

Memorial to Clem Rogers • *CLAREMORE* Rogers County was named for **Clement Vann Rogers**, a member of the Sequoyah Statehood Commission and the Oklahoma Constitutional Convention. This Centennial memorial pays homage to the heroic Cherokee's unique role in Oklahoma history. The monument is located at the memorial honoring **Will Rogers**, son of Clem Rogers. Project coordinator: **Claremore Main Street, Inc.**

Centennial Plaza • *COLLINSVILLE* The Collinsville Centennial Plaza includes new roadwork, period lighting, landscaping, decorative enhancements, utility relocation, outdoor music/sound system, a lighted fountain, park benches, a stage, brickwork, trees, trash receptacles, ballards, walkway/curb modifications, drainage/gutter and planters. The infrastructure and landscaping of the park site have also undergone extensive modifications and renovations. Project coordinator: **City of Collinsville**

Centennial Plaza • *COMANCHE* The centerpiece of the Comanche Centennial Plaza is a horseshoe-shaped reflecting pool, backdropped by a waterfall running over rocks shaped in the state of Oklahoma. Illuminated flags and commemorative plaques that illustrate statewide historic events, people, cattle, oil wells, American Indian culture, the state flower and the state bird surround the pool. Project coordinator: **City of Comanche**

Benches and Park Art • *FAIRVIEW* A total of 40 life-size metal silhouettes comprise six scenes depicting the western and frontier culture of the area. Located east of Fairview on Highway 58, the Major County Historical Property also offers benches and an 1896 rock house with modern restroom facilities. Project coordinator: **City of Fairview**

Centennial Park • *GUYMON* The Guymon Centennial Park spans five acres and is located at the intersection of Highways 54 & 3. Centennial-funded enhancements include a clock, park benches, a fountain in the park pond and a Centennial grove. Project coordinator: **Guymon Community Enrichment Foundation, Inc.**

Centennial Plaza and Clock • *HENNESSEY* The new Hennessey Centennial Plaza includes a Centennial clock, park benches and granite pavers. Clock plaques dedicate the time piece to late local businessman **Kenneth Lott**, and a third plaque marks a Centennial time capsule to be opened in 2057. Project coordinator: **Hennessey 2010 Association**

Gazebo • *JAY* A new gazebo on the courthouse lawn in downtown Jay evokes an earlier time in Oklahoma history and invites residents and visitors to relax and reflect. Project coordinator: **City of Jay**

Centennial Park and Pavilion • *MARIETTA* The new Centennial Pavilion, complete with tables and benches, in popular Shellenberger Park provides shelter and a meeting place for families and groups. Project coordinator: **City of Marietta**

Landscaping and Outdoor Furniture • *OKEMAH* Centennial benches, tables and landscaping have been installed throughout the town of Okemah to enhance park, library and recreation areas. Project coordinator: **City of Okemah**

Oklahoma Press Association Plaza • *OKLAHOMA CITY* A year-by-year history of Oklahoma from its establishment in 1907 to the Centennial Commemoration in 2007 is provided by 100 newspaper headlines engraved on plaza pavers. Just north of the State Capitol, the plaza is located at OPA headquarters on North Lincoln Boulevard. Project coordinator: **Oklahoma Press Association**

State Capitol Park Signage • *OKLAHOMA CITY* Large bronze and granite signs have been installed to mark the entrances and welcome visitors to State Capitol Park. Project coordinator: **Oklahoma Department of Central Services**

Centennial Park Project • *PRYOR* The Pryor Centennial Park project included adding a restroom to a 10-acre park being developed in downtown Pryor. Project coordinator: **Pryor Rotary Club Foundation, Inc.**

Centennial Parks • *SPENCER* Centennial funds provided for park benches and picnic tables, children's playground equipment, and signage for Spencer's Clover and Silver Creek Centennial Parks. Project coordinator: **City of Spencer**

PARKS & PLAZAS
OKLAHOMA CENTENNIAL

Centennial Fountain at United Way Plaza • *OKLAHOMA CITY*
The Centennial Fountain is a popular meeting place in the Bricktown entertainment district. The fountain's 40 jets shoot water 40 feet into the air and interact with music, performing a "dancing" water show for the public. Oklahoma City Centennial sponsors and the City of Oklahoma City funded the fountain. The plaza is paved with bricks containing the names of the Oklahoma United Way's Alex de Tocqueville members.

Oklahoma State Fair Park Waterfall • *OKLAHOMA CITY*
*This 11-foot-tall, 24-foot-wide lighted waterfall is located between the Centennial Building and the Cox Pavilion at State Fair Park. Several stone patio areas with Centennial park benches border the fountain and provide State Fair visitors a quiet spot to relax. Centennial sponsors were **Chesapeake Energy Corporation**, **Jeannette** and **Richard Sias**, **LaDonna** and **Herman Meinders** and the **Freede Family**.*

Leaping Waters Fountain at Norick Library • *OKLAHOMA CITY* (right and below)
*Located on the plaza in front of the downtown metro library, the Leaping Waters Fountain is a computer-controlled display of varied bursts and streams of water launched into a central basin. The fountain is a beautiful spectacle and an intriguing play area for children, and was funded by the **Oklahoma City Downtown Rotary Club**.*

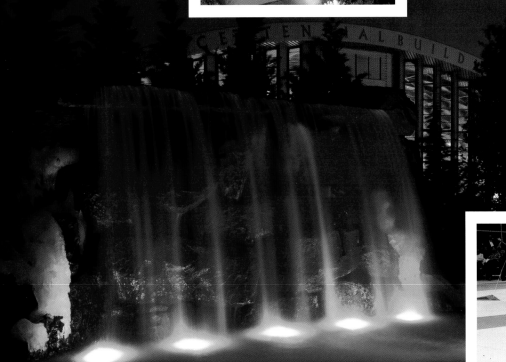

NOT SHOWN:
Centennial Fountain • *HOLDENVILLE*
*The Centennial Fountain is a round brick structure featuring a strong, steady burst of water in the center, surrounded by smaller, varying jet streams. Project coordinator: **City of Holdenville***

Oka Kapassa Centennial Fountain • *SULPHUR*
*The Honor Garden, located at the Chickasaw Cultural Center, celebrates Chickasaw citizens who have had the honor to be inducted into the Chickasaw Nation's Hall of Fame. A beautiful Centennial fountain is the focal point of the garden and serves as a peaceful place of remembrance for the entire Chickasaw community. Project coordinator: **Chickasaw Nation***

Oklahoma City-Tulsa Gift Exchange *In November 2006, Oklahoma City Centennial Sponsors presented the citizens of Tulsa with an Oklahoma Centennial Clock, which was installed at the corner of 3rd Street and Boston Avenue. This goodwill gesture was reciprocated when the Tulsa Oklahoma Centennial Committee presented Oklahoma City with two Centennial Spirit Poles. These 20-foot works of art feature an array of multi-colored streamers atop a light pole and are located in the Myriad Gardens.*

Participating in the gift exchange are (below, left to right) **Jim Davidson**, *project contractor, Traffic & Lighting Systems, LLC;* **Wendel Whisenhunt**, *director, Parks and Recreation Department, City of Oklahoma City;* **Don Walker**, *co-chair, Tulsa Oklahoma Centennial Committee;* **Lou Kerr**, *president, Oklahoma Centennial Commission;* **Lee Allan Smith**, *chairman of projects and events, Oklahoma Centennial Commission;* **Nancy Leonard**, *vice president, Oklahoma Centennial Commission;* **Jim D. Couch**, *manager, City of Oklahoma City; and* **J. Blake Wade**, *executive director, Oklahoma Centennial Commission.*

Standing behind the CenTOONials are (above) **Howard Barnett**, *Tulsa Oklahoma Centennial Committee;* **Sharon King Davis**, *co-chair, Tulsa Oklahoma Centennial Committee;* **Lee Allan Smith**, *chairman of projects and events, Oklahoma Centennial Commission; and* **William D. "Bill" LaFortune**, *mayor of Tulsa.*

NOT SHOWN:

Historic Walk • *BLANCHARD This multi-faceted project included murals painted on buildings alongside Highway 62, attractive gateways on the four corners of Highways 62 and 76, and a historic walkway in downtown Blanchard. Project coordinator:* **City of Blanchard**

Centennial Projects • *CLAREMORE*
With an eye on the past and a vision for the future, Claremore undertook a series of projects that capitalized on the area's history while also preparing the Rogers County city for the future: new and expanded exhibits at both the Will Rogers Memorial and the JM Davis Arms & Historical Museum; repair and renovation of the historical Belvidere Mansion; community event signage and equipment; tourism signage; and bike racks, planters and benches in historic downtown. Project coordinator: **Claremore Main Street**

Centennial Street Lamps and Library Walkway • *DUNCAN*
The 1907-style lighting provides both safety and charm to a new section of Elk Avenue, one of Duncan's major thoroughfares. A lighted, covered walkway lined with seasonal foliage provides a safe and pleasant link between City Government offices and the Duncan library, two of downtown's most frequented sites. Project coordinator: **City of Duncan**

Historic Building Renovation • *McLOUD A renovated historic building in downtown McLoud has become the attractive home of the McLoud Heritage Center, which houses community artifacts and offers educational programs on local history. Project coordinator:* **McLoud Historical Society**

Ben Johnson Memorial Gateway • *PAWHUSKA*
A heroic-size bronze is the Centennial addition to the Ben Johnson Memorial Gateway in downtown Pawhuska. The 30-feet-long, 15-feet-high sculpture depicts the Academy Award-winning actor roping a steer from horseback. Created by Oklahoma artist **John Dale Free**, *the monument pays tribute to an authentic Oklahoma cowboy who brought the American West to movie screens worldwide. Project coordinator:* **Ben Johnson Memorial Gateway Project – Pawhuska Community Foundation, Inc.**

Centennial Projects • *SHAWNEE*
Public art and city and park enhancements were all part of Shawnee's Centennial project: 10 horses representing the area's equine industry were decorated by local artists and placed throughout the city; 12 decorative park benches bearing Centennial plaques were installed downtown; and a popular city park received a decorative wrought iron fence. Project coordinator: **City of Shawnee**

Botanical Gardens • *TULSA One of America's most diverse botanical gardens is being created in the Osage Hills, northwest of downtown Tulsa. Sixty of the 300 acres will be converted to new gardens and features, while the other 240 acres of ancient forest and prairie are being preserved for their historical and ecological significance. From wide-open spaces to woodlands, to rolling hills and wildflowers, Tulsa's new Botanical Gardens is a stunning addition to Oklahoma's rare and unique attractions, and is expected to attract more than 300,000 visitors per year. State Centennial funds supported the construction of a visitors center, roads and a lake. Project coordinator:* **Oklahoma Centennial Botanical Garden/Research and Education Center**

Oklahoma's Beginning • *TULSA Council Oak Park, the historic meeting place of the Osage, Creek and Cherokee Nations, pays tribute to Tulsa's extensive American Indian heritage. A bronze piece depicts three children playing stickball, a popular game among many Native American cultures.* **Sandra Van Zandt** *is the artist and Centennial funding supported this project. Project coordinator:* **City of Tulsa**

Red Fork Derrick Park • *TULSA A 150-foot-tall replica of an oil derrick will include an observation deck with a panoramic view of Tulsa and will anchor an antique railroad park. Project coordinator:* **Southwest Tulsa Chamber of Commerce**

Landscaping and Outdoor Furniture • *VINITA New landscaping and 29 Centennial park benches were installed in parks throughout the city, and landscaping elements and lighting were installed in both parks and at City Hall. Project coordinator:* **City of Vinita**

Oklahoma Centennial Plaza and Clock • *WEATHERFORD At the main entrance to Weatherford, a 1,000-square-foot plaza serves as a reminder of the state's Centennial. Native plants and boulders reflect the local terrain, while an eloquent Centennial clock is the focal point of the plaza. Project coordinator:* **City of Weatherford**

Chisholm Trail Park and Centennial Bridges • *YUKON Recent enhancements to Chisholm Trail Park include two new stone bridges that will be part of a walkway planned to encircle the entire park and connect with other city trails. Project coordinator:* **City of Yukon**

233

PARKS & PLAZAS
OKLAHOMA CENTENNIAL

Oklahoma Centennial Clocks *In 1907, at the time of Oklahoma's statehood, beautiful clocks graced main streets and public areas throughout numerous cities and towns. The 2007 Centennial Clock Project was devoted to bringing these period clocks back to the sidewalks, boulevards and neighborhoods of our state.*

Communities were offered the opportunity to purchase vintage replicas that were fully modernized and virtually maintenance-free. Available in a variety of colors – midnight black, royal blue, reflective silver, brilliant gold, forest green, candy-apple red and chrysanthe-mum brown – the clocks serve as attractive, lasting enhancements to neighborhood areas. A total of 79 communities participated in this project and more than 100 clocks were installed.

All of the clocks feature illuminated faces and daylight savings/power savings failure correction, with optional accent paintings or color, chime system and turnkey installation. Available in small, medium or large, each of the three designs displays the name of the sponsoring entity and "Oklahoma Centennial 1907-2007." **Bezdek + Associates**, *an Oklahoma City firm, served as the Centennial's official clock representative.*

KAY COUNTY COURTHOUSE • NEWKIRK

DOWNTOWN TULSA

DOWNTOWN EDMOND

NICHOLS HILLS

FIRST NATIONAL BANK • TONKAWA

CAPITOL HILL • OKLAHOMA CITY

INTEGRIS Baptist Medical Center

STATE FAIR PARK • OKLAHOMA CITY

BRICKTOWN • OKLAHOMA CITY

INTEGRIS BAPTIST MEDICAL CENTER • OKLAHOMA CITY

CITY HALL/LIBRARY • PERKINS

OKLAHOMA CITY UNIVERSITY

Tom McDaniel, *Oklahoma City University president, and* **Art Cotton**.

OKLAHOMA PUBLISHING COMPANY • OKLAHOMA CITY

CITY LIBRARY • SHAWNEE

CITY LIBRARY • PERRY

Clock Locations

COX CONVENTION CENTER • OKLAHOMA CITY

STATE CAPITOL PARK • OKLAHOMA CITY

TOWN CENTER PLAZA • MIDWEST CITY

Shown at left are (left to right) **Joe Castiglione**, **Tim Brassfield**, Oklahoma City Mayor **Mick Cornett**, **Royce Hammons**, **Tim Allen**, **Lee Allan Smith** and **Brett Hamm**.

STATE CAPITOL COMPLEX • OKLAHOMA CITY

N.W. EXPRESSWAY • OKLAHOMA CITY

CITY HALL • OKLAHOMA CITY

CITY PARK • CHEYENNE

EARLYWINE PARK • OKLAHOMA CITY

PARKS & PLAZAS
OKLAHOMA CENTENNIAL

Oklahoma Centennial Groves *What better tribute to a community than a living tribute? The Oklahoma Centennial Groves project was designed to provide just that – a grove of 100 trees that would serve as an everlasting, commemorative monument representing the state's first 100 years.*

Centennial Groves were coordinated through the **Greater Oklahoma City Tree Bank Foundation, Inc.,** *under the leadership of* **Mary Caffrey,** *executive director. Groves were purchased by municipalities, county governments, state agencies, nonprofits and civic organizations across the state. Trees enhanced community entrances, bordered main thoroughfares, complemented parks and medians, and served as shady respites at a school or playground.*

This statewide volunteer effort included the free services of a professional forester, who was available for assistance with design, tree selection and training in proper planting and maintenance. The Tree Bank also lent a helping hand with fundraising, signage design and dedication of the completed grove.

Grove Locations

Del City
Sooner Road between S.E. 29th & S.E. 44th

Edmond (4)
On I-35, downtown, Bickham-Rudkin Park and Santa Fe High School

Guymon
City Park

Idabel
1st Bank & Trust

Kingfisher
Kingfisher Middle School

Midwest City
Tinker Air Force Base

Norman
Sooner Road & Franklin Road

Oklahoma City (6)
N.W. 63rd Street, North MacArthur & Memorial, two along the Oklahoma River (one in memory of Stanley Draper Jr.), Oklahoma

City Zoo, and Kilpatrick Turnpike & Highway 66

Pauls Valley
Southern Oklahoma Resource Center

Seminole
City Park

Shawnee
I-40 & Kickapoo Street

Warr Acres
Northwest 39th Expressway

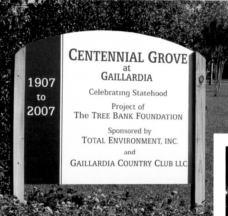

CENTENNIAL GROVE at GAILLARDIA

1907 to 2007

Celebrating Statehood

Project of The Tree Bank Foundation

Sponsored by Total Environment, Inc. and Gaillardia Country Club LLC

Shown at the N.W. 63rd St. and N.W. 58th St. grove in Oklahoma City is **William J. "Bill" Kopplin,** *a member of the Tree Bank Foundation Board of Directors and chairman of the Centennial Groves Committee.*

The SandRidge Energy Bridge

Aduddell Industries Bridge

The Noble Foundation Bridge

The Freede Family Bridge

Canal Bridges • *OKLAHOMA CITY Oklahoma City made major improvements to the south end of the Bricktown Canal in 2004. These included the installation of a majestic fountain and several pedestrian bridges. The project was going to be scaled back considerably due to budgetary concerns, but the Centennial Commission stepped in and secured additional funding to complete the projects.*

The Devon Energy Bridge

Oklahoma Centennial Benches *A variety of communities across the state chose to honor Oklahoma's benchmark anniversary with a Centennial bench. Each came with a lifetime guarantee, which included the spruce-green powder coating finish. All of the benches were cut, welded and finished by an Oklahoma Department of Corrections program that provides job-training skills for incarcerated Oklahomans. The win-win program offered hundreds of organizations, municipalities, schools and individuals the opportunity to purchase reasonably priced, long-lasting benches. Seventy-three communities participated in the program, purchasing 471 benches and another 100 complementary pieces bearing the Centennial logo (bike racks, picnic tables, etc.)*

Bench Locations

Altus (1)	Cushing (2)	Hinton (2)	Okemah (18)	Stillwater (1)
Alva (11)	Cyril (1)	Idabel (2)	Oklahoma City (51)	Stilwell (5)
Ames (7)	Del City (7)	Jay (2)	Pawhuska (5)	Tahlequah (1)
Anadarko (7)	Duncan (12)	Keyes (1)	Pawnee (1)	Taloga (9)
Ardmore (1)	Edmond (9)	Kingfisher (3)	Perry (1)	Texhoma (1)
Arnett (2)	El Reno (2)	Laverne (1)	Ponca City (3)	Tulsa (8)
Barnsdall (4)	Enid (16)	Lawton (1)	Pryor Creek (7)	Tuttle (2)
Broken Arrow (4)	Frederick (1)	Mangum (19)	Purcell (2)	Vinita (31)
Buffalo (1)	Freedom (6)	Marietta (4)	Sallisaw (8)	Wagoner (17)
Chandler (2)	Granite (1)	McLoud (28)	Sapulpa (5)	Watonga (3)
Checotah (1)	Grove (2)	Medford (4)	Seiling (1)	Westville (1)
Cheyenne (9)	Guthrie (2)	Meno (3)	Seminole (18)	Woodward (1)
Choctaw (4)	Guymon (1)	Midwest City (4)	Sparks (1)	Yukon (2)
Cleveland (29)	Harrah (14)	Muskogee (11)	Spencer (8)	
Collinsville (8)	Hennessey (6)	Oakland (1)	Stigler (1)	

Built with a 14-gauge steel frame, the benches carry the Oklahoma Centennial logo on the center of the backrest, along with a bronze plaque bearing the name of the town, organization or individual donor.

MUSEUMS & MEMORIALS

On November 1, 2005, a day-long "ground blessing" prepared the American Indian Cultural Center & Museum for construction. Representatives from Oklahoma's 39 Indian Tribal Nations prepared the site with culturally appropriate activities including songs, dances and the building of a new fire as thousands looked on.

American Indian Cultural Center & Museum • OKLAHOMA CITY

The American Indian Cultural Center & Museum (AICCM) will stand as a vibrant international forum where the values of American Indian life will be expressed through arts, language, dance, music, literature and other traditions thriving in Indian communities throughout Oklahoma.

AICCM attractions will include Smithsonian collections, permanent and temporary exhibits, the Family Discovery Center (for activities such as storytelling and beadworking), film and performance venues, a gathering and performance forum, an orientation theater (educating visitors about the history and importance of Oklahoma tribes), an oral history theater, a cafe and a visitors center.

Visitors to AICCM will hear first-hand accounts from American Indian tribal members. They'll be immersed in cultural celebrations, contemporary events, and activities such as film screenings and community performances – each revealing the importance of vibrant and continuing Native American cultures throughout Oklahoma.

The 300-acre AICCM complex will be located in a wooded site at the geographic center of the continent, in the heart of Indian country, where I-35 and I-40 intersect in Oklahoma City. AICCM is a project of the **Native American Cultural and Educational Authority**.

Scheduled for completion in 2008, the visitors center will serve as a centralized information center that connects and complements arts and cultural destinations across the state. Oklahoma's newest earthen architectural landform, the "Central Promontory Mound," will be dedicated in 2008. This 21st-century mound, inspired by the mound-building cultures in Oklahoma and eastern North America, will become one of the most iconic architectural features of the site.

Standing Bear Museum and Education Center • *PONCA CITY*

The Standing Bear Museum and Education Center honors and preserves the Native American culture of six area tribes and recounts the experience of the namesake Ponca chief whose efforts brought about increased human rights for American Indians. A multi-use facility features both permanent and changing exhibits of art and artifacts, and offers workshops and classes. The 63-acre park includes a one-acre pond with a central arrowhead-shaped island, a walking trail winding through native grasses and wildflowers, and a shaded memorial grove. Project coordinator: **Standing Bear Native American Foundation, Inc.**

A majestic 22-foot bronze statue of Standing Bear depicts the Ponca Chief overlooking the ancient Arkansas River Valley. Located at the feet of Standing Bear is a 60-foot diameter circular viewing court. Large sandstone boulders around the court's perimeter display official seals of the six area tribes: Kaw, Osage, Otoe-Missouria, Pawnee, Ponca and Tonkawa. A reflecting pool at the center includes an eternal flame, "Grandfather Fire," that burns on a large round sandstone pedestal. These previously installed elements provide a dramatic setting for the Standing Bear Museum and Education Center, a major Centennial project.

239

MUSEUMS & MEMORIALS

Cherokee National Historical Society Exhibit • *TAHLEQUAH (right)*
Located in the old community of Park Hill, three miles south of Tahlequah, the Cherokee Heritage Center features permanent exhibits on Cherokee heritage, culture and history, including the Trail of Tears. The Centennial Commission funded a new Cherokee National Historical Society Exhibit (not pictured), which includes artifacts and depictions of Cherokee history, culture and art since 1907. Project coordinator: **Cherokee National Historical Society, Inc.**

Choctaw Nation Capitol Museum • *TUSKAHOMA (above) The Choctaw Nation Capitol Museum preserves tribal history through a Trail of Tears exhibit; Choctaw history, culture and family life exhibits; and the Choctaw Code Talker Memorial exhibit. Displays pay homage to the Choctaw Light Horsemen, who were the law enforcement arm of the historic Choctaw Nation. The Centennial Commission funded renovations to the museum. Project coordinator:* **Choctaw Nation of Oklahoma**

NOT SHOWN:
Kiowa Cultural Center and Museum • *CHEROKEE The Kiowa Tribal Museum was expanded into a cultural center in honor of the Centennial. The center further preserves and shares the traditions, language, art and music of the Kiowa people. Project coordinator:* **Kiowa Culture Preservation Authority**

Seminole Nation Museum • *WEWOKA The Centennial Commission funded the construction of a new Centennial garden on the museum's front façade to serve as a public art space, community gathering space, and teaching and education venue. Plantings significant to Oklahoma Seminole medicine and ceremonialism were included in the garden. Project coordinator:* **Seminole Nation Museum**

Cherokee Strip Regional Heritage Center • *ENID*
(above) A Smithsonian-quality museum in the making, the Cherokee Strip Regional Heritage Center will feature state-of-the-art exhibits interpreting the Cherokee Strip Land Run of 1893 and the history of northwest Oklahoma. Slated to open in spring 2009, the 24,000-square-foot facility will also house gallery space for traveling exhibits and a technologically advanced research center. Project coordinator: **Cherokee Strip Regional Heritage Center**

NOT SHOWN:
Transportation Museum • *CHICKASHA This museum offers displays, antiques and artifacts that depict the history of transportation. The sponsored expansion of the museum includes a new parking lot and a decorative fence surrounding the grounds. Project coordinator:* **City of Chickasha**

Freedom Museum's Burnham Site Exhibit • *FREEDOM*
One of the most exciting archaeological finds in the world is spotlighted in this new exhibit featuring 30,000-year-old artifacts uncovered at a site on a Woods County ranch. Scientists have declared the Burnham Site "an unprecedented discovery that is unique (in the entire world) to Woods County, Oklahoma." The museum's extensive collections of house wares and memorabilia from the late 1800s and early 1900s, antique farm equipment and a large barbed wire display depict more recent Oklahoma history. Project coordinator: **Freedom Museum, Inc.**

NOT SHOWN:

Museum of the Western Prairie • ALTUS The Museum of the Western Prairie is designed in the form of a half-dugout, and houses two galleries and the Bernice Ford Price Memorial Reference Library. Galleries display vignettes and dioramas on fossil remains, Native American life, cattle trails, frontier life, agriculture, the Altus-Lugert Irrigation Project and Altus Air Force Base. The Oklahoma Centennial Commission contributed funds for improvements to the museum. Project coordinator: **Oklahoma Historical Society**

Museum Project • BUFFALO The Buffalo Museum received a new look for Oklahoma's new century. Stucco siding, awnings, windows, and doors with period handles and bison heads etched into the glass brighten the exterior of the local history museum. A sign by area artist **Jason Yauk** completed the transformation. Project coordinator: **Buffalo Beautification Committee**

NOT SHOWN:

Heartland Heritage Center • CHECOTAH The Heartland Heritage Center was developed to celebrate and preserve the history of Checotah with a focus on the impact of the Creek Nation, railroad, rodeo and steer wrestlers. The Centennial Commission funded improvements to the museum. Project coordinator: **Checotah Public Works Authority**

Centennial Community Museum • CHEYENNE A new building housing the Cheyenne Centennial Community Museum contains original community displays and historical memorabilia from the early 1900s on, commemorating the area's early pioneers and its war veterans. Project coordinator: **Historic Roger Mills Preservation Foundation**

Cyril Museum • CYRIL The Cyril Museum displays memorabilia and exhibits that depict the history of the city including bank memorabilia, military uniforms, post office and cotton patch scales, a barber shop, period rooms, fine china, school memorabilia and more. The Centennial Commission funded the construction of a new roof and renovations to the museum. Project coordinator: **Cyril Historical Society**

Cherokee Strip Museum • PERRY The Centennial Commission contributed funds to the conceptual drawings of the site plan, site preparation for the new complex and the installation of the fence at the property line for Perry's expanded Cherokee Strip Museum. Project coordinator: **Cherokee Strip Historical Society, Noble County Chapter**

Transportation Center • WAYNOKA (below and right) The Waynoka Transportation Museum and Regional Interpretive Center recreates a unique period in Oklahoma history when first-class east-coast-to-west-coast travel consisted of a series of plane and train rides, with an overnight in Waynoka. The museum is housed in a renovated 1910 Santa Fe Depot and Harvey House Hotel, which hosted an international who's who from 1910 to 1930. Its artifacts and state-of-the-art exhibits depict a short-but-exciting era in Oklahoma's transportation history. Project coordinator: **Waynoka Historical Society**

MUSEUMS & MEMORIALS

Oklahoma Heritage Association Museum Complex • *OKLAHOMA CITY The opening of the Gaylord-Pickens Oklahoma Heritage Museum on May 10, 2007, began a new journey for its 80-year-old parent organization, the Oklahoma Heritage Association. The museum features custom technology and interactive touch-screens. Influential Oklahomans like aviation innovator* **Wiley Post***, BMX rider* **Mat Hoffman***, astronaut* **Shannon Lucid** *and country music superstar* **Reba McEntire** *are captured in video-driven displays. Everyday Oklahomans representing all walks of life are also honored. The Oklahoma Hall of Fame Gallery provides information on all 621 inductees from across the years via computer touch-screens and trivia games. Project coordinator:* **Oklahoma Heritage Association**

Carl Albert Museum • *POTEAU Carl Albert, former Speaker of the U.S. House of Representatives, reached many prestigious milestones throughout his life. A new museum located in the Carl Albert State College library conveys Albert's early childhood, education and political career. Exhibits include artifacts donated by the late speaker's family and friends. Project coordinator:* **Carl Albert State College**

MUSEUMS & MEMORIALS

Nellie Johnstone Oil Well

BARTLESVILLE (right)

A gushing 84-foot-high oil well is the centerpiece of Discovery 1 Park, the site of the Nellie Johnstone, the first commercial oil well drilled in Indian Territory in 1897. The well reproduction is a one-of-a-kind exhibit and features full movement of all mechanical components, "conversations" among life-size figures, authentic mechanical sounds and a spectacular gusher that substitutes water for oil. The Path of Petroleum Pioneers winds around the derrick and showcases the entrepreneurs, inventors, companies and organizers who were propelled by the discovery of oil in Oklahoma. Project coordinator: **City of Bartlesville** and the **Discovery 1 Park Project Team**

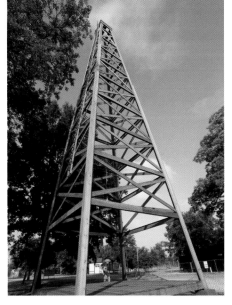

Harn Homestead • *OKLAHOMA CITY (right)*

In August 2007, the ribbon was cut to a new entryway and parking lot for the Harn Homestead Museum. The 9.4-acre site on which the museum stands includes what remains of William Harn's 1889 Land Run homestead, and the exhibits on the property serve as a unique interactive educational experience for visitors and patrons who are curious about early Oklahoma life, from the family farm to the one-room schoolhouse. This project was funded in part by the Oklahoma City Centennial sponsors. Project coordinator: **Harn Homestead Entryway Committee**

Wildlife Heritage Center Museum • *ANTLERS (above)*

Oklahoma's only wildlife heritage center showcases southeast Oklahoma's natural diversity, and promotes quality wildlife and natural resources management. This attractive facility spreads across 3,100 square feet and is constructed of native pine and flagstone. The center offers numerous educational exhibits, a media and research center, and a lounge area for visitors to enjoy. Project coordinator: **Deer Capital Tourism Association**

Pioneer Townsite • *FREDERICK (below)*

The Centennial Commission funded improvements and renovations to this expansive site that included a historic school, depot, church, farm house, barn and other structures from life on the 1920s plains. The on-site museum offers exhibits and a new interactive presentation. Project coordinator: **Tillman County Historical and Educational Society**

NOT SHOWN:

Spudder Rig • *ARDMORE* Spudder Rig is a new addition to the Greater Southwest Historical Museum. This large wooden oil derrick played an important part in the Carter County oil boom in the 1920s and 1930s, and remains an icon to the state's number-one oil-producing county. Project coordinator: **Greater Southwest Historical Museum, Inc.**

J.M. Davis Arms and Historical Museum • *CLAREMORE* The Centennial Commission funded an addition to the already expansive collection, which features some of the most memorable firearms in history, such as a Chinese hand cannon from the 1350s, a seven-barreled goose-hunting gun and the small muzzle-loading shotgun that was J.M. Davis' first firearm. Project coordinator: **Claremore Main Street, Inc.**

Chisholm Trail Heritage Center and Sculpture Garden • *DUNCAN* The 260-foot-long "Chisholm Trail Walkway" invites visitors to walk along a representation of the historic cattle trail as it stretches from Texas, across Oklahoma to Kansas. The walkway features important Oklahoma creeks, rivers and towns, as well as 13 brass plaques containing route information provided to cattle drovers in 1874 by the Kansas Pacific Railroad. Inside the facility, exhibits depict life during the era. An interactive film offers an on-the-trail adventure, complete with stampeding cattle, a rainstorm and other cattle drive experiences. Project coordinator: **Chisholm Trail Heritage Center Association**

Oklahoma Labor and Mining Museum • *HENRYETTA* The Oklahoma Labor and Mining Museum is a new museum that will exhibit artifacts and displays depicting the labor and mining history of Oklahoma. The Centennial Commission contributed to the completion of a new visitors center for the museum as a first step toward honoring the role of the mining industry in Oklahoma's past, present and future. Project coordinator: **Oklahoma Museum of Labor and Mining**

Oklahoma Firefighters Museum • *OKLAHOMA CITY* The Oklahoma Firefighters Museum and Memorial is recognized as one of the nation's outstanding museums dedicated to the preservation and display of antique firefighting equipment. The museum commemorates the heroism of Oklahoma firefighters and features a Civil War-era cabin, the Fort Supply Firehouse, antique fire engines, the "Last Alarm" mural, and interactive exhibits. Located on N.E. 50th Street in Oklahoma City, the museum is owned and operated by local volunteer and paid firefighters. The Centennial Commission contributed funds for improvements and additions to the museum that included a 20-foot Spirit Pole, a Centennial clock, an audio tour system, touch-screen computers with kiosks and a pavilion with pre-manufactured playground equipment. Project coordinator: **Oklahoma State Firefighters Association**

Pawnee Bill Museum • *PAWNEE* Pawnee Bill, partner of the legendary Buffalo Bill Cody, was a pioneer in the development of the traveling wild west show. The two Bills revolutionized this performance art in the early 1900s with demonstrations of trick shooting, bronco busting and choreographed dramas. The museum on Pawnee Bill's ranch features colorful displays of cowboy costumes, boots, guns, saddles and swords that were used by wild west show performers. The Centennial Commission contributed funds for improvements to this historic site. Project coordinator: **Oklahoma Historical Society**

Oklahoma Fish and Wildlife Exhibit at Oklahoma Aquarium

JENKS Swimming otters, raccoons and beavers join native fish and beautiful plant life to create the Hayes Family Ozark Stream Exhibit, named after the late Mark Hayes. Hayes, a native Oklahoman, proudly promoted the restoration of the Ozark habitat in northeastern Oklahoma. This exciting exhibit allows visitors to watch and learn about local wildlife. Project coordinator: Oklahoma Aquarium

Jasmine Moran Children's Museum Maze and History Street Projects • *SEMINOLE (above) The Jasmine Moran Children's Museum contains 28,000 square feet of indoor exhibit space with interactive educational experiences and entertainment, and a huge outdoor space with a ride, statuary, animals and beautiful landscape. The Centennial Commission funded the construction of a 12,000-square-foot "Oklahoma Centennial Castle Maze" and new comprehensive exhibits including "Brickstreet," "Classroom on Track," "Amazing Play," "Dancing Waters," "Education Pavilion," a health exhibit and a rotating science education exhibit. Project coordinator: Jasmine Moran Children's Museum Foundation*

Oklahoma Science Museum Gadget Tree • *OKLAHOMA CITY*
(left) The Centennial Commission sponsored the addition of an exhibit featuring a giant Oklahoma oak tree that serves as a mainstay of an interactive science and history experience for visitors to the Oklahoma Science Museum. Project coordinator: Oklahoma Science Museum Board of Directors

RESTORATIONS
HERITAGE ACTIVITIES

Nowata County Courthouse • *NOWATA (left)* Centennial funds helped support restorations and enhancements to this attractive 1912 courthouse, listed on the National Register of Historic Places. Improvements were made to the roof, front stairs, eaves and overhangs, as well as the plumbing, heating, cooling and electrical systems. Project coordinator: **Nowata County Board of Commissioners**

Virtual hotel rooms at Chandler Interpretive Center.

Washita County Courthouse • *CORDELL (right)* Designed in 1910 by **Solomon Andrew Layton**, architect of the Oklahoma State Capitol, this domed courthouse is one of Oklahoma's most recognizable structures. Centennial funds supported the renovation of the landmark dome. Project coordinator: **Washita County Commissioners**

NOT SHOWN:

Atoka Confederate Museum – Inge Home Restoration
ATOKA This historic 1881 home was restored to its original appearance. The addition of a rock foundation, vintage siding, period windows and doors, and new porches complemented interior restorations. Project coordinator: **Atoka County Historical Society**

Alfalfa County Courthouse • *CHEROKEE* The cleaning, restoration and preservation of the exterior masonry provided this prominent northwest Oklahoma structure with a renewed appearance. Project coordinator: **Courthouse Improvement and Preservation Committee**

NOT SHOWN:

Fort Washita • *DURANT* Located on State Highway 199, the famous Oklahoma fort was declared a National Historic Landmark in 1965. Improvements were made to the historic site. Project coordinator: **Oklahoma Historical Society**

Fort Towson • *FORT TOWSON* Established in 1824, Fort Towson was a frontier outpost located approximately two miles northeast of the current town of Fort Towson. The fort was added to the National Register of Historic Places and is currently undergoing facility improvements. Project coordinator: **Oklahoma Historical Society**

NOT SHOWN:

Tillman County Courthouse • *FREDERICK* The Tillman County Courthouse, built in 1921, is a notable building located in the heart of Frederick. The courthouse underwent facility improvements to preserve the building's rich historical past. Project coordinator: **Tillman County**

Wagoner City Hall • *WAGONER* A Centennial grant, matched by local funds, provided significant upgrades to this busy historic structure. A new roof, interior painting, carpeting, remodeling and even exterior murals of past scenes were included. Project coordinator: **City of Wagoner**

Fort Reno Historic Restoration • *EL RENO (below) Fort Reno, built from stone, wood and brick, was established as a permanent post in 1875. Named after **Jesse L. Reno**, who died in the Civil War Battle of South Mountain, the fort supported the U.S. Army in WWI and WWII. Restoration of building number four, "Commander's Quarters," and building number three, "1891 Victorian House," are underway. Project coordinator: **Historic Fort Reno, Inc.***

Chandler Route 66 Interpretive Center • *CHANDLER*

*(above and below) Renovations to a 1937 National Guard armory created meeting and convention areas, as well as space for the Route 66 Interpretive Center. This entertaining and educational museum offers a one-of-a-kind cruise through the history of America's Main Street. Visitors can experience exhibits and artifacts that feature classic cars, unique lodging (left), roadside attractions and music from the Mother Road's heyday through present day. Project coordinators: **Old Armory Restorers** and **Chandler Community Development Trust Authority***

Fort Reno Commander's Quarters.

Fort Reno 1891 Victorian House, Officers' Quarters.

U.S. Army Field Artillery Museum • *LAWTON/FORT SILL (left) The new U.S. Army Field Artillery Museum provides 23,000 square feet of exhibit space housing artifacts dating from the 1800s to present that tell the story of this essential component of the U.S. military. Project coordinator: **U.S. Army Field Artillery Museum***

247

RESTORATIONS
HERITAGE ACTIVITIES

Lawton High School: Restoration of the Original Building • *LAWTON/FORT SILL (below and right)*
Restoration of the historic 1909 Lawton High School is currently underway. Upon completion, the restored facility will be used to house city offices and a large conference space. Project coordinator: **Lawton Public School District**

Grady County African-American Museum and One-Room School • *CHICKASHA (below and right)* Discovered in a field on the **Kaye Loveless Lee** farm, the 1910 Verden Separate School was moved by flatbed truck to Chickasha, where it has been restored and opened to the public. Project coordinator: **Loretta Y. Jackson African American Historical Society**

Dwight Mission • *VIAN (below)* Beginning in the early 1800s as a Presbyterian mission, Dwight Mission served as an Indian boarding school for 125 years. Located in a scenic rural setting, the historic mission buildings now serve as a year-round conference and retreat center. The first phase of restoring the historic building that houses the conference center was completed as a Centennial project. Project coordinator: **Dwight Presbyterian Mission, Inc.**

On June 24, 2004, as the Verden School was being moved to its new location in Chickasha, a crowd of hundreds awaited the school's arrival at 315 East Ada Sipuel Avenue. Formerly used as a work shed, this historic structure proved to be the most intact school in the nation built by African-Americans on African-American land.

On February 24, 2007, Chickasha Chamber of Commerce Ambassadors helped **Loretta Y. Jackson** (third from right) cut the ribbon for the restored school. Jackson headed up the project.

First Public Schoolhouse in Oklahoma Territory • EDMOND

(left) Dating back to 1889, the first public schoolhouse in Oklahoma Territory, located in Edmond, has recently been renovated and restored. Visitors to the schoolhouse learn about the history of the area, write on chalkboards and ring the antique school bell. The schoolhouse is a popular destination for school and youth group field trips. Project coordinator: **Edmond Historic Preservation Trust**

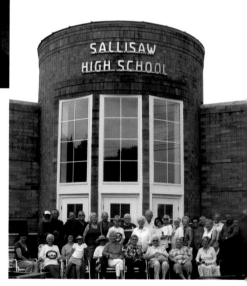

School Restoration • CRESCENT (above and left)

The Alpha School is a single-room schoolhouse located at the Frontier Country Museum in Crescent. Currently under renovation, the school is being restored to its original 1893 appearance. Centennial funds helped support the installation of a windmill, well, swings, flagpole, walkways and even an outhouse on the schoolhouse grounds. Many of the authentic furnishings in the school have been donated by area residents. Project coordinator: **Frontier Country Historical Society**

NOT SHOWN:

Historic School Restoration • COLCORD

Talbot Library and Museum purchased a 1920s one-room school building that was moved from Springtown, Arkansas, to Colcord, and has been renovated and restored. The picturesque building has become a popular site for weddings, community activities and classes. Project coordinator: **Talbot Library and Museum**

Laing School Project • FREDERICK

Laing School District was the first consolidated school district in Oklahoma, and Camp Radziminski was an important stop along the Base Line, a route followed by 1901 Oklahoma Land Lottery pioneers. Projects included production of an anthology of historic and contemporary articles relating to Camp Radziminski, Laing School and the area, and installation of a historical marker. Project coordinator: **Laing School Association**

Historic School Community Building • SKEDEE

An outdoor recreational area was added to the site of the historic Skedee School. The school is currently being used as a community center. Project coordinator: **Town of Skedee**

Historic High School Renovation and Centennial Park • SALLISAW

The former Sallisaw High School, listed on the National Register of Historic Places, received a facelift in 2004 when community volunteers raised funds to renovate the school for use as a community center. Tragically, just one week after completion, the school was set on fire and experienced substantial damage. The Centennial Commission then stepped in and provided funds to help with the second renovation. Today, the center houses reunions, art shows, club and civic meetings, banquets, weddings and memorial services. Project coordinator: **Old Sallisaw High School Association**

RESTORATIONS
HERITAGE ACTIVITIES

Dewey Hotel • *DEWEY (right)* The Dewey Hotel is a three-story Victorian building, completed in 1900 by **Jacob H. Bartles**, an area farmer, rancher and civic leader. Thanks to a grant from the Centennial Commission, the turn-of-the-century hotel has been reopened and renovated as a museum, featuring period furnishings, clothing and photographs of early life in Dewey. Project coordinator: **Washington County Historical Society**

Travis Mansion • *TULSA (above and left)* The renovation of the 11,000-square-foot Travis Mansion into galleries, public meeting spaces and offices for the Tulsa Historical Society completed a two-phase project that included the addition of a 17,000-square-foot wing housing galleries, a great hall and storage areas. Project coordinator: **Tulsa Historical Society**

NOT SHOWN:

Belvidere Mansion • *CLAREMORE* The Belvidere, a three-story Victorian mansion built in 1907, has been restored and decorated in period furnishings. Centennial enhancements include interior and exterior paint and trim work, as well as the rebuilding of an expansive front porch. Project coordinators: **Claremore Main Street** and **Rogers County Historical Society**

Harrah History Center • *HARRAH* When the refurbished 1895 Rock Island Train Depot, which served as a small museum, was set afire in 1999, the Harrah Historical Society set out to once again provide residents a place to experience local history. The society's Centennial project produced the Harrah History Center, an attractive complex that includes a small museum, the renovated depot, a historical marker, Centennial park benches, two railroad coal cars and a caboose. Project coordinator: **Harrah Historical Society**

Peter Conser House • *HEAVENER* This two-story, eight-room house was built in 1894 for Choctaw tribal leader **Peter Conser**, his second wife and his nine children. It was donated to the Oklahoma Historical Society in 1967 and has been restored to reflect life in the Choctaw Nation prior to statehood. The barn was restored by the **Friends of Peter Conser Historic Site Society** in time for the Centennial celebration.

Runnymede Hotel • *ALVA (right)* The Runnymede Hotel, built in Kansas in 1886, began as a facility to train English immigrants in the skills of the gentleman farmer. The three-story building was purchased in 1893 and transported via horse and wagon to Alva. Once reconstructed, the building became the premier area hotel. After a period of neglect and deterioration, the property was purchased in 1999 by the Runnymede Renovation Committee. Now Alva's community and arts center, it hosts weddings, receptions, parties, exhibits and concerts. As part of the statewide celebration, a Centennial courtyard was added adjacent to the hotel, featuring a mural depicting a 1907 statehood parade. Project coordinator: **Nescatunga Arts and Humanities Council, Inc.**

Murray Lindsay Mansion • *LINDSAY (left and below)*
This three-story stone-and-stucco home was built in 1879
for landowner and rancher **Frank Murray**, an Irish immigrant
from Londonderry, his Choctaw wife, Alzire, and their eight
children. It was once the largest and most ornate house in
the western Chickasaw Nation, containing 15 rooms, two
baths and four fireplaces. Dedicated on December 1, 2007,
after extensive renovation, the classic revival-style mansion
is now open to visitors. Period furnishings include
family photos and a 187-piece teapot collection. Project
coordinator: **Lindsay Community Historical Society**

W.T. Foreman House • *DUNCAN (above and left)* This
two-story house, listed on the National Register of Historic
Places, was built in 1918 for one of Duncan's first citizens and
is recognized as an early example of **Frank Lloyd Wright**'s
prairie-style architecture. Extensive restorations, funded in part
by the Centennial Commission, restored the house for use as
a historic attraction and a public gathering place. The house
hosted several community events in 2007 as Duncan's official
Oklahoma Centennial site. Project coordinator: **The Prairie
House Foundation**

Perry Church • *PERRY (above)* Affectionately known as
the "church on a perch," Perry's oldest church was built over
a century ago to house the local Episcopal congregation.
After decades of service, it was replaced by a modern brick
building and the historic landmark was moved to a temporary
foundation of steel beams, giving the church its nickname.
The church was then moved to a permanent location, which
includes a historically correct sandstone foundation, in CCC
(Civilian Conservation Corps) Park. Centennial enhancements
include landscaping, fencing and signage. Project coordinator:
Cherokee Strip Centennial Corporation

HERITAGE ACTIVITIES

NOT SHOWN:

Oklahoma Centennial Plus Five Celebration • *CEMENT* Though
Oklahoma was celebrating 100 years of statehood, the town of Cement had
five more to celebrate. To honor their 105-year-old heritage, the town put on
a slam-bang parade and hosted a broad variety of local entertainment. Project
coordinator: **Cement Community Association, Inc.**

Lincoln County Territorial Militia Ball • *CHANDLER* The Centennial
Lincoln County Territorial Militia Ball featured a Native Amercian color guard and
a live orchestra for dancing. Guests were encouraged to don period dress and
celebrate their Oklahoma heritage and pride. The ball was held in the drill hall
of the recently renovated Chandler armory, another Centennial project. Project
coordinator: **Old Armory Restorers**

Centennial Marker • *FLETCHER* A granite marker in the Fletcher
Centennial Plaza commemorates the 100th anniversary of Oklahoma statehood
and the century mark of the arrival of outlaw **Frank James**, who became a
long-time Fletcher resident. Project coordinator: **Town of Fletcher**

Centennial Reenactments and Pow-wows • *GRANDFIELD*
Downtown Grandfield hosted a Centennial event showcasing Native
American dancers, street dance demonstrations, a talent contest, historical
interpretations, demonstrations, exhibits and a performance of Oklahoma!.
Project coordinator: **City of Grandfield**

Constitutional Convention Exemplifications • *GUTHRIE* Presented in
April and October 2007, this extraordinary event featured high school seniors from
throughout the state portraying the 112 delegates to the 1907 convention which
drafted Oklahoma's constitution. Selected from the same districts as the original
delegates, students spoke from prepared scripts and debated the actual issues
that helped form our state. State funds helped support the event, and the
Masonic Charity Foundation provided travel and lodging for students,
in addition to awarding each student a $1,000 scholarship. Project
coordinator: **Guthrie Scottish Rite Masonic Center**

Early Bird Bluegrass Festival • *HUGO* Oklahoma bluegrass legend **Bill Grant**
served as festival program director and emcee for the decade-old Early Bird Bluegrass
Festival. Bluegrass enthusiasts travel to Hugo from throughout the region to celebrate
and enjoy the rich musical tradition of Oklahoma. Project coordinator: **Little Dixie
Community Action Agency**

Centennial Celebration • *MOUNTAIN VIEW* Festivities for the Mountain View
Centennial celebration included a parade on Main Street with floats, riding clubs and
more. Other features included displays of antique farm machinery, an antique auto
show, blacksmithing demonstrations, a chuck wagon, and all the rides and attractions
of the Mountain View Free Fair. Project coordinators: **Town of Mountain View** and the
Mountain View Oklahoma Centennial Celebration Committee

Chautauqua Series of Oklahoma Themes • *STATEWIDE* A partnership of the
Oklahoma Humanities Council and the **Arts & Humanities Council of Tulsa**, the
Chautauqua Series features local scholars touring the state in educational re-creations
of people and events from history. Each year offers a different theme – the 2007 version
was "100 Years of Oklahoma Heroes." Tens of thousands of Oklahomans gathered
under the big Chautauqua tent to experience keystone moments in state history.

NOT SHOWN:

Wintersmith Amphitheater • *ADA In response to the Great Depression, President Roosevelt created the Civilian Conservation Corps as a way for young men to earn wages by working on improvement projects around the country. One such project was established in Ada: the construction of Wintersmith Park and Amphitheater. The project was completed in 1934 and became a popular setting for concerts, plays and public events. After years of disuse, the city worked with the Centennial Commission to restore the amphitheater to its original condition, once again giving the community an outdoor venue for entertainment and social activities. Project coordinator:* **City of Ada**

Rose Hill Cemetery • *ARDMORE Two impressive new entrances constructed of massive hewn stones and black wrought iron gates were among the several enhancements to this historic cemetery. Other improvements were new landscaping with irrigation and widened paving at entries. Project coordinator:* **Ardmore Cemeteries Beautification Council**

The Harrah Amphitheater • *HARRAH The theater was constructed as a Centennial project on a small lake surrounded by a popular city park. The open native-stone and wood structure provides a scenic venue for special events, while a state-of-the-art sound system is an additional asset for community and school productions. Project coordinator:* **City of Harrah**

Historical Building Renovation • *McLOUD An empty historic building and a historical society looking for a museum site became a successful Centennial project. The McLoud Historical Society renovated a 1920s downtown structure into a pleasant heritage center for local history and artifacts. Retaining the original interior brick walls and other unique features while incorporating energy-efficient windows and other modern amenities, volunteers and contractors worked side by side to blend the historic with the new. Project coordinator:* **McLoud Historical Society**

Black Cultural Center • *OKMULGEE From 1922 to 1956, the Okmulgee Black Hospital provided medical services to Okmulgee County African American residents. The building was eventually condemned and had rapidly deteriorated when a group of local citizens formed the Okmulgee County Multi-Cultural Heritage Association to restore the structure and preserve its cultural history. Joining forces with the City of Okmulgee, the Creek Nation and the Centennial Commission, the association made significant restorations to the exterior of the former hospital and has begun work on the interior, with the intent of converting the 18-room building into a cultural center. Project coordinator:* **Okmulgee County Multi-Cultural Heritage Association**

Old Towne • *SAND SPRINGS Sand Springs' historic downtown center, or Old Towne, received many facelifts and false façades between 1950 and 1970. As part of the Centennial renovation program, Old Towne was restored to its original splendor with the removal of these modifications. The town also completed enhancements to the community center. Project coordinator:* **City of Sand Springs**

Plaza Theater • *OKLAHOMA CITY (above and right) The Plaza Theater opened its doors in 1935 as the first air-conditioned theater in Oklahoma and quickly became a popular area attraction. The theater remained in operation until 1979 and then fell into disrepair. As part of the Plaza District renovation, this landmark theater has been brought back to life for the production of musicals and plays, as well as a venue where students of Lyric Theatre's Thelma Gaylord Academy can hone their talents. The Plaza Theater also featured the play* Oklahoma! *as part of the Centennial celebration. Both the Oklahoma City Centennial sponsors and the Centennial Commission contributed to this project. Project coordinator:* **Lyric Theatre of Oklahoma, Inc.**

Ritz Theater • *SHAWNEE (above) As the oldest building on Main Street, the Ritz Theater dates back to 1897. After serving as a vaudeville theater, the venue became a motion picture theater where the first "talkies" in Shawnee were shown. While work remains to be done, the "Grand Old Lady" has undergone extensive restoration, while preserving the original art deco house lights and other architectural features. Centennial funds supported the installation of heating and cooling systems and a refurbishment of the exterior marquee. The Ritz currently serves as a community performing arts center. Project coordinator:* **Society for Revitalization of Downtown Shawnee, Inc.**

Route 66 Round Barn • *ARCADIA (above) This Route 66 icon has been fascinating travelers since 1898. Renovations completed with the assistance of the Centennial Commission include new sidewalks, restrooms, a machinery display area and signage. Project coordinator:* **Arcadia Historical and Preservation Society, Inc.**

Korns Building • *NEWKIRK Named after Newkirk newspaper editor and civic leader* **Ed F. Korns**, *this historic building serves as offices for Newkirk Main Street and as a community center for holidays and special events. Centennial funds helped support second-floor restorations. Project coordinator:* **Newkirk Community Historical Society**

Oklahoma Centennial Rodeo Opry Theater • *OKLAHOMA CITY (left) A renovated historic theater in Stockyard City has become the brand new home of the Oklahoma Centennial Rodeo Opry. While retaining many features of the original building, project sponsors installed modern seating, lighting and environmental controls, and the latest in sound technology. Traditionally the starting place for many of Oklahoma's most popular country and western performers, the Opry continues to provide a platform for the state's promising young talent. Oklahoma City Centennial sponsors contributed to this project. Project coordinator:* **Opry Heritage Foundation of Oklahoma**

Sayre Fire Truck • *SAYRE (above) Owned by the City of Sayre since 1924, this 1923 American La France Pumper engine underwent an extensive restoration. One of only two trucks of this model and year known to exist in the entire United States, the Sayre fire truck is a popular attraction throughout the region. Project coordinator:* **City of Sayre**

NOT SHOWN:

Frisco Depot • *HUGO This 1914 depot has served since 1978 as a museum for artifacts from Hugo, Choctaw County and southeastern Oklahoma. This Centennial project included restoring a 1918 World War I Saving Stamps building, repairing the depot roof and stage, and upgrading ADA access. Project coordinator:* **Choctaw County Historical Society**

The River Center • *MUSKOGEE Centennial funds helped to construct The River Center at Three Forks Harbor, a $3.4 million multi-use public facility that showcases the diverse cultural, historical, economic, ecological and geological significance of the Three Forks region in the development of today's Oklahoma. Project coordinator:* **Muskogee City-County Port Authority**

Route 66 Cyrus Avery Centennial Plaza • *TULSA The Route 66* **Cyrus Avery** *Centennial Plaza pays homage to the mythic Mother Road and her landmarks across Oklahoma. A statue sculpted by* **Robert Summers** *depicts a horse-drawn carriage meeting a horseless carriage at the crossroads of U.S. history, reflecting the spirit of the historic highway and the visionary who helped create it. Project coordinator:* **City of Tulsa**

253

COMMUNITY & CIVIC CENTERS

Memorial Park Boys and Girls Clubs • *OKLAHOMA CITY (below and right)*
Donations from Oklahoma City Centennial sponsors helped construct three classrooms – music, fine arts and drama – for the facility at Memorial Park. The Boys and Girls Clubs of Oklahoma County provide after-school and summer educational programs to underprivileged, inner-city children and young adults. Project coordinator: **Boys and Girls Clubs of Oklahoma County, Inc.**

Studio Mid-Del • *MIDWEST CITY (right)*
Studio Mid-Del is a community creative arts center for citizens of all ages and talent levels. Offering specific courses in art, dance, drama and music, it's a great cultural arts addition to eastern Oklahoma County. The first development stage has been completed and the second phase is underway. Project coordinator: **Studio Mid-Del, Inc.**

Memorial Pavilion • *NEWALLA (right)*
Located on cemetery grounds, Newalla Memorial Pavilion serves as a peaceful place of remembrance. Primarily serving as an on-site location to conduct funeral services, the pavilion also provides a serene setting for a host of community-based gatherings throughout the year, such as Memorial Day and Veterans Day events. Project coordinator: **Newalla Pilgrim's Rest Cemetery Association**

The award-winning Altus High School band performed a series of numbers at the dedication of the Altus center.

NOT SHOWN:

Community Center • *BRISTOW* To keep up with the community and its growing needs, the Bristow Community Center underwent a renovation that now enables it to better serve city residents. *Project coordinator:* **City of Bristow**

Bristow VFW • *BRISTOW* Just off Route 66 lies a beautifully landscaped municipal park complex that is a great community attraction with its meandering running and walking trails, picnic tables, docks and lake. The complex also holds the Veterans of Foreign Wars National Wake Island War Memorial and VFW Post 3656, which was renovated with Centennial funding. *Project coordinator:* **Veterans of Foreign Wars Post 3656**

Community Center • *ERICK* The center has become one of pride for the citizens of Erick. New signage, landscaping design, ADA-compliant restrooms, an advanced sprinkler system, tables and chairs, and a kitchen equipped with all major appliances have helped transform this once-tired center into a warm home for community events and gatherings. *Project coordinator:* **City of Erick**

Amphitheater • *HARRAH* The Harrah Amphitheater was built to serve as a venue for local community events and school productions. Sitting on a small, tranquil lake, it was constructed from native stone and natural wood, and features a state-of-the-art sound system. *Project coordinator:* **City of Harrah**

Grand Lake Visitors Center Kiosks • *LANGLEY* Grand Lake's 46,500 surface acres of pristine water are a perfect outdoor venue for fishing, swimming and skiing. In addition to its popular sporting appeal, Grand Lake is one of 2,000 publicly owned electric utility systems in the nation that serve millions of people daily. Kiosks explaining the economical significance of Grand Lake have been placed in businesses in nearby Langley. These kiosks will eventually be placed in the Grand River Ecosystems and Education Center to inform the public about energy importance and conservation. *Project coordinator:* **Grand Gateway Economic Development Association**

Oklahoma Life and Ecology Center (Boy Scouts) • *LAWTON* The Oklahoma Life and Ecology Center is an ideal learning environment that educates people of all ages about history and preservation in Oklahoma. This ecological learning center includes beautiful nature areas, running and walking trails, and numerous hands-on outdoor activities in which the community can participate. *Project coordinator:* **Last Frontier Council, Boy Scouts of America**

Oklahoma Music Hall of Fame • *MUSKOGEE* Since 1997, Muskogee has been home to the Oklahoma Music Hall of Fame, which celebrates and honors the talents of Oklahoma-born musicians. From hard-biting country western legend Merle Haggard to "Big Dog Daddy" Toby Keith, Oklahoma stars shine bright in Muskogee. Envisioned as becoming one of Oklahoma's top musical attractions, this facility is being updated with lighting, graphics and collection items donated by the inductees themselves. The first phase of development, including an exhibit space for special events and a multi-purpose performance room, is now complete. *Project coordinator:* **Oklahoma Music Hall of Fame and Museum, Inc.**

Southern Plains Conference Center • *WOODWARD* The City of Woodward has played an integral role in the growth, development and history of northwestern Oklahoma. Beginning as a railroad supply trade point, the city emerged into a leading energy provider and will soon be home to the Southern Plains Conference Center. Currently in development, the center will be a state-of-the-art facility for community gatherings, events and various other functions. *Project coordinator:* **City of Woodward**

Centennial Memorial Center • *ALTUS*
(above and right) The Altus Centennial Memorial Center is a beautifully designed native-stone building with large elegant windows and a small convenient kitchen. Located in a historic cemetery, the center possesses a warm family atmosphere and is open to all community members for private gatherings. Project coordinator: **City of Altus**

MILITARY
&VETERANS SITES

USS Oklahoma, Pearl Harbor Memorial Model

BARTLESVILLE (right) A memorial scale model of the USS Oklahoma has been built in the city of Bartlesville. The memorial honors the bravery and loss of life of 429 military personnel aboard the USS Oklahoma on December 7, 1941. Project coordinator: **Bartlesville Community Foundation – Wall of Honor**

Hinton Veterans Memorial • *HINTON (above and right)*

The City of Hinton donated one acre of land to serve as a memorial ground honoring all local war veterans. It is home to a wall of honor, flagpoles, benches and retired United States military equipment. This will be a sacred place where the local community can pay tribute to the brave soldiers who have risked their lives for our nation. Project coordinator: **City of Hinton**

Broken Arrow Women's War Memorial

*BROKEN ARROW (below and right) It was the dream of **Jene Pointer**, president of the Veterans of Foreign Wars (VFW) Post 10887, Broken Arrow Ladies Auxiliary, to honor American women who have served during times of war. On December 7, 2007, after much hard work, her dream finally came true when a black marble memorial was dedicated to the courageous women who have selflessly served their country. The Broken Arrow Women's War Memorial is the only war monument in the nation specifically dedicated to women.* Project coordinator: **Veterans of Foreign Wars and Ladies Auxiliary Post 10887**

Rush Springs Veterans Project • *RUSH SPRINGS (above)*

A granite monument has been dedicated to all the war veterans of Rush Springs – past, present and future. Accompanying the monument are three flagpoles that are lit at night, ensuring the American flag is always visible. Project coordinator: **Town of Rush Springs**

Purcell Veterans Memorial • PURCELL

(right) The City of Purcell is paying respect to war veterans with a life-sized statue of a patriotic American soldier kneeling on one knee with his hand on his helmet. On the ground surrounding the soldier are granite tablets that list the names of the brave men and women from the local community who have served our country. Project coordinator: **City of Purcell**

Northwest Oklahoma Veterans Centennial Memorial • SHATTUCK

The Northwest Oklahoma Veterans Centennial Memorial celebrates the heroic services of area veterans from the Civil War to the present with a granite wall displaying their names. The focal point is a bronze eagle sculpture (left) that gracefully sits in the middle of the memorial. The local chapter of the Future Farmers of America raised funds for the sculpture. Project coordinator: **City of Shattuck**

Apache Veterans Memorial Park • APACHE

(above) A scenic spread of countryside between the junction of State Highway 19 and US 281 has been beautifully transformed into a memorial park that honors the passion, bravery and spirit of hundreds of local veterans. A granite memorial honoring those killed or missing in action and those who died as prisoners of war anchors a plaza paved with bricks bearing the names of almost 300 local veterans. Benches offer visitors the opportunity to reflect and remember. Project coordinator: **Apache Economic Development Authority**

NOT SHOWN:

Tony K. Burris Congressional Medal of Honor Memorial • BLANCHARD

Tony K. Burris, a native of Blanchard and a sergeant first class in the United States Army, posthumously received the Congressional Medal of Honor for his courageous actions in Korea on October 8 and 9, 1951. The memorial plaza honoring Burris stands downtown at the intersection of Highway 62 and Main Street. The landscaped plaza displays a statue of Burris and is accompanied by written narratives about his integrity, courage and heroic efforts. A classic Centennial clock is incorporated into the overall plaza design. Project coordinator: **Tony K. Burris VFW Post 145 and the City of Blanchard**

Veterans Memorial at Choctaw • CHOCTAW

A memorial honoring Oklahoma veterans who courageously risked their lives for their country in war efforts is currently in development in the city of Choctaw. The memorial will feature an arched hallway that will serve as the focal point of the memorial. Surrounding the arch will be four walls that recognize the names of the charitable donors involved in this memorial project. Beautiful landscaping, sidewalks and an informational area with benches are also included in the design. Project coordinator: **Veterans Memorial at Choctaw and the City of Choctaw**

"Local Heroes" Monument • HAMMON

A special monument to pay respect to all local veterans has been built in Hammon. The monument includes three freestanding granite sections that contain the names of local Oklahomans who have proudly served their nation. The monument has the capacity to commemorate up to 1,200 veterans' names. Project coordinator: **Hammon American Legion Post 185**

Love County Military Museum • MARIETTA

Love County Military Museum is currently under restoration. The museum recognizes the United States military dating back to the Civil War and contains family military history records, more than 700 photos of Love County men and women who have served the United States, a memorial room honoring Love County soldiers who lost their lives in battle and area law enforcement displays. The museum is housed in a two-story 1910 jail. Project coordinator: **Love County Military Museum, Inc.**

Veterans Memorial Park • MOORELAND

A huge mural depicting previous wars, a large bronze eagle and a life-size bronze of a military helmet, rifle and boots were added to this park on Main Street as part of the Centennial commemoration. Project coordinator: **Town of Mooreland**

Cleveland County Veterans Memorial • NORMAN

Cleveland County Veterans Memorial will honor and proudly pay tribute to approximately 22,000 Cleveland County war veterans. Centennial funding supported the architectural planning for the memorial. Project coordinator: **Norman Park Foundation, Inc.**

Payne County Veterans Memorial • STILLWATER

The city of Stillwater is now home to the Payne County Veterans Memorial that honors all military personnel who have lost their lives courageously serving our country. The focal point of the memorial is an abstract design of a flame. Surrounding the flame are numerous panels that represent the different branches of the U.S. military. Plants native to Oklahoma enclose the memorial. Project coordinator: **American Legion Carter C. Hanner-Mamon G. Sharp Post 129**

Veterans Memorial • MINCO

(left and right) A historic 1945 flagpole stands at the center of the Minco Centennial Veterans Memorial, a project of American Legion Post 215. The new plaza now surrounding the original flagpole contains granite monuments honoring local veterans. Additional flagpoles proudly display military service flags and the state flag. Project coordinator: **American Legion Post 215**

Chesapeake Boathouse • *OKLAHOMA CITY (below) The state-of-the-art Chesapeake Boathouse sits on the banks of the Oklahoma River. Sixteen columns of light illuminate the structure, giving the illusion that the boathouse is floating on water. The boathouse is home to as many as 124 boats, a covered observation deck, a spacious lobby, a panoramic 24-foot wall of glass and a multi-purpose meeting room that accommodates up to 60 people. Oklahoma City Centennial sponsors contributed significantly to this project. Project coordinator:* **Chesapeake Boathouse Foundation**

Oklahoma Sports Hall of Fame & Jim Thorpe Museum • *OKLAHOMA CITY*

(left) This all-star museum will honor the athletic prowess of Jim Thorpe, plus exceptional state athletes and those who have supported Oklahoma athletics. Known as America's greatest athlete, Thorpe won Olympic gold medals in both the decathlon and pentathlon. He also played professional football, basketball and baseball. Both the state of Oklahoma and Oklahoma City Centennial sponsors financially supported this project. Project coordinator: **Jim Thorpe Association, Inc.**

Officially christening the boathouse are (left to right) **Aubrey McClendon**, **Clay Bennett**, *Mayor* **Mick Cornett** *and* **Rand Elliott**.

Centennial Oklahoma Derby • *OKLAHOMA CITY*

(right and below) The stakes are always high at Oklahoma City's premier racetrack, Remington Park. The special Centennial edition of the 19th annual Oklahoma Derby featured a $300,000 purse and a classic matchup of three-year-olds. The race offered a thrilling come-from-behind victory with "Going Ballistic" winning in dramatic fashion.

Centennial Soccer Park • *ELK CITY*

(right) Elk City is home to a brand new soccer park that the entire county will benefit from year-round. In addition to the beautiful green pitch, the soccer-specific complex is equipped with bleachers, paved parking, a concession area and ADA-approved restrooms. Project coordinator: **City of Elk City**

Lawton Rodeo Facility • *LAWTON*

(right) The Lawton Rangers' rodeo facility has recently undergone various improvements and renovations. This historic rodeo is an integral element to the city of Lawton and continues to bring the community together year after year. Project coordinator: **Lawton Rangers, Inc.**

NOT SHOWN:

Kerr-McGee Trails • *OKLAHOMA CITY* This newly paved, one-half-mile trail is perfect for walking, running and biking. Located on the north side of the Oklahoma River, the Kerr-McGee Trails will eventually link up with the various trails located within Regatta Park, making for great outdoor activities. Oklahoma City Centennial sponsors donated to this project which was coordinated by the **City of Oklahoma City**.

Mickey Mantle Sculpture • *COMMERCE* Commerce High School is home to a bronze statue honoring hometown sports legend Mickey Mantle. The "Commerce Comet" was an all-star athlete and an inspiration to all who watched. In 1949, Mantle took his first step toward becoming a legend by signing with the New York Yankees. He played with them for 18 years and earned three American League MVP titles, 16 All-Star game appearances, seven World Championships and became a distinguished member of the Baseball Hall of Fame in 1974. Local artist **Nick Calcagno** designed the piece that was sculpted by **R.C. Hunt**. Project coordinator: **Mickey Mantle Memorial Trust**

Seminole Centennial Recreational Complex • *SEMINOLE* The Seminole Centennial Recreational Complex is a new 42-acre, state-of-the-art complex for the local sporting community to enjoy. The complex includes four softball fields, movable fences, top-notch lighting equipment and sprinkler systems. This Centennial project has become a popular venue for weekend activities and various family and community gatherings. Project coordinator: **Seminole Chamber of Commerce**

American Legion Youth World Series • *BARTLESVILLE*

(left) This Centennial project brought baseball to Bartlesville in the form of the American Legion Youth World Series. The eight-day event included the World Series plus a Centennial parade, a home run derby, a golf tournament and a banquet of champions. Project coordinator: **2007 American Legion Youth World Series Committee, Bartlesville**

BOOKS & MEDIA
SPECIAL EVENTS

Dream No Little Dream:
The Legacy of Robert S. Kerr

The inspiring story of the "father of modern Oklahoma" is the subject of this Emmy Award-winning documentary, narrated by actor **Keith Carradine**. Written and directed by Oklahoma City Community College film and video professor **Greg Mellott**, and produced by OCCC artist-in-residence **Gray Frederickson**, scenes were filmed and edited by OCCC film and video faculty, students and graduates.

The **Oklahoma City Philharmonic** performed during a red carpet premiere held November 6, 2007, at the Oklahoma City Civic Center Music Hall, and Carradine introduced the film. After a November 12 television debut over OETA, the documentary was released nationwide.

Documentary underwriters were the **Robert S. Kerr** family; the **Aubrey M. Kerr Sr.** family; **Mr. and Mrs. Aubrey K. McClendon**; Chesapeake Energy Corporation; and the Oklahoma Centennial Commission.

Horseshoe Road
International Tour Documentary

Horseshoe Road is an Oklahoma City-based band that took the Oklahoma Centennial spirit to Japan and Thailand. The band's three-week journey was made into an hour-long documentary – shot by Oklahoma filmmakers **Alan Novey**, **James Payne** and **Jeremy Long** – that was aired on OETA, as well as national and international PBS stations. The tour and documentary were official Centennial projects and were funded by the Oklahoma City Centennial sponsors. Band members included violinist **Kyle Dillingham** of Enid, bassist **Brad Benge** of Sallisaw and guitarist **Dustin Jones** of Yukon – a trio that **J. Blake Wade**, executive director of the Centennial Commission, called "great ambassadors for our state."

Oklahoma Rising CD Set

The "Oklahoma Rising" anthem was featured on a limited edition Oklahoma Centennial CD set that was released in September 2006. Included were songs by many famous Oklahomans: **Vince Gill**, **Reba McEntire**, **Garth Brooks**, **Carrie Underwood**, **Toby Keith**, **Brooks & Dunn**, **The Flaming Lips**, **Hanson**, **Sandi Patty**, **Kristin Chenoweth**, **Woody Guthrie**, **Roger Miller**, **Roy Clark**, **Patti Page**, **Gene Autry**, **Leon Russell**, **Byron Berline**, **Gordon MacRae**, **Restless Heart**, **Rascal Flatts**, **Joe Diffie**, **Bryan White**, **Blake Shelton**, **Katrina Elam**, **The All-American Rejects** and many more.

The Oklahoma Rising CD was originated by **Lee Allan Smith**, with coordination from **J. Blake Wade**. **Jeff Gwaltney** served as executive producer, Gov. **Brad Henry** was chairman, and **Reba McEntire** and **Vince Gill** served as honorary co-chairs. Proceeds from CD sales benefited Central Oklahoma Habitat for Humanity.

Oklahoma Centennial Poem *BY N. SCOTT MOMADAY:*
"The Land," "Settlement" and "Statehood"
*Pulitzer Prize-winning author **N. Scott Momaday** was named poet laureate of the state of Oklahoma in 2007. His poem titled "Centennial: 1907-2007" traces the evolution of Oklahoma from 1907 to today. Momaday read the work at a reception held November 9, 2007, at Chase Tower. The poet prefaced his reading by noting, "I'm an Oklahoman, and I'm proud to be one." He calls himself "a storyteller" and said, "Story is something I've been interested in all my life. My father read to me when I was growing up. The Indian people have a wonderful tradition of story."*

The Land

The first people to enter upon it
Must have given it a name, wind-borne and elemental,
Like summer rain.
The name must have given spirit to the land,
For so it is with names.
Before the first people there must have been
The profound isolation of night and day,
The blazing shield of the sun,
The darkness winnowed from the stars –
The holy havoc of myth and origin,
True and prophetic, and inexorable,
Like summer rain.

What was to become of the land?
What was the land to become?
What was there in the land to define
The falling of the rain and the turning of seasons,
The far and forever silence of the universe?

A voice, a name,
Words echoing the whir of wings
Swelled among the clouds
And sounded on the red earth in the wake of creation.
A voice. A name.
Oklahoma.

Settlement

And there was the flow of migratory blood,
Rising from time and glacial mist
From the four directions,
Touching story and music to the Plains,
Red men dancing, chanting prayer:
    Give us the pounding hooves of horses and buffalo,
    Give us the plumage and paint of ceremony,
    Give us bravery, steadfastness, generosity, and virtue,
    Give us beauty. Give us the heart of hunting and roving.

Then came homesteaders in wagons,
Muledrivers with hammers and plows,
Cattlemen and sheepherders,
Pastors and schoolmarms,
Bankers and doctors and soldiers of fortune,
All bringing definition to the land,
All shaping a destiny, a geometry of camps within camps.
There came about a harvest of community,
An American story, a miracle play,
An enactment of civilization.
They came with the force and energy of driving rain.
Oklahoma.

Statehood

Along the old hunting trails
There sprang up towns and town squares,
The stark architecture of churches and cemeteries on the prairie,
The machinery of settlement and industry,
The stitching of railroads to the horizons.
All the rude and rustic monuments
That became the gleaming glass and metal of upstart cities,
And at last the immersion into a field of stars
On the unfurled flag of liberty and union.
The coalescence of hope and passage,
Of sacrifice and triumph,
A becoming as bold as thunder above a confluence of rivers,
Roaring between luminous banks of rain –
Oklahoma.

— N. Scott Momaday

BOOKS & MEDIA
EDUCATIONAL PROGRAMS

Oklahoma City National Memorial & Museum Centennial Education Program

(below) The program, supported by Oklahoma City Centennial sponsors, included numerous special exhibits, programs and other educational offerings throughout 2007.

Oklahoma Centennial Book Festival

(above) The fair and festival at **Oklahoma City University** were created as a celebration of reading, writing and the printed word. Its intent was to engage state and local citizens in promoting literacy, as well as celebrating the talent of Oklahoma's huge array of authors and poets. Literary workshops and lectures were conducted during the event, and craft displays, as well as puppet and fashion shows, were included. This multi-year event was created and led by Oklahoma City resident **Ann Lacy**. It was funded by the Oklahoma City Centennial sponsors.

Oklahoma Reads Oklahoma

(left and below) This project encouraged Oklahomans to celebrate the state's diverse heritage by reading, discussing and enjoying Oklahoma-themed books. Each year from 2004 through 2007, Oklahomans reviewed a slate of six books and voted for the one book the entire state would read and discuss. Libraries, book clubs, community groups, schools and correctional institutions took part. The **Oklahoma Department of Libraries** and the **Oklahoma Humanities Council** served as project coordinators.

NOT SHOWN:
4-H and FFA Centennial Celebration

The Centennial Commission partnered with the 4-H Foundation and the 4-H Youth Development leadership program to enhance the 2007 Oklahoma 4-H Roundup, and joined with the Oklahoma chapter of the Future Farmers of America Association to bring Centennial attractions to the 2007 FFA annual conference. In addition, Centennial park benches recognizing the two organizations were installed at Oklahoma State Fair Park. Project coordinators: **Kent Boggs** and **Charles Cox**

Oklahoma Centennial Marionette Traveling Play

This educational and entertaining play was designed to commemorate Oklahoma's first 100 years of statehood. The cast consisted of two-foot-tall, hand-carved marionettes. The show was performed in classical theater style and featured highlights of Oklahoma history. Project coordinator: **Children's Historical Resource Center**

ONEOK/Oklahoma Arts Institute Centennial Writing Project

Diverse facets of Oklahoma's rich heritage and compelling history are the intriguing subjects of three books written by Oklahomans and produced by this project: Equal Justice: The Courage of Ada Sipuel, by First Lady **Kim Henry** and **William Bernhardt**; From the Blue Devils to Red Dirt: The Colors of Oklahoma Music, by **John Wooley**; and Four Arrows & Magpie: A Kiowa Story, by Pulitzer Prize winner **N. Scott Momaday**.

Route 66: the Mother Road Series

Legendary Route 66 was the focus of a multi-year series by **Redlands Community College** in El Reno. The college hosted concerts, exhibits and lectures – most were free to the public and several traveled the area. Final offerings in 2007 included presentations by two Oklahomans, historian **John Dwyer** and author/celebrity **Michael Wallis**, and an exhibit, "Signs of the Road: Route 66," by **Anthony Ross**. Wallis also served as guide for "Route 66 Today," a sold-out tour of Oklahoma sites along the Mother Road.

Shown holding musical instruments are (left to right) **Kyle Hawkins**, **Brian Dunning** and **Bart Weilburg** of Brian Dunning & The Rock n Roll Trio. Dr. **Juanita Krittenbrink**, second from left, serves as division director of Liberal Studies & Management Sciences at Redlands Community College. **Denise Wynia-Wedel**, second from right, is a fine arts coordinator, professor and gallery curator at Redlands Community College.

Centennial Collage Project *For seven years, Oklahomans created visual interpretations of Oklahoma themes as part of the* **Hideaway Pizza** *Centennial Collage competition. Classrooms, organizations and individuals entered the contest which was judged by educators, artists, historians and others. The winning entries were exhibited at Hideaway restaurants, the* **Oklahoma History Center** *and various locations around the state – and earned their creators cash prizes.* **Janie Harris**, *of Hideaway, headed up the project.*

Student Poster Contest

The Oklahoma Centennial Commission awarded 30 prizes to students in the Centennial poster contest. The contest was open to all Oklahoma students grades four to 12 and more than 1,800 entries were submitted. The posters reflected the theme "Celebrate Oklahoma! A Unique History. An Extraordinary Future." Winning posters were displayed in the Creative Arts Building during the 2007 Oklahoma State Fair Centennial Expo. The **Oklahoma Publishing Company** *and the Oklahoma City Centennial sponsors underwrote the contest.*

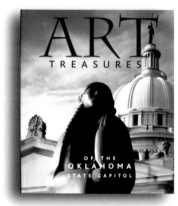

Art Treasures of the Oklahoma State Capitol

BY BOB BURKE, BETTY CROW AND SANDY MEYERS
The Oklahoma State Capitol contains more than 100 works of art that range from beautiful bronze sculptures to magnificent murals, portraits and paintings. It's a stunning collection that has been documented for the first time in this book.
Art Treasures of the Oklahoma State Capitol *is a collaboration of the* **Oklahoma State Senate Historical Preservation Fund***, the* **Oklahoma Arts Council***, the* **Oklahoma Heritage Association** *and* **Friends of the Capitol, Inc.** *All proceeds are used for the conservation, maintenance and commission of works for the State Capitol.*

Celebrate 100: An Architectural Guide to Central Oklahoma
Representing the architecture of the past 100 years in central Oklahoma, this book by the Central Oklahoma Chapter of the American Institute of Architects also recognizes AIA's 150th anniversary.

Chihuly: Oklahoma City Museum of Art
In 2002, a special exhibition of glassworks by internationally acclaimed artist **Dale Chihuly** *so captured Oklahomans' imaginations that the Oklahoma City Centennial sponsors donated a significant sum to the successful fundraising effort to permanently secure the collection.*

The same sponsors helped fund a stunning coffee-table-size book on the Oklahoma City Chihuly collection. Chihuly: Oklahoma City Museum of Art *features full-color images of collection pieces, as well as a chronology of Chihuly's life and career.*

The Artwork of Tulsa
BY JOHN BROOKS WALTON
With a grant from the Tulsa Oklahoma Centennial Committee, 78-year-old **John Brooks Walton** *compiled* The Artwork of Tulsa, *a full-color book that highlights private and public art in the Tulsa area. Photos and articles spotlight pieces as diverse as the hunk of metal on City Hall Plaza ("Amity") and the terra cotta designs at the Tulsa Fairgrounds Pavilion to the Ten Commandments on the exterior of Temple Israel and the "Appeal to the Great Spirit" on the grounds of Woodward Park.*

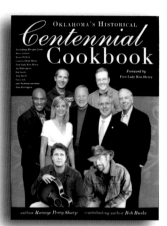

Oklahoma's Historical Centennial Cookbook
Ronnye Sharp *edited this colorful compilation of history and recipes that showcases the state's unique history and flavors. Included are recipes from Oklahomans such as* **Joe Washington**, **John Herrington**, **Hal Smith***, Gov. and Mrs.* **Brad Henry**, **T. Boone Pickens**, **Barry Switzer**, **Vince Gill** *and* **Toby Keith**.

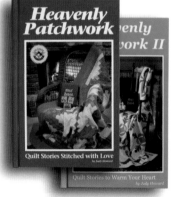

Heavenly Patchwork: Quilt Stories Stitched With Love
AND
Heavenly Patchwork II: Quilt Stories to Warm Your Heart
BY JUDY HOWARD
The Heavenly Patchwork *books recount the role of quilts and quilting in the lives of Oklahomans and their fellow Americans.*

The W. T. Foreman Prairie House Cookbook
More than 300 recipes, tips, tricks and home remedies make this cookbook from the **Prairie House Foundation** *an Oklahoma essential.*

Oklahoma Almanac 2003-2004
An essential reference work on Oklahoma, this edition of the almanac features updated sections on state and county government, education, agriculture and more. The State Capitol Dome is the feature for this edition which includes the history of the capitol building and the creation and building of its dome.

Sights and Sounds of Oklahoma Politics DVD
Produced by the Political Communications Center at the University of Oklahoma, this is a one-of-a-kind resource that provides easy access to 100 years of Oklahoma political campaigns through state-of-the-art technology. Print, radio, and television ads and campaign promotional materials reflect Oklahoma's changing political landscape.

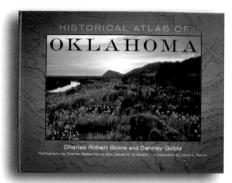

Historical Atlas of Oklahoma
For more than 40 years, the Historical Atlas of Oklahoma *has been an indispensable reference tool. This fourth edition, issued on the eve of the Oklahoma Centennial, is a greatly expanded and updated version.*

The book includes a foreword by **David L. Boren** *and features 17 contributing scholars, including natural and physical scientists and other professionals, on 119 topics. The authors* **Charles Robert Goins** *and* **Danney Goble** *have paired each topic with an interpretive essay. Maps, explanatory legends, tables and graphs are also presented.*

More than 170 new, full-color maps (cartography by **James H. Anderson***) chart Oklahoma's rich and varied history along with current population trends. New to this edition are various aspects of the state's economy and its diverse society, including black history, women's experiences, and the artists and musicians identified with the state.*

Celebrating Oklahoma! The Oklahoma Centennial Photographic Survey
PHOTOGRAPHY BY MIKE KLEMME
This oversized 288-page volume boasts hundreds of spectacular photos depicting Oklahoma's land, people, economy and communities. **Mike Klemme***, an official photographer of the Oklahoma Centennial, captured these striking images during a 20-month journey across the state. Also included are surprising facts about Oklahoma, as well as insights of nearly 50 famous Oklahomans.*

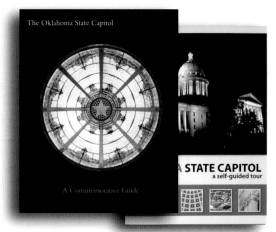

The Restoration and Decoration of the Oklahoma State Senate

*The Oklahoma State Senate Historical Preservation Fund, a non-profit organization founded by Oklahoma Sen. **Charles Ford**, commissioned more than 60 pieces of original art for the Oklahoma State Capitol and the Oklahoma State Senate. The organization, under Sen. Ford's direction, has restored and preserved these works of art, which represent various moments in Oklahoma's rich and colorful history, all at no cost to the state.*

Oklahoma State Capitol Guide
This official visitors' brochure offers historical background on the Capitol (including construction of the dome in 2002), an overview of the building and basic information.

Uncrowned Queens: African American Women Community Builders of Oklahoma
*The Uncrowned Queens Community Builders project was created to honor African-American women and their contributions to their communities, as well as provide an educational resource for local history. This comprehensive volume includes biographies and photos of 106 deserving women. The introduction was written by **John Mark Rhea**, University of Oklahoma Ph.D. candidate in history. Langston University President **JoAnn Haysbert** wrote the foreword. Written and edited by **Peggy Brooks-Bertram** and **Barbara Seals Nevergold** and published in May 2007, the book enjoyed an enthusiastic response from the Oklahoma community.*

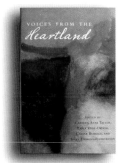

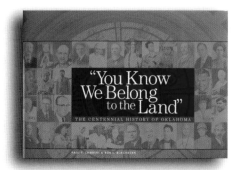

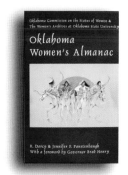

You Know We Belong to the Land – The Centennial History of Oklahoma
*This keepsake coffee-table-size book tells the story of the Sooner State through the lives of 33 fascinating individuals. Written by historians Dr. **Bob Blackburn** and Dr. **Paul Lambert**, it utilizes biographies, sidebars and photographs to bring the Oklahoma experience to life.*

Oklahoma Women's Almanac
CO-AUTHORED BY DR. BOB DARCY AND DR. JENNIFER F. PAUSTENBAUGH At an impressive 564 pages, this is the first almanac to focus exclusively on the women of Oklahoma. It consists of five article-length chapters that describe the policy issues that have had a major impact on women. Included are statistics, the records of Oklahoma female high school athletes, and brief biographies and photos of distinguished Oklahoma women and female members of the Oklahoma Hall of Fame. The book received the 2006 Outstanding Achievement Award given by the National Association of Commissions for Women.

Voices From the Heartland
EDITED BY EMILY DIAL-DRIVER, CAROLYN ANNE TAYLOR, CAROLE BURRAGE AND SALLY EMMONS-FEATHERSTON
*This is a celebration of women's contributions to Oklahoma's recent past. Women from a wide range of professions, lifestyles and backgrounds describe how the defining moments of their lives helped them develop and grow from ordinary girlhood into extraordinary women. From former Cherokee Chief **Wilma Mankiller** to prima ballerina **Maria Tallchief**, the authors share their personal experiences and convey the wisdom they've unearthed on their journeys thus far.*

The Oklahoma Scranimal
BY LARRY DERRYBERRY
*"What happens when a tornado picks up Papa Derryberry's barn, shakes it up and puts it down? Oh, the Oklahoma Scranimal will be loose on the town!" This sing-along book about an Oklahoma farm will enchant children and the young at heart. The CD features legendary Oklahoma voices including Gov. **Brad Henry**, Miss America 1967 **Jane Jayroe Gamble**, **Barry Switzer**, **Nadia Comaneci** and four-star General **Tommy Franks** as the Scranimal.*

Oklahoma Women: Creators of Destiny
BY GLENDA CARLILE This three-book set details the lives of Oklahoma women from territorial days to the present. The volumes included are Buckskin, Calico and Lace: Oklahoma's Territorial Women; Petticoats, Politics & Pirouettes: Oklahoma Women from 1900-1950; *and* Astronauts, Athletes & Ambassadors: Oklahoma Women 1950-2007.

NOT SHOWN:
The Clinton People, Yes!
BY JOANNA THURSTON ROPER
Created as part of Clinton's 100-year celebration, this is a play covering 10 decades of characters who made a difference in the quality of life in this western town.

Oklahoma Today *A series of special issues of* Oklahoma Today *was produced in honor of the state's Centennial. These eight magazines highlighted Centennial people, projects and places, and featured noteworthy moments in our state's history.* **Louisa McCune-Elmore** *serves as editor-in-chief and* **Joan Henderson** *is publisher.*

Regional Magazines *Statewide publications provided numerous cover features and in-depth articles about Oklahoma Centennial activities.*

Annual Reports *Many state agencies included Centennial images and themes in their yearly reports.*

Centennial Ads *Throughout 2007, the Oklahoma Press Association created and distributed bi-weekly ads on Centennial events around the state. More than 200 OPA member newspapers participated in the initiative, which was overseen by OPA Executive Vice President* **Mark Thomas***.* **Jennifer Gilliland** *created the eye-catching ads.*

Magazine Ads

Oklahoma Today ran several two-page ad spreads that promoted both the Centennial in general and specific events from the anniversary celebration. These ads were written, designed and produced by Centennial Commission staff members **Colin McEwen** *and* **Jeanie McCain Edney***.*

BOOKS & MEDIA
SPECIAL EDITIONS & EDITORIAL CARTOONS

Regional Newspapers *Oklahoma dailies played a large part in the Centennial celebration, as they helped keep readers up to speed on the latest 100th anniversary happenings in their town and across the state.*

Editorial Cartoons *Even newspaper cartoonists got in on the action, drawing up several Centennial-related illustrations. These cartoons are by **Jim Lange** of The Oklahoman.*

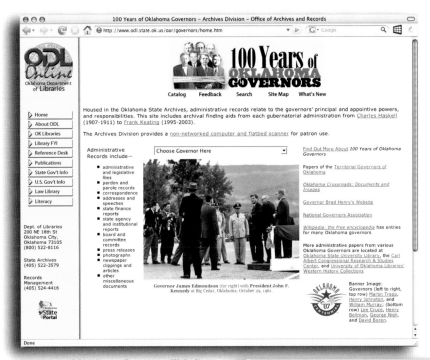

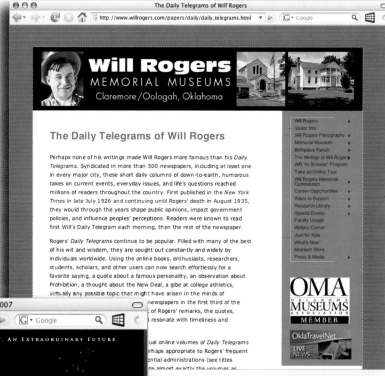

100 Years of Oklahoma Governors Website

This digital gubernatorial database, which is accessible online through the Oklahoma State Archives (www.odl. state.ok.us/oar/governors/home.htm) and in the records section of the Oklahoma Department of Libraries website, contains easily accessible information on Oklahoma's governors from Charles Haskell, the state's first governor, to Brad Henry, Oklahoma's current chief executive. **Tally Fugate** *– of the State Archives Division of the Oklahoma Department of Libraries – is responsible for the database.*

Will Rogers Historical Newspaper Articles

Readers worldwide are now able to access the four volumes of Will Rogers' Daily Telegrams, *arguably his most famous and recognized body of work. The database at www.willrogers.com includes Rogers' quotes on the famous and not-so-famous events that captured our nation's headlines at the time, as well as the causes and concerns of everyday people. The full text of the writings of Will Rogers and his weekly radio broadcasts will also be available online. The database is a project of the* **Will Rogers Memorial***.*

Oklahoma Centennial Website

Prepared for and maintained by the Oklahoma Centennial Commission, this website (www.oklahomacentennial.com) provided information on the more than 1,000 projects and events that were planned to commemorate Oklahoma's Centennial.

CELEBRAT

1907-2007

Spirit Poles *These 20-foot-tall decorative poles were designed to symbolize Oklahoma's colorful cultural heritage. Topped with swirling ribbons of yellow, red, blue, purple and green, several of these eye-catching pieces have been installed in Oklahoma City and Tulsa.*

JUL OKLAHOMA
OKLAHOMA
001 OKS
1907-2007
CELEBRATE OKLAHOMA!

License Plates *Many drivers proudly demonstrated their state pride by displaying this special-edition plate commemorating Oklahoma's statehood.*

Hot Air Balloon *The official hot air balloon of the Oklahoma Centennial stands 62 feet tall by 52 feet wide. This balloon was used to promote several Centennial events across the state and also flew in the Albuquerque Balloon Festival.*

A UNIQUE HISTORY.

AN EXTRAORDINARY FUTURE.

1907

2007

Pole Banners *A series of street pole banners in Oklahoma City depicted several different scenes along with the Centennial logo – serving as yet another reminder to residents and visitors of the state's historic year.*

OKLAHOMA!

Outdoor Boards *With the intent of creating awareness and pride, Oklahoma's Centennial celebration was promoted on outdoor boards that were posted throughout the Oklahoma City metro area.*

Centennial Markers *The Oklahoma Department of Transportation installed 902 of these markers along Oklahoma's highways, including major entrances to the state.*

Signs & Flags *As a complement to the billboards, street signs, pole signs and flags could also be seen in cities and towns statewide.*

Discover Sallisaw

Jeannette and Richard Sias

271

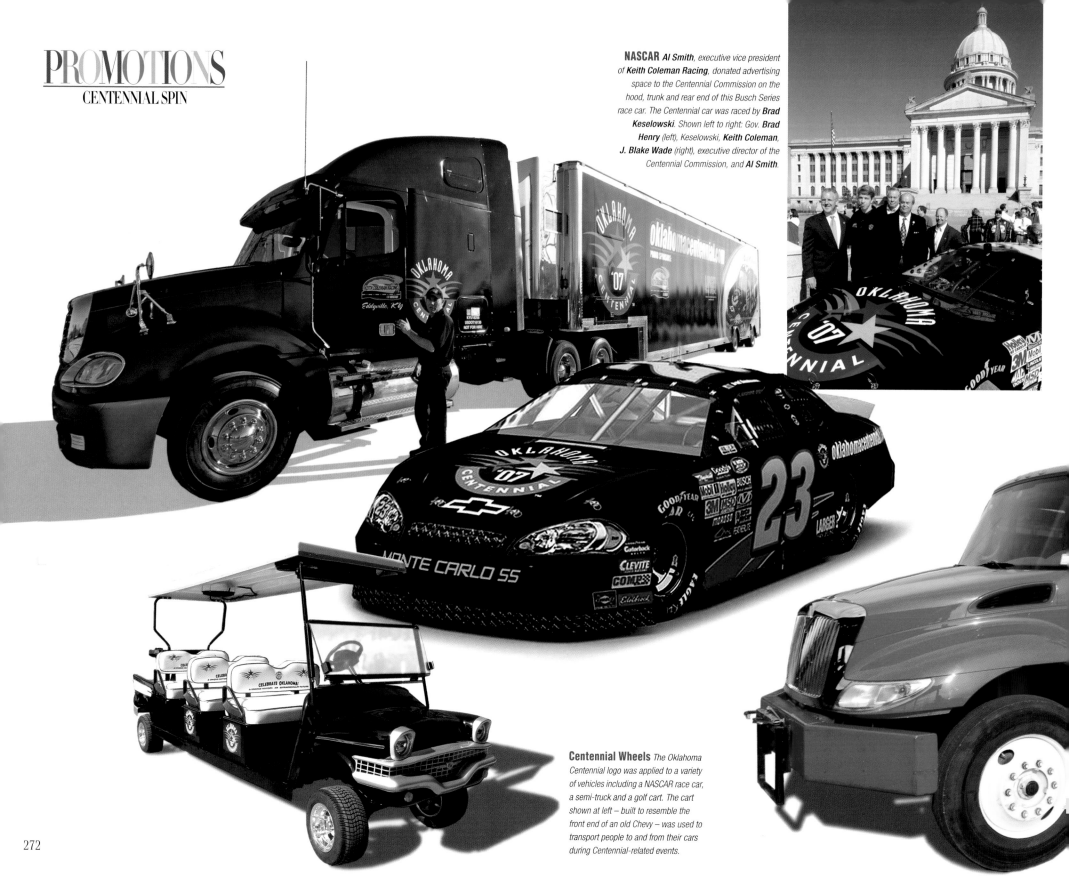

PROMOTIONS
CENTENNIAL SPIN

NASCAR *Al Smith*, *executive vice president of* **Keith Coleman Racing**, *donated advertising space to the Centennial Commission on the hood, trunk and rear end of this Busch Series race car. The Centennial car was raced by* **Brad Keselowski**. *Shown left to right: Gov.* **Brad Henry** *(left), Keselowski,* **Keith Coleman**, **J. Blake Wade** *(right), executive director of the Centennial Commission, and* **Al Smith**.

Centennial Wheels *The Oklahoma Centennial logo was applied to a variety of vehicles including a NASCAR race car, a semi-truck and a golf cart. The cart shown at left – built to resemble the front end of an old Chevy – was used to transport people to and from their cars during Centennial-related events.*

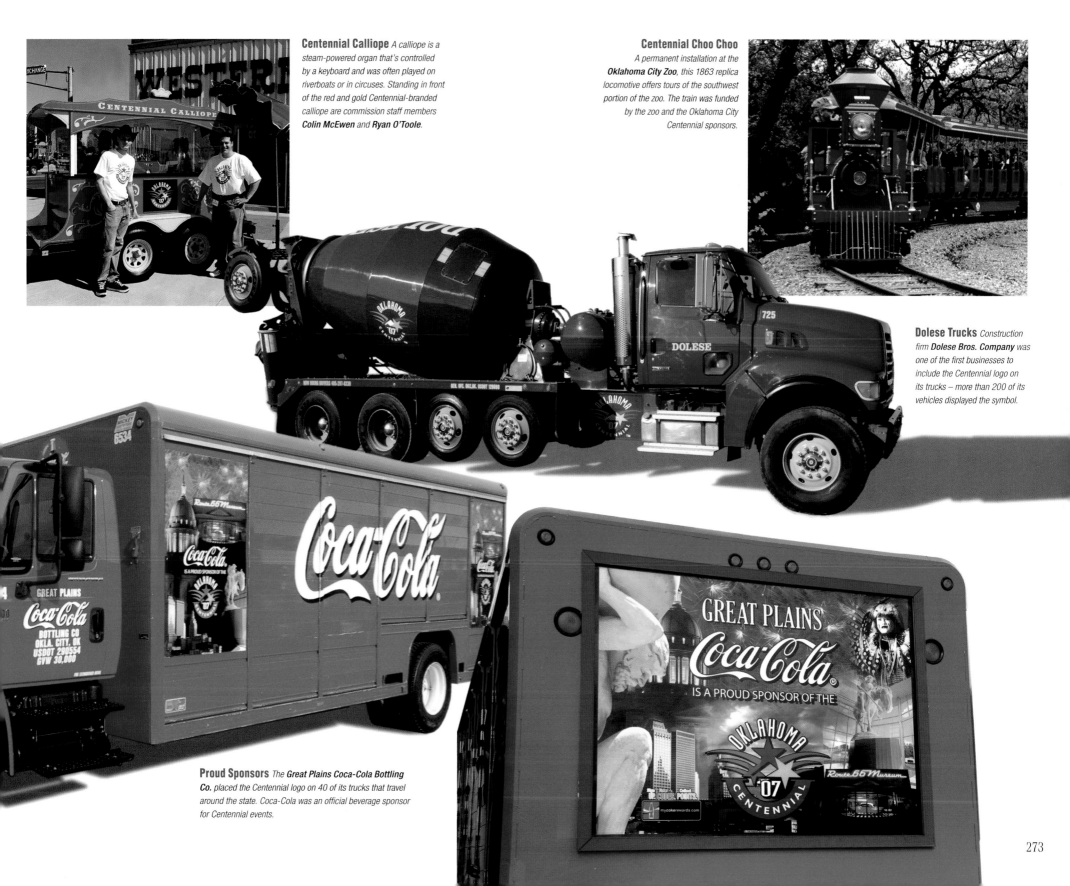

Centennial Calliope *A calliope is a steam-powered organ that's controlled by a keyboard and was often played on riverboats or in circuses. Standing in front of the red and gold Centennial-branded calliope are commission staff members* **Colin McEwen** *and* **Ryan O'Toole**.

Centennial Choo Choo *A permanent installation at the* **Oklahoma City Zoo**, *this 1863 replica locomotive offers tours of the southwest portion of the zoo. The train was funded by the zoo and the Oklahoma City Centennial sponsors.*

Dolese Trucks *Construction firm* **Dolese Bros. Company** *was one of the first businesses to include the Centennial logo on its trucks — more than 200 of its vehicles displayed the symbol.*

Proud Sponsors *The* **Great Plains Coca-Cola Bottling Co.** *placed the Centennial logo on 40 of its trucks that travel around the state. Coca-Cola was an official beverage sponsor for Centennial events.*

State Fair Park Signage *As part of Oklahoma's Centennial year activities, State Fair Park in Oklahoma City added new fencing around the facility and put up signs with the Centennial logo and 1907-2007 dates.*

Centennial Expo *The 2007 Oklahoma State Fair was billed as the Centennial Expo. It featured a historical exhibit in the Spirit of Oklahoma Plaza that showcased each decade of the state's 100 years and displayed items of significant cultural and historical relevance.*

Oklahoma State Fair Centennial Expo *In honor of the state's anniversary, the Oklahoma State Fair introduced a new attraction in 2007 – the Centennial Frontier Experience. It's an entertaining step back in time to Oklahoma's extraordinary past and features performers, exhibits, demonstrations and shows including Indian dancers, Chisholm Trail Chuck Wagon Camp, Trick Ropin' Extraordinaire, Wild West Stunt Riders, Square Dancers of Oklahoma and OK Kids Corral.*

Zoltar • *OKLAHOMA CITY The fortune-telling Zoltar machine in* **Penn Square Mall** *is a replica of that used in the movie* Big, *starring Tom Hanks. All proceeds from this permanent machine benefit the* **Children's Medical Research Institute** *– an affiliate of the* **Children's Miracle Network**. *The institute works to improve the health of children through research and education in Oklahoma.*

Zoltar was unveiled and dedicated on June 5, 2008, by special guests that included **Barry Switzer** *and* **Jacob Stoepker**, *age 11. Diagnosed with diabetes in 2003 and brain cancer in 2004, Stoepker has since been declared cancer-free and dubbed a "Miracle Child" by the Children's Medical Research Institute. Zoltar hopes to help many more children like Stoepker.*

Wall of Winners *Winners of the Oklahoma Centennial Poster Contest had their work displayed at the Oklahoma State Fair, as well as on the websites of* The Oklahoman, Tulsa World *and the Centennial Commission.*

Centennial Memorabilia
Proceeds from the sale of branded merchandise went toward covering the costs associated with the Centennial celebration.

CenTOONials *Rascal the Raccoon, one of the four CenTOONial mascots, poses with fair-goers. Second-grader* **Trey Terry** *(not pictured) of Choctaw submitted the name "Rascal" in a contest for children to name the mascots.*

Antique Tractors *Several historical tractors were on display at the fairgrounds during the Expo.*

Centennial Mural *The Mega Mural Painting Station, set up in front of the Creative Arts Building, encouraged fair-goers of all ages to demonstrate their creativity. The mural will be on display at the 2008 Oklahoma State Fair.*

Sweet Success *Created by* **Donna Fields** *of Jones, this cake depicting Oklahoma's historic Round Barn on Route 66 took home Best of Show and blue ribbon honors.*

PROMOTIONS
MEMORABILIA & MERCHANDISE

Centennial Merchandise *USA Screen Printing & Embroidery Co. produced a wide range of items and apparel in commemoration of Oklahoma's milestone anniversary. Merchandise was sold in shopping malls and at special events, and was also available online.*

Holiday Ornaments *These treasured keepsakes came from the collections of two of America's foremost holiday designers: Michael Storrings and Christopher Radko.*

Centennial Rifle *Only 101 of these .45-caliber Colt long rifles were produced, one for each year of Oklahoma statehood. They were sold to the public by Miles Hall, president of H&H Gun Range in Oklahoma City.*

Meet the CenTOONials *These entertaining mascots appeared at many Centennial events. Behind the costumes were K.C. Glyckherr as Lizzy the Mountain Boomer Lizard, John Helstein as Scissy the Scissor-Tailed Flycatcher, Chad Tolle as Buckley the Buffalo and Jina Tolle as Rascal the Raccoon.*

Pendleton Blanket and Frankoma Plate *These items were both designed by Oklahoman Harvey Pratt, a Cheyenne-Arapaho. The limited-edition plates and signed, numbered blankets were available for public purchase, and Centennial Commission members presented blankets to dignitaries.*

Centennial Cuvée *The official wine of Oklahoma's Centennial, these wines were vinted by* **Ridge Watson**, *winemaker, at* **Joullian Vineyards** *in Carmel Valley, California. The vineyard is owned by Oklahomans* **Jeannette** *and* **Richard Sias**.

Frankoma Pottery *These collector's edition casserole dishes were produced by Oklahoma-based Frankoma Pottery. Located in Sapulpa, Frankoma is in its 75th year of producing distinctive ceramics that are reflective of the American west.*

Centennial Mascots *These dolls are pint-sized replicas of CenTOONials, bigger than life mascots who appeared at Centennial-recognized events throughout the state. Representing the Oklahoma state symbols of the mountain boomer lizard, raccoon, scissor-tailed flycatcher and the buffalo, they helped teach children about Oklahoma history and heritage.*

Centennial Guitar *The spirit of the Centennial stretched far and wide, and included individuals who sought to participate in the celebration by customizing unique items, like this prized guitar, with the Centennial logo.*

Refreshments *National brands got involved in the Centennial as well:* **Budweiser** *and* **Coca-Cola** *produced commemorative Centennial bottles. Oklahoma City's* **Great Plains Coca-Cola Bottling Company**, *headed by CEO* **Robert Browne**, *distributed the "retro" six-bottle carton shown above. Budweiser distributors and retailers also displayed their Centennial pride. The best way to enjoy the drinks, of course, was in Centennial-branded glasses with logo-themed coasters.*

PROMOTIONS
MEMORABILIA & MERCHANDISE

Halftime Shows *Many high schools and universities featured special football halftime entertainment that was dedicated to the Centennial. The University of Oklahoma's Pride of Oklahoma performed the "Oklahoma Rising" anthem in a couple of halftime shows.* **Dan "Rocketman" Schlund** *also made a surprise appearance during one of the games.*

Centennial Patches *To encourage participation among schools and universities across the state, Centennial patches were given to all high school teams – including pom squads – and to universities. Patches were provided courtesy of the* **Payne Family**.

Yahoo! *By early 2007, it was clear that the Oklahoma Centennial Commission's effort to raise awareness of the state's celebration had been successful – "Oklahoma Centennial" appeared as one of the top 10 most-searched-for items on Yahoo!, demonstrating worldwide interest in the landmark celebration.*

Airport Announcements
Oklahoma native sons and daughters welcomed travelers arriving at **Oklahoma City Will Rogers World Airport** *and* **Tulsa International Airport** *and informed them of the 2007 Centennial. Some of the celebrities included in these PA announcements were* **James Garner, Johnny Bench, Reba McEntire, Barry Switzer, Vince Gill, Shannon Miller, Toby Keith, Eddie Sutton** *and* **Bob Stoops**.

Today's Top Searches

1 Ruth Graham
2 Whale Shark Pictures
3 Prince Harry
4 Thomas the Tank Engine
5 Father's Day Poems
6 Lisa Ann Walter
7 Daytime Emmy...
8 Flag Day
9 Sammy Sosa
10 Oklahoma Centennial

Oklahoma Statehood Stamp

On January 11, 2007, the U.S. Postal Service debuted the Oklahoma statehood stamp, a commemoration of the state's 100th anniversary. Oklahoma City officials first unveiled the stamp in September 2006 at the National Cowboy and Western Heritage Museum. Former Oklahoma Governor **George Nigh** and **Bert Mackie**, an Enid banker, were co-chairmen of the stamp project.

1907 "Oh, what a beautiful mornin'..."

Oklahoma

USA 39

2007

Left to right: **Martha Larsen**, **Mike Larsen**, *former Gov.* **George Nigh** *and Gov.* **Brad Henry**.

FIRST DAY OF ISSUE

OKLAHOMA CITY OK JAN 11 2007 73125

CENTENNIAL STATION FIRST DAY OF SALE JANUARY 11, 2007 OKLAHOMA CITY OK 73125-9998

Left to right: former Gov. **George Nigh**, **Bert Mackie**, **Julie Gosdin**, *Sen.* **Glenn Coffee**, **Lee Allan Smith**, *Gov.* **Brad Henry** *and* **J. Blake Wade**.

Artist Mike Larsen *The stamp's design is a painting by Oklahoma artist Mike Larsen and features the morning sunlight as it touches the water of the Cimarron, one of several rivers that meander through the state. Written in the right corner are the words "Oh, What a Beautiful Mornin'," a popular song from the Rogers and Hammerstein musical* Oklahoma!.

First Day of Issue *More than 250,000 stamps were sold the first day of issue, and many post offices across the state sold out. One of the first sheets was reserved for display in the Oklahoma History Center.*

Oklahoma State Quarter *The Oklahoma State Quarter was unveiled January 28, 2008, in Oklahoma City. As the nation's 46th state, Oklahoma was the 46th coin produced in the Mint's 50 State Quarters Program, which began in 1999 and has been releasing a new state quarter every 10 weeks. The commemorative coin features the state bird, the scissor-tailed flycatcher, in flight. More than 500 million Oklahoma quarters were placed into circulation.*

4
SPECIAL
THANKS

OKLAHOMA CENTENNIAL

–Special Thanks–

SPONSORS

OKLAHOMA CITY CENTENNIAL SPONSORS

Ackerman McQueen

American Airlines,
Official Airline of the Oklahoma Centennial

AT&T Foundation

BancFirst

Budweiser

Chesapeake Energy Corporation

City of Oklahoma City

ConocoPhillips

County of Oklahoma County

Cox Communications

Devon Energy Corporation

The Freede Family

Bob & Nedra Funk,
Express Personnel Services

Great Plains Coca-Cola Bottling Company

Kerr-McGee Corporation

The Meinders Foundation

Noble Corporation

The Noble Foundation

OGE Energy Corp.

Oklahoma Industries Authority

The Oklahoman

PowerSmith Cogeneration

SandRidge Energy, Inc.

7-Eleven Stores

Jeannette & Richard Sias

Dorchester Capital
Integrated Medical Delivery
INTEGRIS Health, Inc.
KWTV News 9
Lamar Advertising
LSB Industries, Inc.
ONEOK, Inc.
Presbyterian Health Foundation
Jim & Jill Williams

American Fidelity Foundation
Anonymous
Arvest Bank, Walton Family
　Foundation
The Benham Companies
Libby & G.T. Blankenship
Blue Cross & Blue Shield
　of Oklahoma
Braum's Ice Cream &
　Dairy Stores
The Chickasaw Nation
Jackie Cooper Family
Dealers Auto Auction
Dobson Communications Corp.
L. Thomas Dulaney Jr.
Richard P. Dulaney
Eddie Foundation Inc.
Jean I. Everest Foundation
Farmers Insurance Group
Hudiburg Auto Group
Inasmuch Foundation
JPMorgan Chase
Aaron & Gertrude Karchmer
　Memorial Foundation
John E. Kirkpatrick
Love's Travel Stops &
　Country Stores
Mercy Health Center
Kyle & Pat Moore
　Cordell, Oklahoma
Mustang Fuel Corporation
Naifeh Family
Norick Investment Company
Oklahoma City University
Oklahoma Historical Society
Oklahoma Today
OU Medical Center
The Payne Family
Sonic, America's Drive-In
Southwestern Stationery &
　Bank Supply
St. Anthony Hospital,
　Bone & Joint Hospital
University of Oklahoma
Western Enterprises, Inc.
M.V. Williams Foundation, Inc.
York International

Aduddell Foundation
Bank of America
Patsy & Jim Brewer
Vicki Clark & J. Leland Gourley
The Dolese Foundation
C.L. Frates & Company
Frontier City
Wayne E. Hirst/Joe Klein/Hirst Imports
The Journal Record Publishing Co.
The Kerr Foundation, Inc.
Masonic Fraternity of Oklahoma
M-D Building Products, Inc.
Meade Energy Corporation
Oklahoma City Renaissance &
　Courtyard Downtown
Pat & Ray Potts
Riggs Abney Neal Turpen
　Orbison & Lewis

Allied Steel Construction
Lettie Branan Douglass
The Braver Family
Jerry & Sherry Cash
The Catering Company/
　Restaurant Row Catering
Crowe & Dunlevy
Doug & Peggy Cummings
Nancy & Edwin deCordova
Dell
Chris & Dana Gordon
Gumerson & Associates
IBC Bank
Lippert Bros., Inc.
J.W. & Connie Mashburn
McAfee & Taft Law Firm
Oklahoma Gazette
Oklahoma Heart Hospital
Oklahoma State Medical Association
Oklahoma Tank Lines
Roy T. Oliver
The John W. & Cecelia A. Norman
　Family Foundation
Penn Square Mall
Phillips McFall McCaffrey
　McVay & Murrah, P.C.
Ford C. Price
Quad/Graphics, Inc.
Jack Sargent
The Family of Robert C. Saunders
Simons Petroleum, Inc.
DeAnn & Lee Allan Smith
UMB Bank Oklahoma
Donna & J. Blake Wade
The Wileman Family

Lou & Ray Ackerman
Nancy & Claude Arnold
ATC Freightliner Group
Billye & Jimmie Lynn Austin
Jane & Paul D. Austin
Balliet's LLC
Bank of Nichols Hills
The Bank of Union
Steve & Sally Bentley
Jeff & Lori Blumenthal
Linda & Morris Blumenthal
Bob Mills Furniture Co., Inc.
Bowers Foundation
The Burbridge Foundation, Inc.
Horace K. Calvert
Cardinal Engineering
Sam & Sandra Cerny
B.C. Clark Jewelers
Cleary Petroleum Corporation
Clements Foods Company
Comanche Resources Company
Coyle Enterprises, Ltd.
J.W. & Julee Coyle
Crescent Market
Marion Briscoe DeVore
Chris & Jill Dobbins
Peggy & Nick Duncan
The Egolf Family
Electro Enterprises, Inc.
Elliott + Associates Architects
Carla & Richard Ellis
Eskridge Lexus & Honda of Oklahoma City
Fellers, Snider, Blankenship,
　Bailey & Tippens, P.C.
Frankfurt-Short-Bruza Associates
Fremont Exploration, Inc.
Gerald & Betty Ann Furseth
Gerald L. & Jane Jayroe Gamble
Charles S. Givens Interests
GMX Resources Inc.
Samuel Gordon Jewelers
Grant Thornton LLP
Melanie & Shan Gray
Ginny & Bob Greenberg
Crosby & Robert Harris
Dr. J. Don Harris
Harrison-Orr Air Conditioning, Inc.
Hobby Lobby
Stanley & Suzie Hupfeld
George W. & Lyda James
Jimmy's Egg Restaurants
Stanley Lee Family
Don J. & Patti P. Leeman
Legacy Communities
Lopez Foods, Inc.
Marianne's Rentals for Special Events
John McHenry Mee Family
Mr. & Mrs. Harry Merson
Metropolitan Auto Dealers Association, OKC
MidFirst Bank
The George & Nelly Miskovsky Family
Northrop Grumman
The Nye Family
The Oppenheim Family
Richard M. & Janis K. Parker
The John R. Parsons Family
Phil & Anita Patterson
The Philip Boyle Foundation
Preferred Hospice of Oklahoma, Inc.
Public Supply Company
Shirley & Ben Shanker
Shawver & Son, Inc.
Sandy & Hal Smith
Stillwater National Bank &
　Trust Company
Gene & Marilyn Torbett
Marilyn Torbett & Kent Potter
Larry Trachtenberg &
　Jeff Trachtenberg Families
Trigen Oklahoma City Energy Corp.
Mr. & Mrs. Joe Dan Trigg
In Honor of Morrison Tucker
U.S. Cellular
Visual Image Advertising
Justin & Marguerite Vogt
Chuck & Ann Vose
W&W Steel Company
Wells Fargo & Co.
Steve & Becky Wetwiska
Willis Granite Products, Inc.
Rebecca & Jack Wilson
Bill & Joan Yinger
Loyce Youngblood

CENTENNIAL PARADE GROUPS

4-H

Hunter Aldridge
Cathy Allen
Kevin Allen
Eric Alspaugh
Wooby Armstrong
Kati Ashcraft
Kimberlie Baab
McKinzey Baab
Kendyl Bailey
Danielle Baker
Katelyn Baker
Chelsea Beck
Steve Beck
Brandon Blankenship
Julie Bragg
Tracy Branch
Danielle Brecheen
Brandi Brown
Charlie Brown
Tyler Burney
Dillon Burns
Maria Burris
Victoria Burris
Samantha Cannon
Cody Clovis
Joshua Coffey
Jaycie Conaway
Joshua Conaway
Charles Cox
Nikki Craig
Katy Crocker
Holley Dennis
Kate Dillsaver
Whitney Dockrey
Tara Drwenski
Samuel Durbin
Sarah Embry
Clarissa Farrow
Sierra Franks
Ashley Fuksa
Greg Furey
Rance Gilliam
Trevor Gilroy
Amber Goddard
Samuel Greer
Mercedes Gregory
Rhiannon Hill

Wendi Holland
Daniel Howard
Scout Jackson
Debra Kime
Raychel Kozik
Tracy Lane
Katy Leimbach
Erin Lindley
Katie Lindsay
Gabriel Loman
Shay Loudermilk
Sierra Loudermilk
Matthew Lowry
Meridith Lowry
Brandi Mack
Sarah Major
Jaimee Malone
Terrie Mangum
Jan Maples
Robbie Maples
Chris Maxcey
Clint Maxcey
Meg McConnell
Amber Nicole McGee
Adam McKay
Casey McKay
Karen McPhearson
Brenda Medlock
Korinne Medlock
Krischa Medlock
Mark Miller
Mitch Miller
Hillary Minick
Tandy Morris
Robert Parrish
Dena Powers
Meredith Rawson
Megan Renner
Meagan Rhodes
Emilee Robbins
Jacob Sanders
Jerret Sanders
Taler Sawatzky
Katherine Schiete
Sarah Schiete
Caitlin Scott
Danielle Segovia
Steffani Silva

Alexandra Smith
Sam Smith
Tanner Stunk
Peyton Swanick
Ryan Swanick
Judy Talley
Kioti Taylor
Matthew Taylor
Rogue Taylor
Ross Taylor
Jenny Thibodeau
Kelsey Thurman
Garrett Totty
Abe Wallace
Andi Will
Nicole Woods
Whitney Woods

45th Infantry Division Museum & G Company, 180th Infantry Regiment
Michael Gonzales, Curator
Clark Brain
Mike Buckendorf
Nathan Buckendorf
Gene Church
Cliff Geisser
Cameron Howerton
Jeff Huston
Kat Katzung
Tim Katzung
Larry Lewis
Kevin O'Keefe
Forest Pruitt
Jammie Romee
Dewey Wilson

ASTD
Rob Anderson
Vonnie Anderson
Jerry Drake
Rebecca Frenchman
Elizabeth Giordano
Todd Giordano
Penny Hampton
Brandon Henshall

Heather Henshall
Lessie Jones
John Kemp
Linda Lumen
Travis Marker
Chris Murlin
Kathleen O'Toole
Stacy Pierce
Susan Ramos
Brischelle Skidmore
Kathy Smith
Bret Streetman
Michael Tull
Suzy White

Astec Charter School

Beta Sigma Phi International Sorority
Pattie Bedlion
Melissa Bowers
Deidra Brown
Mary Ellen Brown
Noreen Bruns
Dona Canterbury
Shannon Casey
Charlotte Cole
Elaine Cox
Peggy Denker
Gail Dutton
Beth Gocke
Jimi Hadley
Burna Hankins
Rachelle Harms
Phyllis Harris
Mimi Hendricks
Elaine Hukill
Lisa Jobe-Elkins
Gwen Jones
Ann Kendall
Denise Leonard
Judee Lyon
Sherry Manor
Sharon Mastrocco
John Mastrocco
Nicolee McCowen
Tara Pagenkops

Liz Parker
Kathy Reynolds
Adele Rowland
Connie Sims
Beverly Smith
Pam Wampler
Billie Willis
Joanna Wills-Bernard

Big Brothers & Big Sisters

Central District Square Dance Association
Ronnie Jackson, Co-Publicity Director
Shirley Jackson, Co-Publicity Director
Henry Israel, Caller
Bernie Bergmann
Lila Bergmann
Glen Bray
Linda Bray
Myron Brown
Shirley Brown
Jean Calhoun
Joann Calhoun
Jim Ford
Ruth Ford
Don Foster
Kathryn Foster
Jim Fuller
Claudia Georgi
Luis Gruntmeir
Renee Gruntmeir
Melissa Harrison
Barbara Israel
Joe Manek
Dick Manley
Dorothy Manley
Greg Mills
Stacey Palmer
Steve Palmer
Bill Patton
Doug Pruitt
Sylvia Pruitt
Michelle Schaffer

Carol Schwake
Richard Schwake
Nikita Sheppard
Wade Sheppard
David Snow
Judy Snow
Barbara Sparks
Gary Sparks
Linda Spaugy
Nolan Spaugy
Mary St. John
Bob Thomas
John Thompson
Teresa Thompson
Don Tremain
Helen Tremain
Vernon Willis
Adeline York

Desk & Derrick Club of Oklahoma City
Kapin Anthony
Jackie Black
Deena Electericiteh
Regina Finney
Marsha Gentry
Teena Hollingshead
Frances Jowers
Toni Kitchell
Sarah Ledgerwood
Mark Loch
Jacque Loch
Ellen Maddon
Maureen Nelson
Jack Shaver
Evelyn Smith
Maria Spano
Gwen Wyatt

Dove Dance Studio

Edmond Memorial High School Varsity Pom
Melinda Moore, Sponsor

Emily Clowdus
Courtney Cox
Katie Daugherty
Alexis Hancock
Madilynn Hillis
Meaghan Hoose
Ashton Laughlin
Amber Leal
Jordan Norton
Abbey Philbrick
Lauren Romano
Annie Runnels
Emily Smitherman
Allison Stafford
Shelby Stone
Emily Swenson

Express Personnel
Vicki English
Ryan Hardy
Amanda Nicklas
Jason Nicklas
Sally Sondker
Scott Sondker
Debbie Zettlemoyer

Fancy Dancers

Farmers Insurance Group
Bernard E. Barber
Greg Beaty
Pam Bolgren
Leashia Briggs
Kristi K. Buchholz
Andrew Calxton
Kathryn Carter
Marc Castle
Tiara Collins
Mark Costello
Thomas S. Davidson
Brant Davis
Scott E. Davis
Kim Decker
Randy Dickerson
Randy Elam
Maria Elam
Staci Flowers

Jayme Goss
David Gouge
Elaine Graves
Sheri Harlow
Cheshire K. Hill
Dan Holcomb
Stephanie Howard
Jessica Isam
Monica Jacks
Chris Jones
Korey Klause
Paula Langley
David A. Leader
Michelle Malone
Victoria McAdams
Tony McClain
Sheri McGuire
Elnita Miller
Don Mullican
Jennifer O'Brien
Stephanie D. Patton
Donna Pershica
Heather Preble
Reba Rivera
Keri Roberts
Jamie Schrick
Stephen Seibel
John D. Slayton
Gina Smith
Patricia Spivey
Cassie K. Tevebaugh
Matthew A. Travis
Brad Valentine
Ben Wheeler
Amanda White
Sean Winget
Ashley Zahrai
Teresa E. Zamarron

Flyover
Richard Burpee
Colonel Gary Harencak (Brigadier General Select)
Major James Price
Captain Anthony Smith

Captain Luke Lucero
Captain Kent Mickelson
Jennifer Avery

Hermetic Switch, Inc.
Kay Bogle
Kristi Bridgers
Elizabeth Byers
Lynda Cantu
Kathy Carden
Ashley Carden
Sara Chaney
Kelly Daniels
Russell Dull
Shannon Ellis
Misty Jenkins
Charlotte Latta
Tina Lee
Kimmy Loggins
Mark Mandrell
Barbara Mandrell
Shane Mandrell
Barbie Mehringer
Shannon Richardson
Marni Ross
Desira Rutledge
Eddie Shearer
Amanda Wakefield
Paula Woodrow
Martha Zubiate

Hilb Rogal & Hobbs
Shirlene Chambers
Larry Chambers
Rebecca Clenn
Katie Conley
Stella Davis
Kim Davis
Vivian Dodson
Teddi Edwards
Nancy Hansen
Thelma Holley
Chris Link
Donna McLean
Larry Mitchell
Patricia Mogg
Duane Mogg
Carolyn Myers

Sharon Reddington
Shelli Samsel
Beverly Smith
David Varner
Sandy Walker
Johnny Walker

Junior League of Oklahoma City
Karla Wallace

Lawton Rangers (Centennial Rangers)
Wayne Bales
Ronnie Caha
David Crank
Richard Crow
Al Dreves
Hank Elling
Bennie Gibson
Joe Hall
Andrew Hayes
Paul Hayes
Richard Hixon
Joe Joiner
Don Jones
Ferrell Large
Chuck Lodes
Ronald Lodes
Mark McDonald
Brian Parks
Eugene Shafer
Randy Spoon
Don Thomas
Greg Mills
Stacey Palmer
Steve Palmer
Bill Patton
Doug Pruitt
Sylvia Pruitt
Michelle Schaffer
Carol Schwake
Richard Schwake
Nikita Sheppard
Wade Sheppard
David Snow

CENTENNIAL PARADE GROUPS

Judy Snow
Barbara Sparks
Gary Sparks
Linda Spaugy
Nolan Spaugy
Mary St. John
Bob Thomas
John Thompson
Teresa Thompson
Don Tremain
Helen Tremain
Vernon Willis
Adeline York

Lyric Theatre's Thelma Gaylord Academy
Colin Anderson
Emily Bendick
Jacob Chancellor
Leah Coleman
Brooks Meyers
Jillian Neville
Haley Schafer
Cliff Synar
Lexie Thompson
Angela Weightbrodt

Moore High School Pom
Kim Barnett, Advisor
Megan Beddo
Shonna Chiles
Emily Crandell
Autumn Garza
Bria Hanlon
Lindsay Haygood
Shelby Heintzelmen
Kayci Hymes
Trent Keel
Kailey Lyda
Mikala Mutchler
Cassandra Nguyen
Amber Ortiz
Kaitlin Reeves
Mackenzie Vines

Norahua Mexican Folkloric Group

OK.gov
Ahmed Anouar

Todd Bevins
Kim Bevins
Kelli Bond
Shauna Cole
Sherri L. Cook
Laura Cooper
Patrick Du
Chad Hester
Marti Hester
Tewfic Kidess
Katie Meadows
Mark Mitchell
Lauri Parker
Pat Pflaum
Katrina Phillips
Johnathon Pregler
Rodney Rollison
Glen Sargent
Derek Stevens
Kirstin Swearingen
Dana Wanzer
Diana Woods

OKC Lightning Women's Football Team
Jenn Archer
Shannon Davis
Jen Demery
Kandace Malena
Stephanie Smith

Oklahoma Art Education Association
Donna Barnard
Teresa Barnes
Valerie Beck
Bob Curtis
Barbara Gabel
Teresa Hutter
Nancy Matheson
Susan McCaughtry
Judy McIntosh
Bob Palmer
Glenda Ross
Gail Sloop
Laura Stewart
Frances Williams
Trish Winnard

Oklahoma City Blazers

Oklahoma City Pi Beta Phi Alumnae Club
Cristi Bullard
Nan Buxton
Julianna Deligans
Sheryl Hines
Debbie McCord
Jan Ette Oakley
Kelsie Orendorff
Mary Reneau
Amber Shelton
Monica Szymanski
Nicole Tintera
Julie Vaughn
Chris Verity

Oklahoma City University Amercian Spirit Dancers
Travis Andrews
Brandt Binkley
Lacy Brown
Kacia Dimick
Ashley Durst
Osagie Ehigie
Roger Ellis
Kimberly Fauré
Kimberly Flanagin
Virginia Fox
Tyler Foy
Steve Gorski
Erika Hebron
Chris Large
Frances Lawrence
Michael McCarthy
Aaron Nedrick
Daniella Ortega
Sam Payne
Aubrey Phillips
Ashley Rivers
Matthew Rivers
Alissa Robinson
Tiffany Schranck
Jacob Sewell
Addie Tomlinson
Emily Turner
Christopher Villegas
Todd Walker
Paige Williams
Chaz Wolcott
Michael Wood

Oklahoma City Yard Dawgz

Oklahoma Department of Human Services Friends & Family Volunteers Balloon Team
Rebecca Bussell
Laura Bybee
Cari Crittenden
Christi Fore
Melody Garneau
Mercedes Lambert
Kathy Marion
Stacie Mayer
Jenny Milner
Ashton Milner
Bailee Milner
David Odle
Kim Sawyer
Gaila Smalley
John Smalley
Taylor Smalley
Joann Yeager

Oklahoma FFA
Kent Boggs,
    FFA Executive Secretary
Austin Akins,
    State FFA President
Charlee Goodwin,
    State FFA Vice President
Kassie Houston,
    State FFA Vice President
Josh Lindsey,
    State FFA Vice President
Cody Nieman,
    State FFA Vice President
Cody Ott,
    State FFA Vice President
John-Kyle Truitt,
    State FFA Reporter
Gary Kirk, Advisor
Wayne Anderson
Cory Boyle
Anthony Buoy
Cade Burns
Chris Cranford

Dayton Gambrell
Chase Hensley
Cooper Hensley
Tiffany Herzbag
Rusty Kenner
Steve Pritchard
Tatum Pritchard
Liz Terry
Brandon Vicknair
Kyle Warden
Dalton Wright
Skyler Wyatt

Oklahoma Heart Hospital
Jane Braden
Renee Cohee
Mary Law
Cindy Miller
Georgiana Pineda
Charla Rhodes
Andy Sanford
Olivia Wilson
The Marcos Hernandez
    Family

Oklahoma Llama Association
Dwight Anderson
Susan Anderson
Colby Bodkin
Pat Bodkin
Emily Buchalla
Lauren Buchalla
Adra Cheek
David Cheek
David Cohenour
Patty Cohenour
Bob Cowles
Shelby Dunkle
Cameron Erdmon
Staci Forshee
Gayliene Lagasse
Keith Miller
Michelle Miller
Sarah Miller
Tracy Mueggenborg
Johnathan Pope
Bethany Sackett
Bryan Salsman
Larry Salsman
Nancy Salsman
Ashleigh Stallcup
David Swihart
Joy Swihart

Lynn Tentou
Eric Thacker
Janelle Wenzel
John Wenzel
Taylor Wenzel

Oklahoma Public Employees Association
Melinda Alizadeh-Fard
Cara Alizadeh-Fard
Christie Biggs
J.D. Biggs
Wyatt Biggs
Wayne Everson
Sherrie Furgason
Melody Hobbs
Austin Zearley
Hunter Zearley

Oklahoma Rodeo Pageants Council
Lynzie Albright
Kallie Sue Baker
Reba Baker
Megan Caldwell
Candice Carper
Keta Gray
Julie Harper
Lauren Heaton
Melissa Heaton
Lauren Holt
Kristin Killion
Morgan Roberts
Calie Jo Sebor
Rachael Smith
Sarah Spears
Lauren Underwood
Bayleigh Warren

Oklahoma State University Rodeo Association
Cathryn Christensen,
    Parade Presentation Chair
Lexi Archer
Ote Berry
Bennie Beutler
Mary Burger
Blair Burk
Barry Burke
Susan Campbell
John Charles

Kamera Charles
Morgan Charles
Bobby Clark
Wayne Cornish
Ashley Cotton
Jennifer Cunningham
Ty Cunningham
Laramie DeBock
Megan Draguesky
Clay Drake
Larry Dry
Margie Dry
Alanna Foley
Madison Freeman
Moni Heinrich
Richard Heinrich
Kelly Herrington
Wendell Hicks
Don Huddleston
Abby Imke
Terry Imke
Tracy Imke
Sherry Johnson
Teddy Johnson
Caitlin Kelly
Andy Kincaid
Georgiana Kincaid
Justin Knowles
Sharen Martin
Shane McAddo
Clem McSpadden
Kris Ranson
Charlotte Razook
Lee Schauffler
Rosie Seaborne
Jackie Sheperd
J.W. Sheperd
Kelly Shumacher
Dan Stein
Jana Stein
Leslea Thurber
Joe Vielma
Rena Vielma
Sally Vielma
Cathy Vinson
Janae Ward Massey
Shoat Webster
Dee Wynn
Marsha Wynn
Florence Youree
Officers of Stillwater
    FFA Chapter
Wild Horse Gang
    of Kremlin, OK

The Pointe Performing Arts Center
Penny Capps, Owner Director
Meghan Alexander
Briana Baker
Faith Baker
Megan Burke
Rachel Cantwell
Riley Cole
Kylie Cowan
Alexa Cutler
Areta Davis
Camden Denton
Courtlan Denton
Madison Ferguson
Kat Gaines
Sarah Jackson
Brienna Laib
Taylor Ledford
Elizabeth McAfee
Becca Newman
Baylee Owen
Megan Patten
Haley Rapacz
Audrey Scheirman
Hannah Scott
Lindsey Scott
Gina Stiles
Megan Storey
Aleisha Williams
Marissa Wolf

Shannon Crites School of Dance Ardmore, Oklahoma "Dancing Scarecrows"
Shannon Crites, Owner Director
Haleigh Aman
Zach Aman
Taryn Callendar
Audrey Cox
Destiny Denney
Andrea Duran
Hannah Fite
Sarah Greufe
Rachel Griesman
Anna Haas
Callie Huddleston
Jordan Hunter
Spencer Jordan
Paige Kriet

Chandler Lemons
M'Kayla Lott
Michelle McGee
Allison Miller
Katelyn Miller
Kaitlin Moore
Maegen Morgan
Kara Moss
Victoria Myers
Cayman Oaks
Katie Parish
Mathew Patrick
Melissa Sluice
Sarah Smith
Danielle Smith
Jade Southerland
Brandon Stahlbusch
Avery Sullivan
Shea Wells
Tandra Worthen

Shawnee Academy of Ballet
Janet Combs, Director
Katherine Adams
Morgan Barnett
Taylor Britt
Ashley Bruner
Casey Carlton
Nicolette Chin
Lauren Clement
Kelsie Collins
Stephanie Currie
Sammie Gasper
Natalie Gates
Sydney Gunderson
Kate Hammons
Libby Hammons
Meagan Hanson
Mackenzie Kelly
Kara Laster
Cassidy Lumry
Kim Marshall
Kurstyn Mills
Bailey McCullar
Bailey Noble
Summer Randell
Tina Roach
Hayley Simpson
Mayci Sparkman
Kendra Standlee
Taylor Stobbe
Katie Tucker
Kaitlin Wiens
Karoline Wiens

Maddie Wilson
Kelsey Winterringer

Sheriff Bob Wire & Deputy Chuck Waggin' (Frontier City)
Stephen Ball
Crystal Bell
Charissa Cothran
Montana Martzall
Jonathon Ortwin
Dorinda Wilmoth

UMB Bank
Cindy Argo
Mary Blankenship Pointer
Nicole Calvert
Cookie Hill
Allen Jackson
Montgomery Jackson
Mariah Livingston
Friend Livingston
Resa Masopust
Shannon Mayahi
Emad Mayahi
Kyla Mooney
Tiffany Mosley-Pierce
Joe Pointer
Natalie Pointer
Todd Sanders
Frank Sewell
Jeanne Shaughnessy
Mike Shaughnessy
Brad Traynor
Natalie Williams

University of Oklahoma Health Sciences Center College of Nursing
Melissa Bales
Tonya Bardsher
Tiffany Black
Christel Byrom
Lacey Doyle
Shawn Elwell
Jonathan Flint
Jessica Fradd
Jennifer Gray
Ann Gregory
Lauren Hamm
Kendra Harmon
Jennifer Helm

286

Abir Hines
Shea Holden
Rhonda Hromas
Maleatha James
Krista Keuchel
Kristin Kidd
Annie Minton
Judy Muskrat
Trisha Nava
Jed Nguyen
Kristen Potts
Krystal Raines
Cheron Rowe
Rachel Schupp
Angela Seddelmeyer
Tracie Summers

**University of
Oklahoma Pom**

**U.S. District Court
of Western District
of Oklahoma**
Debbie Bare
Bruce Bare
Christopher Bare
Dixie Becktold
Denise Bergner
Lesa Boles
Rosene Coleman
Brien Detamore
Kelly Edwards
Lori Gray
Ehteshamul Haque
Brock Johns
Andrew Leasau
Michelle Matthews
Barbara Montague
John Norberto
Robert Payao
Rhonda Reynolds

Zachary Reynolds
Murphy Reynolds
Anne Ross
Faith Sampier
Carmelita Shinn
Burle Steelman
Vanessa Thurman
Penny Wallis
Karen Worth
Jeff Yowell

Venture Crew 291
Jessica Beedle
Leslie Davenport
Amelia Dethloff
Misti Dethloff
Carmen Dethloff
Barry Dethloff
Tina Kelly
Larry Kelly
Shawn Kelly

Patrick Kelly
Amy Kelly
Cody Logston
Fonda Logston
Shelbee Millwee
Julie Millwee
Lea Mote
Morgan Patton
Kimberly Rogers
Emiley Schwin
Kayla Warner
Vonda Warner
Emiley Wiley
Katie Williamson
Todd Williamson
Brandon Woodam

**Victory School
of the Arts**
Lynne Allred
Hayden Bingaman
Amanda Boggs
Courtney Bryce
Mindy Cash
Bethany Clay
Emily Clay
Sara Clay
Rachael Dickson
Carisa Douglas
Kelsey Douglas
Jennifer Epperson
Emma Greenback
Jennifer Haddock
Mariah Haxton
Bethanie Head
Jenny Hester
Elizabeth Hinojos
Rebekah Magbee

Jessica Matallana
Karen Ortiz
Kelli Ortiz
Hannah Pierce
Natasha Schmid
Carol Seay
Daniel Tardibano
Allie Ward
Providence Ward
Elizabeth Wolfe
Miles Yeung
Christy Zondlo

**Wells Fargo
Stagecoach**
Bradleigh Bell
Laura Burns
Alan Cartwright
Georgia Cartwright
Allie Dodson
Cady Dodson

Bruce Leach
Alexandra Munger
Rebecca Smith

**Western Heights
High School**
Jean M. Adams
Roberto Alba
Shelly Borrelli
Brett Bowers
Amy Bowers
Amanda Campana
Mariel Davenport
Lindy Heller
Katie Helms
Elizabeth Ho
Lacreitia Jemison
Alisha Jenkins
Quanna Kennedy
Kathryn Kicenski
James McCurtain

Rita McCurtain
Cheney McCurtain
Curtis Mullenax
Casey Mumme
Davin Newsom
Devin Newsome
Chung Nguyen
Michael Nguyen
Tim Nguyen
Karen Parra
Amanda Price
Spencer Rooker
Emily Sanders
Melissa Spitler
Elisha Tetreault
April Zamora
Anthony Zarate

**Westmoore
Pom Squad**
Deborah Christian,
Head Advisor
Laura Walker,
Assistant Advisor
Kaci Ballard
Jensen Bryan
Maci Cameron
Jessica Cody
Rachel Cunningham
Sarah Davidson
Valerie Dycus
Megan Ferguson
Abbie Freeman
Sheridan Fulkerson
Courtney Hoffman
Brittany Hubbard
Yancee Lyles
Kayle Marshall
Karissa Miles

Bailee O'Brian
Krystle Pierce
Rachel Soult

145th Army Band of the Oklahoma National Guard

Scott Sanders,
    Commander
Barbara Atkinson,
    1st Sergeant
Timothy Vermillion,
    Drum Major

Scott Ashpaugh
Jack Baker
Chad Bratton
Andrew Brooks
Joshua Buxton
Anthony Campbell
Gregory Clifton
Jerry Cooper
Kenneth Coward
Thomas Durman
Cordell Ehrich
Sean Feroli
Carley Flowers
James Friedemann
James Gaston
Prisicillia Gray
Drey Hawkins
Dakota Horn
Tammy Johnston
Michael Kissick
Cody Lathrop
James Leckie
Eugene Morrison
Christyn Raincrow
Julie Reeves
Randall Smith
Zechariah Smith
Jason Tiger
Albert Trochesset
Jonathan Twilley
Danny Vaughn
Lena Vermillion
Harold Wilson

Altus High School Band

LaFrancis Davis,
    Band Director
Jeff Hastings,
    Band Director
Mary Runyan,
    Band Director

Drew Ahrens
Carlos Aleman
Jamie Anderson
Megan Baker
Lindsay Barnes
Stephanie Barnes

Seth Barton
Daniel Boggs
Travis Bourgeois
Jordan Brickhouse
Reagan Brickhouse
Kelsey Brown
Kevin Burns
Krista Carraway
Chelsea Chargualaf
Chris Cheaney
Kern Clarke
Krys Clarke
Tracie Coats
Taylor Cole
Jesse Coronado
Justin Davidson
Vanessa Delgado
Chloe Deweese
Rafael Escobar
Tommy Finch
Lemmy Fojut
Cassie Glover
Katrina Gonzales
Alex Green
Gabriela Guerra
Robert Guerra
Lindsey Guyette
Kiersten Harvile
Cerrah Hembroff
Jacob Hobbs
Breanne Holley
Danielle House
Sarah Hubner
Elizabeth Humpula
Kelsey Husband
Lesli Kelly
William Kime
Lisa Kiniry
Michael Knight
Bailea Kosbau
Connor Long
Morgan Looney
Rebecca Lupton
Keyon Martin
Gustavo Martinez
Karissa McClain
Maria Mendez
Amy Middaugh
Justin Miller
Lance Mock
John Morrow
Jonathan Nails
Linda Nolley
Ashley Panagopoulos
Lucely Pantoja
Grecia Peralta
Caitlin Pierce
Stacie Price

Nickole Ragsdill
Karalyn Rawlings
Angela Reinhardt
Rebecca Reyes
Michael Rogers
Preston Runyan
Gina Sarabia
Sarah Sewell
Kristina Sharpe
Kristen Shreiner
Stephanie Smith
Travis Smith
A.J. Soliven
Ericka Sollis
Bonnie Stallman
James Studdard
Becca Surles
Taylor Timmons
Baron Tockey
Courtney Tuttle
Tia Vega
John Veirs
Breanna Wagnon
Micah Ward
Mylan Ward
Micah Webb
Dale Whitehead
Jesse Winters
Bobby Wolfe
Anthony Yeager
Jessica Zuccarelli
Rachael Zuccarelli

Antlers Band

Broken Arrow High School Band

Kristin Stephens,
    Instrumental Music
    Secretary
Scott Tomlinson,
    Director of
    Instrumental Music

Chris Adams
Rebecca Adams
Leanna Albaqamy
Katherine Alexander
Ann Marie Almeida
Daniel Anderson
Miranda Anderson
Katelyn Anderson
Justin Anderson
Jill Arnold
Jordan Aschkenas
Kayla Aud
David Bacher
Samantha Bachman
Stephanie Bahara

Brandon Bahara
Brian Baker
Reba Balch
Sammi Jo Barker
Gianna Barolin
Taylor Bartmier
Ryan Beeman
Alex Bell
Tyler Bell
Anna Bennett
Chris Bennett
Reid Bennett
Miranda Bentley
Zac Bettinger
Blake Birmingham
Josh Blaho
Benjamin Bland
Jessica Bogue
Emily Borgstrom
Blaire Bothell
Daniela Bravo
Amber Broberg
Erin Brockway
Josh Brucculeri
Aaron Bryant
Robbie Buckinger
Kateri Burris
Jayson Burscough
Amanda Burt
Katie Buynak
Chris Buynak
Braden Calhoun
Amanda Campbell
Brionne Cannon
Wes Cartwright
Danielle Chavez
Matthew Clark
Zac Cockrell
Adam Colon
Ethan Cooper
Paul Cornell
Stefanie Cottrell
Lacey Craig
Morgan Croft
Matt Curlee
D.J. Darais
Darrin Davis
Noren Davison
Jessica Detar
Kayla DeVault
Ravyn Divine
Gianna Dixon
Joe Domeier
Elizabeth Doring
Ethan Dougherty
Tyler Downes
Levi Duethman
Kayla Dunn

Ashley Dykes
Amber Dykes
Josh Edmonson
Drew Egli
Elizabeth Ellis
Ben Ellis
William Ely
Kyleigh Embrey
Kaiti Embrey
Hannah Estes
Anna Factor
Kristin Finley
Alaiszia Fobbs
Caleb Forbes
Eric Gammenthaler
Garrison Gillham
Lindsey Gilstrap
Kyle Goralczyk
Chad Graves
Jill Graves
Emily Graves
Travis Gunnells
Michael Hackney
Bruce Haiduk
Monica Hakes
Samantha Hammock
Quint Hancock
Jennifer Hanford
Brittni Hauser
Rhiannon Hays
Nick Hegdale
Tyler Heiss
Jalynn Helberg
Kason Helberg
Jordan Hendon
Brooke Hendricks
Kaylah Higgins
Emalie Hoar
Pat Hodge
Chris Hodge
Erin Hood
Kasey Hood
Jesse Hopper
Jake Huddleston
Jennifer Huggard
Sarah Hull
Natalie Hundley
Billy Hutcheson
Olivia Jacobs
Chase Johnson
Demontra Jones
Samantha A. Jones
Samantha Jones
Greg Jones
Jesse Kaiser
Greg Kettlewood
Natalie Killingsworth
Lauren Kimball

Bryant Kimball
Trina King
Alex Kochan
Shannon Kohake
Ben Korzelius
Stephany Kuxhausen
Sam Larzalere
Arantxa Lasa
Gaizka Lasa
Brittany Leak
Jared Ledgerwood
Cheryl Lee
Zach Lewis
Sherrill Little
Nick Livingston
Jacob Long
Jacob Mares
Acen Marinov
Whitney Martin
Amberlee Martin
Geoff Martin
Ryan Martin
Tia Martinez
Lauren Mason
Morgan Matlock
Jeff McCarter
Jenny McClain
Braden McCready
Tom McGillen
Sean McKinney
Jessica McKissic
Grace McKnight
Kevin McLean
Wynton McNary
Hayley Melvin
Dustin Merries
Mandi Michalski
Brooke Mickelson
Jacob Miller
Michelle Miller
Elise Moore
Ashley Morton
Ceirra Moses
Alexandra Moulton
Ahmad Mustafa
Henry Nally
Erin Nally
Amanda Nelson
Ryan Nossaman
Sarah Nowotny
Darrian Noyes
Katy Nye
Melissa Oliver
Ashlea Owens
Kevin Oyler
Blake Pace
Katie Paine
Jeralle Parrish

Johnathon Parrish
Theresa Partner
Julie Partner
Heather Peden
Kayla Pendergraft
Cole Penrise
Chris Phelps
Melissa Picard
Molly Priebe
Kara Ratzlaff
Jordan Raymer
Derek Reece
Kathryne Reed
Garrett Relja
Andrew Rhinehart
Sarah Rillo
Kelsi Rolland
Heather Rost
Hannah Rost
Shelby Russell
Aaron Russell
Jacob Ruzicka
Aaron Salisbury
Briana Sallee
Keighley Sallee
Kaitlen Sanders
Amanda Sappington
Dillon Scott
Hannah Scrimsher
Brittany Seale
Kasey Searles
Kristin Shepard
Matthew Sheppard
Heather Sherwood
Carissa Shideler
Brooke Shimp
Sabrina Slatcher
Amy Smith
Cassie Smith
Michael Smith
Kirby Smithe
Craig Spencer
Nick Spriggs
Alisha Stafford
Ian Stansell
Ashley Starkey
James Stephens
Sami Stretesky
Josh Tackett
Michael Talley
Natalie Tankersley
Nathan Tankersley
Amber Taylor
Caitlin Thomas
Michelle Thomas
Kyle Thompson
Joshua Thompson
Jessica Tinsley

Michael Tinsley
Alyssa Tomlinson
Kory Trent
Chris Trimble
Kelsey Tully
Audra Turner
Lynna Van
Kim Vento
Lanie Varvel
Chad Waken
Joel Walden
Kaylynn Ward
MacKenzie Ward
Dayton Weatherford
Casey Weber
Sarah Weber
Evan Westbrook
Shayna White
Ben White
Justin Whitekiller
Arrielle Wilbanks
Blake Wilhelm
Eric Williams
Tyler Williams
Taylor Wolters
Khyra Young

Byron Berline Band

Byron Berline
Greg Burgess
Jim Fish
John Hickman
Barry Patton
Richard Sharp

Konawa High School Band

Donny Longest,
    Director

Meggie Akerman
Ashley Barber
Dellana Bingham
Justin Boissenin
Kim Caldwell
Ashley Carter
Derien Christensen
Bryce Clark
Jessica Coats
Kassi Coffey
Haylee Crawley
Michael Cummings
Travis Cummings
Raechel Davis
Easton Denton
Erin Fixico
Chelsea Fleming
Robin Floud
Brendon Foreman

Chelsea Foreman
Cylas Foster
Destini Foster
Tiffany Gamble
Jalan Garner
Jacob Garner
Brianna Gattenby
Janey Glover
Travis Harjo
Taylor Henderson
Jeremy Herriman
Morgan Hicks
Sarah Johnson
Riley Jones
Ashleigh Khoury
Kaleb Kiker
Kendra Kiker
Miles Klupenger
Ciara Kuestersteffen
Hilary Kuestersteffen
Amanda Larney
Jessica Leslie
Catherine Longest
Anna Mocabee
Emily Mocabee
Elisabeth Morris
Sarah Morris
Tashina Narcomey
William Narcomey
Stephanie Neely
Chelsey Oglesby
Courtney Oglesby
Destinie Palmer
Chelsey Patterson
Chelsea Peters
Wayne Phillips
Keelan Prewett
Sara Reeves
Heather Renolds
Krishta Rhodd
Stormy Rhodd
Kirstie Schur
Cody Sexton
Justin Shannon
Josh Sharber
Dillon Snow
Kellie Snow
Cody Stinnett
Brittany Stokes
Sydney Stoup
Chad Thomas
Shay Thomas
Jeremy Tooley
Chalin Vaughn
Jamie Walker
Natalie Walker

Voney Warrior
Jessie Wheeler
Nikki Wheeler
Courtney White
Hailey Wilson
Kaci Wilson
Lindsey Wilson
Madison Wolf
Samantha Yott

Langston University Band

Albert Jackson,
    Band Director

Courtney Alexander
Justin Allen
Charles Anderson
Candace Antwine
Je'Netta Ausbie
James Baker
Brandon Barber
Damon Beasley
Lovli Bell
LaKisha Black
Sherrell Bowen
Claude Bradshaw
LeDaniel Bradshaw
Jeremy Buller
Timia Butler
Taylor Byrne
Jamela Carrell
Jermaine Carter
Heather Chapel
Leon Christian
Pilar Clark
James Cooper
Micheal Cullom
Celeste Dabney
Ashton Davis
Tenecia Davis
Tenivia Davis
Braylon Dedmon
Napoleon Dumay
Gregory Elmore
Gevon Finklea
Kristie Gales
Kelvin Garrett
Jason Gilley
Brandon Golston
Kelvin Hadnot
Kayvryelle Harmon
Braxton Harris
Justin Hawkins
Princess Hays
Randel Holiday
Justin Holloway
Zachary Holmes

Bryant Hopkins
Irene Howard
Rochelle Howard
Tamara Hughes
Alexandria Hutchinson
Terrance Jackson
LeDelia Jackson
Jackie Jackson
Steven Jackson
Brandon Jenkins
Carolyn Jones
LaJuana Jones
DeAia Kaigler
Katrina Kane
Reginald King
Talasheia King
Marzett Kirk
Harnecia Kirk
De'Vin Lewis
Rashawn Mance
Victor Martin
Donterrio Marzett
Angelica McBee
Derek McBee
Kristen McClellan
Lovell McCord
Jeryme McCrary
Michiel McMillian
Chelsea Murrey
Whitney Nicholas
Derrick Norman
Jeanese Outlaw
Timothy Parker
Akeem Prince
Terrance Pugh
Kimberly Rainger
DeMario Reynolds
Gary Reynolds
Gabriel Rhone
Tshaka Rivers
Tara Robinson
Tramikca Robinson
Sharonda Royal
Crystal Scott
Kenyelle Session
Bethany Sherman
Whitney Smith
Sasha Spikes
Lacey Summerville
Kevin Tarver
Gerald Thomas
Britney Thomas
Kenneth Thomas
Carla Thompson
Whitney Traylor
Qeisha Vaughn
LaMesha Wade
Delisia Walker

Sasha Watts
Kymberli Whayne
LaKeese Wickes
Pattrick Wilborn
Courtney Williams
Princess Williams
Chester Woods
Stacia Worley

Oklahoma City Centennial Massed Pipes and Drums

Oklahoma State University Band

Tinker Air Force Base Marching Troops
Willie Barkley,
  Petty Officer 2nd Class
Scott Blair,
Justin Butler
  Staff Sergeant
Kristin Gasaway,
  Tech Sergeant
  Honor Guard Lead
Melissa Naas
Amy Schiess, Coordinator
Captain Brenden Shaw
Jodi Abbott
Jose Aguilar
Clinton Ashley
Bradley Barnes
Jeffrey Bradford
Melissa Brooks
Mark Crespo
Jessica Defalco
Erica Eldridge
Justin Fife
Jamie Fife
Kenneth Fontano
Richard Gravely
Kevin Gustafson
Charles Hamilton
Steven Hammock
Daniel Hammonds
Justin Hernandez
Elizabeth Holder
Fabio Horton
Christopher Hughes
Amanda Janetski
Christopher Jensen
Kyle Johnson
Michael Johnson
Jeffrey Keating
Sean Kent
Aaron Kirby
Katrina Ledig
Christopher Lenhart
James Luna
Stanley Mandelin
Maury Miles

Andrew Moulton
Thomas Murray
Milette Palanca
Kristina Paliwoda
Sarah Pena
Rockford Pierini
Christopher Ray
Vickie Reed
Jeremy Reid
Charles Riney
Charles Rivera
Dusty Roberts
Natasha Sanders
George Shallis
Charles Shands
Nathan Sobolewski
Christine Stone
Dexter Sweeting
Summer Talbott
Erik Thacker
Lee Tillman
Jose Tomlinson
Miranda Wallace
Justin Wine
Bryan Winters
John Wolf
Christopher Yepes
Robert Young

University of Oklahoma "Pride of Oklahoma"
Chauvin Aaron
Mallory Adams
Justin Allen
David Allums
Fred Alonzi
Patricia Anderson
Jon Annesley
Stephanie Ansell
Jose Armendariz
Nick Aspero
Bruce Bacon
Jared Bailey
Alyssa Baker
Thad Baker
Alisa Baldwin
Jess Ballard
Paige Bannecker
Michael Barber
Adam Basset
Josh Batty
Alan Beall
Celeste Beasley
Justin Beck
Micah Berman
Ana Besore
Mark Billy
Michael Birdsey
Zach Blankenship
Zack Blocker

Sarah Blosch
Andrew Boes
Mark Bove
Caitee Boxeur
Sarah Boyd
Kim Bramblett
Melissa Broaddus
Lauren Brockman
Andrew Brown
Chase Brown
Brittany Buckner
Ryan Bunyan
Justin Burkhart
Catie Byrd
Mady Byrne
Krista Cannicott
Chris Cannon
Andrew Cao
Chris Carlson
Lynzi Carlson
Josh Carter
Jacob Carter
Brandon Cave
Addison Chandler
Carrie Cheaney
Kiley Christian
Morgan Clarke
Megan Coatney
Nikki Cobb
Hailee Cocanougher
Harrison Cohen
Brandon Collins
Jeff Collins
Steven Collins
Talitha Cook
Samantha Coppedge
Cortney Cormier
Alex Couch
David Couch
Matt Courtney
Tricia Cranfield
Jamie Cyr
Micah Dail
Shelley Davidson
Katie Davis
David DeWitt
Trent Degray
Katie Del Regno
Brian Deshazer
Clayton Dodds
Brigitte Doughty
Megan Douglas
Jason Downing
Brittany Duffin
Sabrina Dufran
Sarah Dumas
Greg Evans
Mina Farzad

Jacob Ferguson
Heidi Fioretti
Katie Fitzharris
Michael Flores
Lauren Fogarty
Shane Folks
Lindsey Foltyn
Allison Foster
Lizz Fowler
Scott Frame
Kami Gallagher
Trevor Galvin
Jeffrey Garza
Geoff Giauque
Tyler Gibson
Mike Gillespie
Courtney Gilless
Vanessa Gillingham
Jacob Gnew
Kimberly Grooms
Lindsey Grotheer
Dani Grumbles
Nathan Hall
Tim Halsor
Katy Hamilton
Jessica Hanes
Courtney Harbaugh
Drew Harnish
Michael Harp
Greg Harrison
Jonathan Harvey
Heather Hatchett
Rachel Haynes
Christy Hebert
Janet Heinzelmann
Jordan Hillin
Beth Hines
Josh Honel
Gina Hooper
Robin Hunt
Amanda Hyde
Cari Ingram
Emma Jahnke
Gage Jeter
Lizzy Johnsen
Erin Johnson
Pam Johnson
Josh Johnson
Nick Johnson
Dan Johnson
Matt Jones
Erin Jones
Kelly Jordan
Steph Kane
Callie Kavourgias
Terry Kavourgias
Madalyn Kearnes
Cameron Kedy

Nick Keepers-Phillips
Rajah Kennedy
Nancy Kenny
Sean Kindley
Alyssa Kruse
Sarah LaFountain
David Larson
Christophe Leblo
Tom Leverich
Nicole Light
Stephen Littlejohn
Daniel Long
Dean Long
Lee Longhorn
Alisha Lynn
Reina Lyons
Tim Major
Spencer Malicki
Drew Mangus
Lisa Mannel
Jason Marshall
Ryan Martin
Trey Mathews
Craig Maucere
Robert Maucere
Michael Russell
Shawna Maxey
Tony McAmis
Ellen McCoy
Michael McEver
Aaron McGeisey
Jennifer McKitrick
Liz McLane
Rachel McLaughlin
Lauren McPhee
Nick McPherson
Jensen Mecca
Garret Merle
Sean Miller
Meredith Miller
Tyson Misak
Amanda Mobbs
Laura Mobley
Erick Moham
Justin Moore
William Moore
Brian Morris
Eric Morrison
Daryl Nagode
Erin Nagode
Maile Naone
Jon Stefanick
Steven Ness
Jay Norris
Katherine O'Hearne
Laura Olson
Emmanuel Osadebey
Jayson Patel
Margaret Perry
Colton Perry

Mallory Phillips
Dara Pickering
Parker Pilkington
Rachel Porter
A.J. Powell
Emily Powell
Mary Powell
Beth Powell
Laura Ramsey
Daniel Reck
Braden Reece
Daniel Reeves
Katherine Reynolds
Jess Reynolds
Shannon Reynolds
Kirsten Rhea
Mike Rhea
Kelsey Richerson
Kristin Robertson
Cameron Robinson
Rosalie Rodgers
Brandon Rodgers
Toni Rodgers
Ari Rooker
Jason Rubin
Michael Russell
Casey Weaver
Grant Wells
Megan Russell
Jose Santiago
Stephanie Santiago
Trey Sargent
Hunter Sargent
Emily Scales
Megan Schafer
Liz Schenk
Mark Schoelen
Nicole Schonberg
Felicia Schwake
Clarence Scott
Richard Shafer
Tristianne Shaw
David Sherman
Meredith Sigler
Joel Siria
Zack Smith
Cameron Smith
Brian Smolinski
Andrew Soliven
Brian Spinner
Jessi Stecker
Jon Stefanick
Krissy Stempf
Sammy Stephenson
Amy Stiles
Brad Stone
Karla Stone
Matt Sumner
Marc Sutton
Allison Synnett

Ronald Taite
Caitlin Tate
Jessica Taylor
Clint Taylor
Dylan Taylor
Matt Taylor
Lacey Taylor
Patrick Tefteller
Courtney Templeton
Travis Thomsen
Vincent Toffoli
Jenna Tow
Richard Tsambikos
John Tucker
Ashley Turner
Christopher Utz
John Van Duyne
Monica Vickers
Jarel Walker
Alisha Walker
Jeff Wampler
Candice Warner
Staci Warren
Steven Watson
Michael Watson
Casey Weaver
Grant Wells
Josh Wesneski
Paul Whaley
Kaity White
Kyle Whitmus
Sam Whitson
Jonathan Wiegner
Kaden Williamson
Steele Willison
Adam Wilson
Jared Wingo
Drew Winters
Kelly Wisley
Gharrett Workun
Dallas Worth
Callie Yeager

U.S. Marine Drum and Bugle Corps.

Wilburton High School Band
Wayne Vog, Director
DeJa Johnston,
  Color Guard Instructor
Shelby Atkinson
Shlyer Bell
Dayna Bills
Regina Bockus
Spencer Bray
Taylor Bray
Shantel Brinkley

Taylor Brinlee
Caitlin Busby
Kattaree Chaowanich
Brittany Chronister
Paige Coffey
Casey Cole
Mitchell Cook
Nathan Cook
Skylar Cravens
Jacob Darby
Lacey Dunlap
Emily Enis
Jayce Ferguson
Ashton Forwoodson
Clint Freeman
Jason Freeman
Spencer Gray
Jessi Green
Jeremiah Gullifer
Jayme Harley
Chuck Hidgon
Jacob Hood
Heather Hudlow
Josh Hunnicutt
Jacob Jiles
Hannah Johnson
Jeremy Johnson
Jessica Johnson
Shelly Johnson
Josh Kelly
A.J. Kendrick
GL Kendrick
Hailey Ketchum
Brandon Mahoney
Kaley Menasco
Sarah Mitchell
Hanna Mooney
Laura Myers
Keith Ott
Jennifer Pearson
Billie Joe Phipps
Casey Pitchford
Jon Ramirez
Lindsey Reager
Kelsey Robsison
Marilee Rowland
John Savage
Marissa Scott
Mandy Sharp
Larissa Sivic
Jake Sparks
Matta Steele
Zach Tate
Caleb Vinson
Zach Vinson
Richard Welsch
Ty Weston
Jerri Wilson

Emily Witt
Chynna Zink
Natassia Zink

Penny Abdullah	Angela Bullard	Kelly Daniels	Katherine Hager	Kevyn Kennedy	Ellen Maddon	Jim Neville	Kortny Rhodes	Pat Snodgrass	Margaret Ann Wickstrom
Sheri Admire	Leni Burrow	Janet Daugherty	Sue Hall	Barbara Kerrick	Jamie Maddy	Pam Neville	Carol Rosacker	Maria Spano	Marci Widmann
Mary Alaoui	Nicole Calvert	Karen Derrick	Leslie Haney	Frances Kersey	Resa Masopust	Sherry Newton	Richard Rowe	Randy Stein	Roy Widmann
Cathryn Allen	Mary Lou Casper	Eileen B. Douglas	Ehteshamul Haque	Anastasia Kilpatrick	Jackie Mattox	Stephanie Nguyen	Sasha Running	Teresa Stephens	Joan Willcox
Helen Allison	Diane Casteel	Aaron Duncan	Sheri Harlow	Taylor Kilpatrick	Emad Mayahi	Kathie Nicoletti	Todd Sanders	Genie Stone	Mary Ann Williams
Cheryl Anderson	Karen Castonguay	Regina Dunn	Anne Hasenfratz	Gay Kirby	Shannon Mayahi	Katie Ogden	Ryan Schaefer	Malcolm K. Stoughtenborough	Natalie Williams
Kapin Anthony	Susan Chambers, MD	Marlene East	Ken Hays	Sandy Kirk	Barbara Mayfield	Laura Ogle	Sydney Schafer	Deanna Taylor	Susie Williamson
Cindy Argo	Robert Chronister	Ray East	Mary Hays	Toni Kitchell	Renee McCollum	Dalawna O'Guin	Ryan Schafer	Michelle Teus	Bonnie R. Wood
Luke Back	Steve Clanton	Meara Eaton	Faye Henson	Jennifer Klos	Lisa McConnell	Kelli Packnett	Jonetta Schrick	Kelli Thornton	Kristen Woodard
Becky Bailey	Robert A. Clark	B.C. Echohawk	Vanessa Hernandez	Wilson Kobel	Maggie McGowan	Kristen Packnett	Rita Scranton	Brad Traynor	Betty J. Worley
Ann Baskin	Ronald Clarke	Deena Electericiteh	Edward L. Hile	Elizabeth Kondor	Keren McLendon	Tonya Pember	Frank Sewell	Vy Trinh	Laura Wren
Patti Bedlion	Andrew Claxton	Regina Finney	Cookie Hill	Kathy J. Kooen	Mary Lou McMartin	Brian Perryman	Jeanne Shaughnessy	Martha Pat Upp	Gwen Wyatt
Gary L. Bennett	Rebecca Clayton	Karen Foster	Floriece Hill	Joanne Kurjan	Amy Million	Jolinda Perryman	Mike Shaughnessy	Richard Vaughn	Susan Wynkoop
Ike Bennett	Shanne Cochran	Kathy Frankenfied	Kelly Hillburn	Lavon Lacey	Cheryl Mims	Alexis Persico	Jack Shaver	Ron Ventresca	Michelle Wynn
Sherry Bennett	Teddi Conley	Melba Frazier	Stephanie Holbrock	Michelle Lashley	Kathy Moffitt	Kathryn Phan	J.G. Shelton	Reagan Vincent	Molly Youngblood
Joanna W. Bernard	Dawrenda Cooper	Laureen Freede	Harold Hollenbeck, Jr.	Sarah Ledgerwood	Chris Moler	Larry Pigeon	Lora Sherman	Joe Wade	Mr. Youngblood
Ashley Black	Jeanetta Cooper	Pamela Freeman	Harold Hollenbeck, Sr.	Hunter Ligon	Judy Moon	Erika Plum	Wendi Shipp	Elizabeth Wagoner	Donna Zawisza
Jackie Black	Deb Corbett	Lynn Garrison	Teena Hollingshead	Friend Livingston	Kyla Mooney	Joe Pointer	Alyssa B. Smith	Kelly Wagoner	
Dayna Blailock	Chad Cosper	Marsha Gentry	Tracie Ann Holsworth	Mariah Livingston	Margot Morris-Dawkins	Natalie Pointer	Ariel Smith	Debora Wallace	
Ruth Blailock	David Cosper	Rebecca Glenn	Cynthia Houghton	Jacque Loch	Tiffany Mosley-Pierce	Joyce Poska	David Smith	Karla Wallace	
Mary Blankenship Pointer	Donna Cosper	David Gouge	Jan Hutchinson	Mark Loch	Bert Mujica	Lois Presley	Evelyn Smith	Darrell Walton	
Dan Boling	Melissa Cosper	Jason Greenwood	Allen Jackson	Deidre Lockwood	Dinorah Mujica	Kristiana Pryor	Gregory Smith	Brian Wandel	
Kay Bradford	Tina Crider	Novalyn Greff	Montogomery Jackson	Georgette Long	Brandelyn Murphy	Ashley Qualls	Jackie Smith	Vonda Warner	
Mary C. Brewington	Rosemary Crouser	Jo Eda Gregory	Christy Johns	Jim Long	Laurie Myers	Haley Qualls	Janna Smith	Joyce Lynn Weber	
Mary Ann Brochowiak	Allen Curry	Paige Gregory	Michael Johns	John Lowe	Sharon Neal	Jessica Reading	Johnny L. Smith	David White	
Denise Brown	Libby Curry	Nancy Groves	Frances Jowers	Christy Mabrey	Maureen Nelson	James Redden	Kimberly Smith		

Centenarian Event(s) Volunteers
- M.J. Alexander
- Richard Amend
- Mary Lou Bates
- Cristi Bullard
- Pam Cullen
- Kerry Fisbeck
- Lauren Humphrey
- Jamie Maddy
- Devin Resides
- Lance Robertson
- Rachel Shortt
- Richard Ziglar

Guthrie BBQ
- Carolyn Alexander
- Patrick Anderson
- Ed Austin
- Barbara Bailey
- Tom Bailey
- Joseph Bennett
- Donna Betchan
- Glen Blair
- Billie Bonner
- Gary Boxley
- Tami Boxley
- Gary Boyles
- Josh Bradley
- Naymon Braggs, Jr.
- Debbie Brewer
- Hazel Burress
- Chuck Burtcher
- Gene Chumbley
- Raymond Cockrum
- Cathie Cordis
- Rusty Crockett
- Cassie Dalton
- Rodney Davidson
- Rick Davis
- Sharon DeVeau
- Damon Devereaux
- Jackie Dodd
- Dot Ellis
- Rob Ferris
- Elaine Ford
- Shirley Ford
- Alexandra Forney
- Mick Fredrickson
- Jarrett George
- Kenny George
- Ric Gorden
- Dallas Greenwood
- A.J. Griffin
- Sheila Guthrie
- Hersey Hammons
- Jim Hanke
- Kari Harris
- Dan Hoffman
- Kenneth James
- Ronnie Jech
- Charlie Jones
- William Jones
- Mary Kelly
- Ken Koch
- Jibu Kuruvilla
- Dan Ladd
- Randy Lewis
- Priscilla Mayberry
- Don McBride
- Tim McBride
- Bill McKnight
- Julie McPeek
- Dan Miller
- Johnny Miller
- Linda Miller
- Reginald Mitchell
- Terry Moore
- Bill Naifeh
- Jacob Nelson
- Dan Newton
- Joy Newton
- David Nolen
- Mitchell Oakes
- Dennis Ochs
- Edward Oliver
- Neel Patel
- Kenny Patterson
- Kenneth Pickering
- Sam Porter
- Richard Price
- Maxine Pruitt
- Amanda Putnam
- Steve Raupe
- Phil Richardson
- Shannon Richardson
- Diana Saenz
- Janet Sanders
- John Sanders
- Tammy Scott
- Brenda Selby
- Parke Selby
- Cindy Short
- Dwayne Smith
- R.C. Smith
- Rosemary Smith
- Verdell Smith
- Tom Stambeck
- Rick Staton
- Juliana Swanson
- Mary Swindall
- Nic Thams
- Becky Tobin
- Billy Tobin
- Phillip Tucker
- John Vance
- Deb VanOverbeke
- Keith Ventris
- Lanny Westbrook
- Raman Westbrook
- Kenneth Will
- Lee Williams
- Montoya Williams
- Pam Williams
- Al Willoby
- Linda Willoby

Guthrie Centennial Committee
- George Watts, Chair
- Michael Bennett
- Paul Blount
- Kim Biggs
- Donald Coffin
- Mary Coffin
- Cathie Cordis
- Lance Crenshaw
- Frank Davis
- Robert Davis
- Dale Depue
- Melissa Fesler
- Jarrett George
- Valerie Haynes
- Melody Kellogg
- A.J. Griffin
- Gary Good
- Richard Hendricks
- Robin Lang
- Kathy Montgomery
- Dan Newton
- Dennis Ochs
- Walter Pitts
- John Vance
- Rose Williams

Guthrie Corporate Volunteers
- ACE Hardware
- Baptist General Convention of Oklahoma
- Burgess Manufacturing
- Central Oklahoma Wakeboard Park
- Delta Epsilon of University of Oklahoma
- Event Productions
- Ford Motor Company
- Four State Meat Processing
- Gooch-Smith Electric
- Guthrie High ROTC
- Guthrie Job Corps Center
  - Carpentry Team
  - Culinary Arts Team
  - Protection Security
  - Investigation Team
  - Team Management Team
  - Welding Team
- Guthrie Parks Department
- Logan County Asphalt
- Logan County Medical Center
- Logan County Health Department
- Logan County Red Cross
- Meridian Technology Center
- OG&E
- Oklahoma State University
- Ozarka Water
- Platte Culinary Arts
- Procter & Gamble
- RDS Shipping
- Regional Food Bank
- Sara Lee Products
- Sysco Foods
- Volunteer Club at University of Oklahoma
- Willoby Wholesale

Guthrie Volunteers
- Betty Atchley
- Gwen Bailey
- Phil Bailey
- Rosemary Barnett
- Kim Bennett
- Pat Brainard
- Steve Brainard
- Barbara Brookshire
- Pam Daniels
- Jim Donoho
- Margie Donoho
- Jack Emerson
- Mae Emerson
- Audrey Humphries
- Brianne Humphries
- Christa Humphries
- Rose Humphries
- Melanie Jenkenson
- Donna Keller
- Frank LaForce
- Mary LaForce
- Jeannine Long
- Joan Maker
- Sylvia Ochs
- Diane Pross
- Ada Roberts
- Joan Robinette
- Barbara Ryan
- Tia Shields
- DeDee Taylor
- Mona Taylor
- Bobbie Thompson

Spectacular Volunteers
- Sandy Alvarado
- Rosemarie Baker
- Julie Barron
- Terrye Bell
- Mike Brashears

ADDITIONAL VOLUNTEER GROUPS

Gwen Brashears
Niki Burch
Mark Burch
Scott Corley
Kristin Dahlgren
Becky Deacon
Viki Donahoo
Robyn Eitelman
Eddie Fuentes
Melissa Gardner
Rhonda Giles
Jennifer Gilliam
K.C. Glyckherr
Lorie Higginbotham
Dylan Higginbotham
Sandra Landgraf
Summer Ledbetter
Carrie Lewis-Crawford
Madeline Mahoney
Rob Martin
Lynn Regouby

Monica Regouby
Ray Rice
Allen Rice
Dee Dee Rice
Joshua Standifer
Darrel Stone
Theressa Taylor
Chad Tolle
Jina Tolle
Kelly Wagoner
Elizabeth Wagoner
Valerie Walker
Brogan Ward
Frank Wheeler
Nancy Wheeler

**Tulsa Oklahoma
Executive Committee**
Sharon King Davis, Chair
Don Walker, Co-Chair
Paula Hale, Co-Chair

**Tulsa Buried Car
Committee**
Sharon King Davis, Co-Chair
John Earling, Co-Chair
Paula Hale, Director
Pamela Bennett
John Biles
Jim Brackett
Jesse Boudiette
Jerry Burch
Rhonda Burch
Joe Cappy
Art Couch
Bill Cox
Elmer Clark
Steve Doede
Phil Eller
Maggie Brown
Lou Fitch
Chuck Fitch
Phil Feist

Jack Frank
Sandy Grossman
Yvonne Hovell
Barby Jobe
Cyndi Koch
Robert Koch
George Kolczun
Randy Krehbiel
Pat Kroblin
Tim Krusmark
Kelly McElroy
Ron McMahan
Pat McMichael
Joshua Peck
Jack Petreikis
Lucinda Rojas
Buck Rudd
Rod Sands
Nancy Schallner

Chuck Schnake
Bruce Shalon
Dianna Smith
Seth Spillman
Laura Stone
Suzanne Stewart
Jim Taylor
Bill Waller

**Tulsa Kickoff
Committee**
Sharon King Davis, Chair
Paula Hale, Director
Karisha Arnett
Nancy Bolzle
Gary Caimano
Yolanda Charney
Nancy Day
Jeanie Edney
Steve Frantz

Debbie Friggel
Clydella Hentschel
Pat Kroblin
Kelly McElroy
Jeff Olsen
Barbie Rainey
Carla Shwadlenak
Barbara Smallwood
Seth Spillman
Barbara VanHenken
Jeremiah Wiley
Tony Winters
Richard Ziglar

**Tulsa Kickoff
Volunteers**
Brooke Battles
Bree Bedsworth
Lesli Blackburn
Paula Blalock
David Brixey

Kathy Brumley
Brandi Burk
Kim Camp
Trapper Charboneau
Jon Davis
Angie Harrison
Heather Hughey
Shana Lindsey
Jim Long
Diana Mann
Jackie Mattox
Chad McMains
Desiree Mitchell
Diane Pressell
Rebecca Reed
Brian Richmond
Jessica Sanderson
Lesa Sheets
Justin Tascier
Amanda Walker
Brian Walker

Amy Ward
Jason Wayne
Kaleb Woolever

**USS Oklahoma
Memorial Executive
Committee**
Greg Slavonic, Co-Chair
Tucker McHugh, Co-Chair
Paul Goodyear
Ed Vezey
Ray Ackerman
Norman Lamb
Jim Reynolds
Gary Banz
Elayne Dennis
Jeff Houpt
Kevin King
Eldridge Luber
Mike McAuliffe
Frank Naifeh

First Lady Kim Henry,
   Fund Raising Co-Chair
Mike McAuliffe,
   Fund Raising Co-Chair
Memorial Design
Don Beck
Beck Designs, Inc.

M.J. Alexander
Mary Ellen Alexander
Altus Air Force Base
AP/Wide World Photos
Jim Argo
Linda Barry
The Cannoneer
Chris Carter
Central Oklahoma Habitat for Humanity
Cherokee Strip Regional Heritage Center
Tim Colwell, Superlative Publications, Inc.
Jordan Dabby
Jeff Dixon, Lawton Constitution
Ross Dixon, OETA
Downtown Cushing Main Street/Tom Cummings
Lynne Draper
Ashleigh Dunham
Kristin Dunn
El Reno Tourism
Elliott + Associates, Photos by Scott McDonald

Gary England, KWTV
John Fain Architects
David Faytinger
David Fitzgerald
Fort Sill Army Base
Frankfurt-Short-Bruza
The Goddard Art Center
Ace Guervo
Bill Gumerson & Associates/Bill Dinger AIA
Michael Hardeman
Drew Harmon, The Edmond Sun
Historic Fort Reno, Inc.
Tinker Hulen
Greg Hursley
Jerry Hymer
Marty Ingels
Michael Ives
John Jernigan
Jones Public Relations
Karen Keith

Keith Kinslow
Todd Kinslow
Mike Klemme Photography, Inc.
Ward Larson
Leisure Photography
Library of Congress
R.E. Lindsey
Jeff Manning, J.A. Manning Construction
Fred W. Marvel
Stuart McDaniel
Scott McDonald
David McNeese
Travis Meyer, KOTV
Terry Michael
Frank Mitchell, KTUL
Andy Moffat, Piedmont, Oklahoma
Todd Moore © Crown Arts Inc. 2008
Mike Morgan, KFOR
The National Archives
Norman Convention & Visitors Bureau

The Nowata Courthouse
Oklahoma Centennial Commission
Oklahoma Department of Human Services
Oklahoma Department of Tourism
  and Recreation
Oklahoma Events
Oklahoma Historical Society Research Division
Oklahoma State Fair
Dustin Orona
Scott Padgett, KOKH
Bill Perry
Pickens Photography
Tamara L. Pinkston
Chris Pribil
Redlands Community College
Rush Springs Gazette
"Rocketman" Dan Schlund
Science Museum Oklahoma
DeLee Smith
Ian D. Swart, Woodward, Oklahoma

Dave Tamez
Greg Tatum, Oklahoma Aquarium
Robert H. Taylor
Joyce Carol Thomas
Dan Threlkeld, KJRH
Tinker Air Force Base
Tournament of Roses Photo Archives
Ann Scaling Tucker, Enid Buzz
Tulsa Historical Society
University of Oklahoma
Vance Air Force Base
Kent Vinyard
Valerie Wakefield
Will Rogers Heritage, Inc.
Mike Wimmer

The Oklahoman
Jaconna Aguirre
Jim Beckel
John Clanton
Steve Gooch
Paul Hellstern
Chris Landsberger
Linda Lynn
David McDaniel
Mary Phillips
James Plumlee
Steve Sisney
Paul B. Southerland
Matt Strasen
Bill Waugh

We extend heartfelt appreciation not only to the names listed
on this page, but to the many Oklahomans who contributed their
time, efforts, passion and creativity. The photographs, illustrations
and renderings so graciously provided have helped forever
document this historic event.

CENTENNIAL BOOK

Ackerman McQueen
Aduddell Foundation
American Fidelity Foundation
Arvest Bank
AT&T
Libby & G.T. Blankenship
Bank of America
Patsy & Jim Brewer
Chesapeake Energy Corporation
The Chickasaw Nation
ConocoPhillips
Luke & Becky Corbett Foundation
Cox Communications
Devon Energy Corporation
Dobson Partnership
Dorchester Capital

Dulaney Brothers
Eddie Foundation, Inc.
Jean I. Everest Foundation
Flintco/Manhattan Construction
C.L. Frates & Company
The Freede Family
Robert A. Funk
Great Plains Coca-Cola
Griffin Communications
　Oklahoma's Very Own
Hudiburg Auto Group
INTEGRIS Health, Inc.
JPMorgan Chase & Co.
Don Karchmer
The Kerr Foundation, Inc.
Lana & Dave Lopez

Love's Travel Stops & Country Stores
LSB Industries, Inc.
McAfee & Taft Law Firm
The Meinders Foundation
Mercy Health System of Oklahoma
Mustang Fuel Corporation
NAIFCO
Norick Investment Company
Oklahoma Centennial Commission
Oklahoma City Community College
Oklahoma City University
Oklahoma Industries Authority
OGE Energy Corp.
OU Medical Center
The Oklahoman
The Payne Family

Ray & Pat Potts
Presbyterian Health Foundation
Carl & Carolyn Renfro
Riggs Abney Neal Turpen Orbison & Lewis
7-Eleven Stores
Jeannette and Richard Sias
DeAnn & Lee Allan Smith
James R. Tolbert III
University of Oklahoma
Donna & Blake Wade
Jim & Jill Williams
M.V. Williams Foundation, Inc.

Special thanks to **Southwestern Stationery & Bank Supply** for their cooperation in the printing of this book.

The Centennial Spectacular, held on November 16, 2007, at the Ford Center in Oklahoma City, earned an Emmy Award for Special Event coverage at the 2008 Heartland Regional Awards. It was a privilege to accept this prestigious award, presented by the Television Academy of Arts & Sciences, on behalf of the city, state, sponsors, celebrities, performers and volunteers who worked countless hours to ensure the event was a success.

Back row, left to right:
Paul Christensen, *Technical Producer*
Steve Dahlem, *Creative Director*
J. Blake Wade, *Associate Producer*
Lee Allan Smith, *Executive Producer*
Bill Thrash, *TV Producer*
Price Wooldridge, *Production Manager*

Front row, left to right:
Melinda Lovelace, *Producer*
DeLee Smith, *Project Coordinator*
Mickie Smith, *Technical Director*
Jennifer Kiersch, *Senior Project Coordinator*
Erica Reid, *Project Coordinator*

Not pictured: **Curt Casassa**, *TV Director*

ACKNOWLEDGMENTS

On behalf of our fellow Oklahomans, the Oklahoma Centennial Commemoration Commission and Oklahoma Events recognizes the Oklahoma State Legislature for its significant financial support of Centennial projects throughout the state. The matching funds provided by the Legislature enabled communities of all sizes to participate in this momentous commemoration and, as a result, generated a sense of pride and optimism that will propel Oklahoma far into its second century.

Oklahoma Centennial Commission
Lou Kerr, Chair
Nancy Leonard, Vice Chair
J. Blake Wade, Executive Director
Jeanie McCain Edney, Deputy Director
Steve Anderson
Mary L. Cole
Pat Downes
Nick Duncan
Kim Gomez
Sarah Hearn
Joan Hess
Terri Humphrey
Colin McEwen
Ryan O'Toole
Theresa Owens
Georgiana Rymer
Amy Weaver
In memory of Dr. Willis J. Wheat and Martin Hagerstrand

Oklahoma Events
Lee Allan Smith, President; Chairman of Centennial Projects and Events
Jennifer Kiersch, Vice-President; Vice-Chairman of Centennial Projects and Events
DeLee Smith
Erica Reid

Ackerman McQueen
Angus McQueen
Bill Winkler
Ed Martin
Jeanette Elliott
Rodney Lipe
Gail Daniels
Sherri Duran
Lael Erickson
Jon Minson
Brett Willison
Jeanne Oden

Christy Allen
Heather Barger
Deidre Barnes
Daniel Benatar
Steve Brite
Jason Bushore
Justin Claborn
Aubrey Coble
Mike Dennehy
Bentley Dill
Andrew Duong
Hillary Farrell
Randall Fransen
Anthony Glass
Kari Griffith
Amy Hall
Dusky Hamm
Dawn Harth
Amy Hearn
Sara Hogg
Becky Hughes
Peyton Hutchison
Michael Ives
Jennifer Jackson
Barbara Johnston

Rory Jones
Don Juntunen
Rick Lipe
Marcus Luellen
Riley Marshall
Kyle Martin
Whitney Meier
Jessica McDaniel
Macy Miller
Jeff Minson
Justin Morris
Danny Murphy
Rob Neatherlin
Jessica Ockershauser
Alecia Owens
Josh Owens
Matt Patterson
Jason Peak
Wes Powell
Melissa Rhodes
Bonnie Rucker
Julie Ruffin
Ed Russell
Trevor Schirf
Jeanette Schreiber
David Scott
Ali Shadfar
Scott Strandberg
Lauren Taylor
Michael Tucker
Clay Turner
Dana Weddle
Dean Wilhite
Darla Willison
Ashley Wilson

Special Thanks
Jim Abbott
Angela Ables
Jane Abraham
George E. Adams
Gerald Adams
Jennifer Adair
Mary Ellen Alexander
M.J. Alexander
The All-American Rejects
Bob Allee
Bill Allen
Deby Allen
John Allgood
Robin Alvis
Ambassadors' Concert Choir
Mark Anderson
Mike Anderson
Tom Anderson
Bill Anoatubby
Bob Anthony
Jim Armagost
Argonne Parades
Jari Askins
Associated Press
Mike Atkins
Alison Auerbach
Michael Bahamonde
Chris Bain
Karen Baker
Mike Baldwin
Howard Barnett
Timothy Beachley
Beacon Club
Larry Bearden
Jeff Becker
Krista Becker
John Bedford
Molly Beffort
Henry Bellmon
Johnny Bench
Phyllis Bennett
Byron Berline
Paul Bethell
Jeff Bezdek
Darlene Bieber
Josh Bertrand

Dave Bialis
Rev. Joseph Bias
Big Events
Matt Bishop
Harlan Bixby
Sally Bixby
Bob Blackburn
Narvel Blackstock
Joe Blough
Scott Booker
David Boren
Molly Boren
Greg Bosler
Don Boulton
Sam Bowman
Deren Boyd
McKinney Boyd
Boys & Girls Clubs
Connell Brandon
Tim Brassfield
Brewer Entertainment
Brent Brewer
Brett Brewer
Jim Brewer
Brian Britt
Tom Britt
Garth Brooks
Brian Brown
Jim Brown
Linda Brown
Jim Bruza
Bubba's BBQ
Dennis Buckley
Ellis Burgoyne
Kimberly Burk
Bob Burke
Greg Burns
Richard A. Burpee
Mary Caffrey
Rick Cain
Virginia Calame
Carol Calcagno
Gini Moore Campbell
Owen Canfield
Canterbury Children's Choir
Canterbury Choral Society
Pete Cappa
Tom Caraway
Lance Cargill

Jenni Carlson
Karen Carney
Joe Carter
Curt Casassa
Susan Cassidy
Tom Cassidy
Joe Castiglione
Carolyn Caudill
Kelly Caviness
Celebrity Attractions
Central District Square Dance Association
Central Oklahoma Transportation & Parking Authority
Stuart Chai
Challenger
Ryan Chase
Kristin Chenoweth
Marc Cherry
Mark Childers
Paul Christensen
Cinemark Tinseltown
City of Oklahoma City
Bill Citty
Civic Center Music Hall Staff
Chris Clifton
Jeff Cloud
Dennis Clowers
Michael Clowers
Sherri Coale
Glenn Coffee
Chris Coffie
Colcord Hotel
Sandy Cole
Nadia Comaneci
Bart Conner
Ed Cook
Jackie Cooper
Steffie Corcoran
Joan Cornett
Mayor Mick Cornett
CorporateMagic Inc.
Fran Cory
Cory's Audio Visual
Clayton Coss
Wayne Coyne
Cox Communications
Chad Cosper
Melissa Cosper

Jim Couch
County of Oklahoma County
Cox Communications
Millie Craddick
Bob Craig
Carolyn Crain
Greg Crane
Crucible Foundry
Harry Currie
Eric Dabney
Jordan Dabby
Steve Dahlem
Valory Dalton
John Daugherty
Dirk Davenport
Gena Davis
Greg Davis
Jamie Davis
Mike Davis
Sandi Davis
Sharon King Davis
Jana Dean
Keith Dean
Michael Dean
Stacey Dean
Bo DeCaulp
Ed deCordova
Tara Deguisti
Denton's
Gary Desjardins
Pat Dennis
Jennifer Dennis-Smith
Department of Central Services
Janie Deupree
Digital Express
Bill Dinger
Jonathan Dodd
Peter Dolese
Mitch Dorger
Pat Downes
Steven Drozd
Bob Doucette
John Dougherty
Roman Dudok
Randy Earhart
Ed Eason
Matt Eaton
Caryn Eaves
Rich Eckhardt

Ann Edelblute
Drew Edmondson
Katrina Elam
EMSA
Tony Emig
Gary England
Ty England
Linda English
Tim Estes
Steve Evans
Eventures
Christy Everest
Expo Design
Express Clydesdales
Christy Factor
Stephan Fagan
David Failor
Teddy Falkenbury
Mary Fallin
George Frame
Ann Felton
Bob Fenimore
David Ferris
Fiesta Parade Floats
Fine Arts Engraving
Bruce Fisher
Russell Fisher
The Flaming Lips
Larry Flener
William Flinn
Flintco/Manhattan
Joey Floyd
Jerry Foshee
George Frame
Frankfurt-Short-Bruza
Jim Franklin
Ryan Free
Brett Freedman
Butch Freeman
Jay Freeman
FRIDAY
Roger Frizzell
Kelly Fry
Jane Jayroe Gamble
Benny Garcia
James Gamer
Linda Garrett
Sandy Garrett
Denzil Garrison

ACKNOWLEDGEMENTS

Chris Gaylor
Jim Gibb
Douglas Gibson
Vince Gill
John Goetz
Chuck Goff
Bob Goins
Juanitta Goins
Gary Good
Jody Gooden
Jennifer Berry Gooden
John Gooden
Garrett Goodwin
Carrie Gordon
Larry "T-Byrd" Gordon
"Lil" Larry Gordon
Julie Gosdin
Steve Gragert
Amy Grant
Shan Gray
David Green
David Griffin
David Groom
Tom Gruber
Gumerson & Associates
Bill Gumerson
Courtney Gutekunst
Jeff Gwaltney
Habitat for Humanity
Eric Hagstrom
Deana Haidary
Paula Hale
Sue Hale
Tripp Hall
Jim Halsey
Jonathan Hamby
Argus Hamilton
David Hamilton
Roy Hamilton
Brett Hamm
Lorie Harned
Jason Harrison
Eddie Hartwick
Jim Hartz
Lee Hawkins
Kris Haynes
Beverly Hedges
Jason Henderson
Joan Henderson

Jenny Hendrick
Richard Heinrich
Governor Brad Henry
First Lady Kim Henry
Dave Herbert
James Hermank
Javier Hernandez
David Herrendeen
John Herrington
Bob Hersom
Robyn Hilger
Carolyn Hill
Ed Hill
Kasie Hill
Mick Hinton
John Hobbs
Mat Hoffman
Toni Hoffman
Randy Hogan
Harold Holden
Paul Holman
Susan Holman
Kay Holt
Don Honiker
Charlotte Houle
Rance Howard
Ron Howard
Kirk Humphreys
Chad Huntington
Ernest Istook
Michael Ivins
John Jamison
Verej Jazirvar
Chad Jeffers
Hotel Jenny
Joe Jondahl
Chris Johnson
Don Johnson
Glen Johnson
Hugh Johnson
Junie Lowry Johnson
Willa Johnson
Jones Public Relations
Brenda Jones
Charles Jones
John Jones
Shirley Jones
Joullian Vineyards

Journal Record
Justice Golf Carts
Kamber's
Don Karchmer
Ben Kates
Ronnie Kaye
KFOR
KOCO
KWTV
Cathy Keating
Frank Keating
Gayleen Keeton
Toby Keith
Ed Kelley
Ronald Skip Kelly
Mike Kennerty
Key Magazine
Leighton Kirkpatrick
Doug Klausen
Fritz Kiersch
Kenneth Kilgore
T.K. Kimbrell
Allen King
Mitch King
Mike King
Mike Knopp
Scotty Kramer
Mark Kranenburg
Rob Krier
Amy Kule
Greg Kunesh
Bob Kurland
Joe Kyle
Kay Lacey
Steve Lackmeyer
Ann Lacy
Suzie Lalone
Marvin Lamb
Paul Lambert
Bob Landeck
Jim Lange
Devonna Landrum
Ron Landrum
Steve Largent
Mike Larsen
Kathy Ledbetter
John Lee
Shirley Lee

In Memory of
  Grant Leftwich
Nicole Leonti
Joel Levine
Tom Lindley
Linda Linn
Tim Linville
In Memory of
  Bill Lofthouse
Chris Lofthouse
Melinda Lovelace
Dick Lowry
Hunt Lowry
Libby Lowry
David Luke
Julia Lyles
Nancy Lyon
Lyric Theatre
Robbie Mackey
Bert Mackie
Laure J. Majors
Marianne's
Gary Marrs
Debbie Martin
J.W. Mashburn
Rex Mauney
Tom Maxwell
Caroline May
Sundae May
Dave McAfee
Larry McAtee
Mike McAuliffe
Jan McCaffrey
Terry McCaffrey
John McCarroll
Trisha McClanahan
Shelton McCoy
Kathy McCracken
Louisa McCune-Elmore
Brenda McDaniel
Tom McDaniel
Reba McEntire
Kathleen McGuire
Sandra McLennan
Matt McMillan
Michael McNutt
Amy McRee
J.E. McReynolds

In Memory of
  Clem McSpadden
Susan McVey
Scott Meacham
Susan Meacham
Kent Meyers
Kirby Middleton
David Milam
Wes Milbourn
Don Miles
Annalee Miller
Bill Miller
Shannon Miller
Josh Mitchell
Leona Mitchell
Chris Moler
N. Scott Momaday
Moonlight Serenade Orchestra
Mary Ann Moore
Paul Moore
Mike Morgan
Linda Morris
Kenny Mossman
Mickey Mulcahy
Megan Mullally
Scott Munz
In Memory of
  Bobby Murcer
C.J. Murphy
Carl Murr
Jim Murray
Music Express Limo
Misty Myers
Shannon Nance
National Cowboy & Western
  Heritage Museum
Earl Neal
Ken Neal
Lauren Nelson
New Leaf Floral
Galen Nichols
George Nigh
Nonna's
Ron Norick
North American Group
North Pole City
Mark Northcutt
Steve Nunno
Oak Ridge Boys

Susan Oden
Tim Oden
OETA
Kelly Ogle
Sean O'Grady
Kelli O'Hara
Oklahoma Art Museum
Oklahoma Centennial Rodeo Opry
Oklahoma City Beautiful
Oklahoma City Chamber of Commerce
Oklahoma City Community College
Oklahoma City Fire Department
Oklahoma City National Memorial
Oklahoma City Philharmonic
Oklahoma City Police Department
Oklahoma City University American Spirit
  Dance Company
Oklahoma City Zoo
Oklahoma Department of Tourism
Oklahoma Department of Transportation
Oklahoma Events
Oklahoma Gazette
Oklahoma Heritage Association
Oklahoma History Center
The Oklahoman
Oklahoma RedHawks
Oklahoma State Chamber
Oklahoma State Department of
  Education
Oklahoma State Fair
Oklahoma State Firefighters Museum
Oklahoma State University
  Marching Band
Oklahoma Today
Jay O'Meilia
Tim O'Toole
Don Otto
Gary Owen
Destan Owens
George Owens
Steve Owens
Patti Page
Russ Pahl
Bryan Painter
Bob Palmer
Paper 'n More
Paris Limousines
Jennifer Paris
Jimmy Paris

Susy Paris
Mark Parker
Sam Parker
Sandi Patty
Jeremy Paul
Bond Payne
Larry Payton
Penn Square Mall
John Perry
Twylia Peterson
Petroleum Club
Russell Pettite
Mary Phillips
Phoenix Decorating
Hobie Pileski
Dave Pitman
Susan Plonkey
Susan Powell
Patricia Presley
Betty Price
Dan Provo
Scott Pruitt
Rainbow Pennant
Rob Rankin
Phillip Ransford
Jeff Raymond
MaryAnn Rea
Red Stone Singers & Eagle
  Spirit Dancers
Chris Reen
Jonathan Beck Reed
Pat Reid
Stuart Reid
Kathy Reitz
Remington Park
Renaissance Hotel
Michael Rhodes
Drake Rice
John Richard
Gary Ridley
John Riggs
Lisa Riggs
Donna Rhinehart
Brett Rinehart
JoAnne Ritchey
Tyson Ritter
Ritz-Carlton Huntington Hotel & Spa
Mica Roberts
Raul Rodriguez

ACKNOWLEDGEMENTS

Rick Rogers
John Rohde
Lynne Roller
Judy Roof
Megan Rossman
Jim Roth
Jo Rowan
Reg Rowe
Willie Roy
Dick Rush
Barkley Russell
Patrick J. Ryan
Dee Sadler
Greg Sadler
Mary Sameri
Brian Sargent
Bill Saxon
"Rocketman" Dan Schlund
Melissa Schleicher
Jessie Schmidt
Willard Scott
Dawn Sears
Paul Sechrist
Angie Sellers
Chase Senge
Karen Schott

Dave Schramm
Chuck Schroeder
Lori Schumaker
Rachelle Schwartz
Louis Schwing
Science Museum Oklahoma
Dwight Scott
Stephanie Seymour
Mike Shannon
Blake Shelton
Daren Shepard
Natalie Shirley
Elaine Shock
Jim Shoulders
Signworks
Joann Silver
Silvertree Productions
Stephen Silvestrl
Brett Skelton
Skirvin Hotel
Ann Simank
Billy Sims
Sam Sims
Stan Sims
Six Flags
SMG

DeAnn Smith
Gary Smith
Jeanette Smith
John Smith
Leroy Smith
Mickie Smith
Patrick Smith
Terry Smith
Wendy Smith
Southwestern Seating
Southwestern Stationery & Bank Supply
Scott Spradling
Darla Stafford
Mark Stansberry
Steve Stavinoha
Bob Stoops
Paula Stover
Martin Stringer
Leonard Sullivan
John Sutter
Eddie Sutton
Sweet Adelines
Barry Switzer
Megan Syzmanski
Brett Syzmanski
Ann Taylor

Kathy Taylor
Nicholas Taylor
Billy Thomas
Clendon Thomas
David Thomas
Mark Thomas
Bill Thrash
Ann Thompson
David Thompson
Sandra Thompson
Tommy Thompson
Bill Thorpe
Jack Thorpe
Gena Timberman
In Memory of Bob Todd
Toucan Lighting
Jim Tolbert
Trish Townsend
Berry Tramel
Robbie Trammell
Tree Bank Foundation
Charlie Trimble
Gene Triplett
Jake Trotter
Shawn Tubbs
Marty Tucker

Tulsa World
Mike Turpen
Carrie Underwood
Unigraph
United States Postal Service
University of Central Oklahoma
University of Oklahoma Marching Band
Marylin Upsher
USA Screen Printing & Embroidery
Scott Vankirk
Stan Van Nort
Ray Vaughn
Susie Vessels
Keven Virgilio
Randi Von Ellefson
Mark Voyles
Donna Wade
Joe Wade
Stacia L. Wake
Bill Wakefield
Waldorf=Astoria
Don Walker
Eddie Walker
Craig Wallace
Helen Ford Wallace
Jay Brian Walters

Lew Ward
Pete Wasner
Shoshanna Wasserman
Waterford Marriott Hotel
Hardy Watkins
Kari Watkins
Ridge Watson
Jimmy Webb
Laura Savini Webb
Roger Webb
Stacey Weddington
Max Weitzenhoffer
Scott Wells
Ted Wells
Paul Westbrook
Rob Westcott
Western Enterprises
Nick Wheeler
John Whetsel
Bryan White
Daniel White
Jason White
Jeff White
John White
Pete White
Wendel Whisenhunt

Janet Wilburn
Wiley Valentine
John Wilhoite
Alexandria Williams
Danny Williams
Jill Williams
Jim Williams
John Williams
Willis Granite
Will Rogers World Airport
Mike Wimmer
Kim Wimmler
Linda Wood
Price Wooldridge
Joe Worley
Shawntel Smith Wuerch
Kurt Wunsch
Yamaha
Tim Zwink

SPECIAL PROJECT SPONSORS

Anthem Preview
Presented by Kerr-McGee Corporation
Cox Communications
KWTV News 9
The Oklahoman

Attorney General Lady of Justice Statue
Chesapeake Energy Corporation
Devon Energy Corporation
Kerr-McGee Corporation
John W. Norman
OGE Energy Corp.
ONEOK
Oklahoma Bondsman Association, Inc.
PrePaid Legal Services
SBC Communications
Smith Cogeneration
The Yaffe Companies Incorporated

Attorney General Mural
Nix, Patterson & Roach, LLP

Attorney General Spilling Pool
Marylin Jones Upsher

Ballerina Statue
Mr. & Mrs. David Rainbolt

Baseball
BancFirst
Kerr-McGee Corporation
Integrated Medical Delivery
The Oklahoman

Beacon of Hope
E.L. and Thelma Gaylord Foundation
Oklahoma City Centennial Sponsors
Presbyterian Health Foundation

Billy Sims Statue
Clayton I. Bennett
The Jackie Cooper Family
Mr. & Mrs. Toby Keith
Hunter & Kathy Miller

Oklahoma University Football
Letterman's Association
Jakie Sandefer
Barry Switzer
Gene Torbett
The University of Oklahoma
Touchdown Club
The University of Oklahoma Department
of Intercollegiate Athletics
Marshall Weir
Bob White
Jim & Jill Williams
The Lee Allan Smith Family

Billy Vessels Statue
Sam Allen
Claude Arnold
Clayton I. Bennett
Gaylord Graham Bennett
G.T. Blankenship
Edwin W. deCordova
Eddie Crowder
Richard Ellis
Buck McPhail
Steve Owens
Oklahoma University Football
Letterman's Association
Sigma Nu Fraternity
Lee Allan Smith
Gene Torbett

Brubeck Concert
Jeannette and Richard Sias

Canal Bridges
Adduddell Foundation
Devon Energy Corporation
The Freede Family
The Noble Foundation
SandRidge Energy

Carillion, Leadership Square
Dorchester Capital

Centennial Parade Floats
Chesapeake Energy Corporation

Devon Energy Corporation
Farmers Insurance Group
OERB
Oklahoma Heart Hospital
SandRidge Energy

Centennial Saddles
The Freede Family

Chesapeake Boathouse
BancFirst
Dobson Communications Corp.
Dorchester Capital
E.L. and Thelma Gaylord Foundation
Kerr-McGee Corporation
Oklahoma City Riverfront Redevelopment
Authority
City of Oklahoma City

Clocks
BancFirst, BancFirst Centennial Clock,
N.W. Expressway & Pennsylvania
The Freede Family, Integris Clock
Hobby Lobby, Oklahoma City National
Memorial Clock
SandRidge Energy, Inc, Oklahoma City
National Memorial Clock
Oklahoma City Centennial Sponsors,
North State Capitol Clock
Oklahoma City Centennial Sponsors &
State Capitol Association, South State
Capitol Clock
The Oklahoman, Oklahoman Clock
UMB Clock, Cox Convention Center Clock
YMCA of Greater Oklahoma City
– Earlywine Clock

Conductor Statue
Jeannette and Richard Sias

Corporation Commission Project
AT&T
OGE Energy Corp.
Oklahoma City Centennial Sponsors

Endowment for the Allied Arts
The Chickasaw Nation
Anonymous
BancFirst
The Freede Family
INTEGRIS Health, Inc.
Kerr-McGee Corporation
Oklahoma City Centennial Sponsors
The Oklahoman
Jeanette & Richard Sias

In Kind Contributions
Lou & Ray Ackerman
Ackerman McQueen
Allied Steel Construction
American Airlines, Official Airlines of
the Oklahoma Centennial
The Benham Companies
Pasty & Jim Brewer
The Catering Company/Restaurant
Row Catering
Jackie Cooper Family
County of Oklahoma County
Cox Communications
Gazette Media, Inc
Vicki Clark and J. Leland Gourley
Gumerson and Associates
The Journal Record Publishing Co.
Aaron and Gertrude Karchmer
Memorial Foundation
Lamar Advertising
Oklahoma City University
Penn Square Mall
Southwestern Stationery and Bank Supply
Western Enterprises

Jason White Statue
Capital West Securities
Chesapeake Energy Corporation
Clayton I. Bennet
Dealers Auto Auction, Oklahoma City
Dr. J. Don. Harris
In Memory of
Sgt. J. Brandon Harris
Kerr-McGee Corporation
Knippelmier Chevrolet, Inc.

Oklahoma University Football
Letterman's Association
Regent Jon R. Stuart
The University of Oklahoma Department
of Intercollegiate Athletics
The University of Oklahoma
Touchdown Club
The Lee Allan Smith Family

Kerr-McGee Bell Tower
Kerr-McGee Corporation

Kerr-McGee Trails
Kerr-McGee Corporation

Mosaic on the Canal
Devon Energy

New Years Eve Celebration in Pasadena
Chesapeake Energy Corporation
Devon Energy Corporation
The Freede Family
The Meinders Foundation
NAIFCO
The Oklahoman
Jeannette and Richard Sias
Jim and Jill Williams

Oklahoma History Center
Devon Energy Corporation
Kerr-McGee Corporation
The Meinders Foundation
Oklahoma City Centennial Sponsors

Oklahoma Rising TV Program
The Clay Bennett Family
The Jim Everest Family
The Freede Family
The Oklahoman

Oklahoma Sports Hall of Fame and Jim Thorpe Museum
The Chickasaw Nation
City of Oklahoma City
The Freede Family

Kerr-McGee Corporation
State of Oklahoma

Rodeo Opry
Chesapeake Energy Corporation
Aubrey and Katie McClendon
Kerr-McGee Corporation
Oklahoma City Centennial Sponsors

Septemberfest
Oklahoma City Centennial Sponsors
Oklahoma State Medical Association

Spectacular Post Show Party
Patsy and Jim Brewer
Chesapeake Energy Corporation
Barbara and Jackie Cooper
Devon Energy Corporation
Dorchester Capital
The Freede Family
The Meinders Foundation
NAIFCO
The Oklahoman
SandRidge Energy
Jeannette and Richard Sias
DeAnn and Lee Allan Smith
Donna and Blake Wade
Jim and Jill Williams

State Fair Centennial Waterfall
Chesapeake Energy Corporation
The Freede Family
The Meinders Foundation
Jeannette and Richard Sias

Steve Owens Statue
Clayton I. Bennett
Don Carlton
Nancy & Ed deCordova
Stan & Joan Deardeuff
L. Thomas Dulaney, Jr.
Richard Ellis
Hal W. & Sandy Smith
Jean I. Everest Foundation
Gary L. Massad, M.D.

Mr. & Mrs. Aubrey McClendon
Oklahoma University Football
Letterman's Association
The Lee Allan Smith Family
Barry Switzer
Gene Torbett

Train Project
The Chickasaw Nation (Engine)
E.L. and Thelma Gaylord Foundation
(The Oklahoman Passenger Car)
The Freede Family (OCU Star Express)
Kerr-McGee Corporation (The Kerr-McGee
Explorer Passenger Car)
LaDonna and Herman Meinders
(OCU Star Express)
OKC Adventure District
Oklahoma City Centennial Sponsors

Tulsa Sponsors
QuikTrip
State of Oklahoma
Williams
Arvest Bank/Walton Family Foundation
The Bama Companies
ConocoPhillips
Grace & Franklin Bernsen Foundation
Senior Star Living
Stuart Foundation
Tulsa Port of Catoosa
ONEOK, Inc.
KOTV News on 6
Tulsa World
JPMorgan Chase
The Barnett Family Foundation
Blue Cross and Blue Shield of Oklahoma
Dollar Thrifty Automotive Group, Inc.
Great Plains Coca-Cola Bottling Company
Mollie Williford
The Oxley Foundation
Robert J. LaFortune
Kathleen Patton Westby Foundation
Farmers Insurance Group
The William K. Warren Foundation

INDEX

INDEX